What Critics and Professionals Say About the "Impact G...

"**THE DEFINITIVE GUIDE** ...
Frommer, The Arthur Fro...

"**THE BEST** travel book I've ...
West

"**AN EXCELLENT, EXHAUS... ...ASCINATING** look at shopping in the East . . . it's dif... imagine a shopping tour without this pocket-size book in hand."—**Travel & Leisure**

"**BOOKS IN THE SERIES** help travelers recognize quality and gain insight to local customs."—**Travel-Holiday**

"**THE BEST GUIDE** I've seen on shopping in Asia. If you enjoy the sport, you'll find it hard to put down . . . They tell you not only the where and what of shopping but the important how, and all in enormous but easy-to-read detail."—**Seattle Post-Intelligencer**

"**ONE OF THE BEST GUIDEBOOKS** of the season—not just shopping strategies, but a Baedeker to getting around . . . definitely a quality work. Highly recommended."—**Arkansas Democrat**

"**WILL WANT TO LOOK INTO** . . . has shopping strategies and travel tips about making the most of a visit to those areas. The book covers Asia's shopping centers, department stores, emporiums, factory outlets, markets and hotel shopping arcades where visitors can find jewelry, leather goods, woodcarvings, textiles, antiques, cameras, and primitive artifacts."—**Chicago Tribune**

"**FULL OF SUGGESTIONS**. The art of bartering, including everyday shopping basics are clearly defined, along with places to hang your hat or lift a fork."—**The Washington Post**

"**A WONDERFUL GUIDE** . . . filled with essential tips as well as a lot of background information . . . a welcome addition on your trip."—**Travel Book Tips**

"**WELL ORGANIZED AND COMPREHENSIVE BOOK**. A useful companion for anyone planning a shopping spree in Asia."—**International Living**

"**OFFERS SOME EXTREMELY VALUABLE INFORMATION** and advice about what is all too often a spur-of-the-moment aspect of your overseas travel."—**Trip & Tour**

"**A MORE UNUSUAL, PRACTICAL GUIDE** than most and is no mere listing of convenience stores abroad . . . contains unusual tips on bargaining in Asia . . . country-specific tips are some of the most valuable chapters of the guidebook, setting it apart from others which may generalized upon Asia as a whole, or focus upon the well-known Hong Kong shopping pleasures."—**The Midwest Book Review**

THE TREASURES AND
PLEASURES OF PARIS
AND THE FRENCH RIVIERA

Books & CD-ROMs by Drs. Ron and Caryl Krannich

THE TREASURES AND PLEASURES OF

Paris and the French Riviera

BEST OF THE BEST

RON AND CARYL KRANNICH, PH.DS

IMPACT PUBLICATIONS
MANASSAS PARK, VA

THE TREASURES AND PLEASURES OF PARIS AND THE FRENCH RIVIERA: BEST OF THE BEST

Library of Congress Cataloging-in-Publication Data

Krannich, Ronald L.
     The treasures and pleasures of Paris and the French Riviera: best of the best / Ronald L. Krannich, Caryl Rae Krannich.
     p. cm. -- (Impact guides)
Includes bibliographical references and index.
ISBN 1-57023-057-9 (alk. paper)
     1. Paris (France)--Guidebooks. 2. Riviera (France) -- Guidebooks.
I. Krannich, Caryl Rae. II. Title. III Series
DC708.K73   1996
914.4'3604839--dc20   96-21753
                                     CIP

For information on distribution or quantity discount rates, Tel. 703/361-7300, Fax 703/335-9486, e-mail impactp@erols.com, or write to: Sales Department, IMPACT PUBLICATIONS, 9104-N Manassas Drive, Manassas Park, VA 22111-5211. Distributed to the trade by National Book Network, 4720 Boston Way, Suite A, Lanham, MD 20703. Tel. 301/459-8696

Contents

iii

PART II
Paris

PART III
The French Riviera

Liabilities and Warranties

While the authors have attempted to provide accurate and up-to-date information in this book, please be advised that names, addresses, and phone numbers do change and shops, restaurants, and hotels do move, go out of business, or change ownership and management. Such changes are a constant fact of life. We regret any inconvenience such changes may cause to your travel plans.

Inclusion of shops, restaurants, hotels, and other hospitality providers in this book in no way implies guarantees nor endorsements by either the authors or publisher. The information and recommendations appearing in this book are provided solely for your reference. The honesty and reliability of shops is best ensured by **you**—always ask the right questions and request proper receipts and documents.

The Treasures and Pleasures of Paris and the French Riviera provides numerous tips on how you can best experience a trouble-free adventure. As in any unfamiliar place or situation, or regardless of how trusting strangers may appear, the watchwords are always the same—watch your wallet! If it's too good to be true, it probably is.

THE TREASURES AND
PLEASURES OF PARIS
AND THE FRENCH RIVIERA

Welcome to Fabulous France

W elcome to Paris, the French Riviera, and Monaco. You're going to have a wonderful time discovering the many treasures and pleasures of these delightful areas. Forget anything negative you've heard about France and the French. It's probably not true. And if there's any truth to it, it's probably not really important to having a great time. We like France, the French, and the many treasures and pleasures they offer. We hope you will too.

A QUALITY ADVENTURE

France offers one of the best quality travel experiences you will find anywhere in the world. It's not particularly cheap but it need not be excessively expensive—if you know what you're doing. You'll find some special treasures, especially in the exquisite jewelry shops of Paris, on which you can literally spend $1 million a minute! And then there are places where you can get by on only $75 a day or even less, including food, accommodations, and transportation. It depends on you.

What Paris, the French Riviera, and Monaco offer in great abundance is **quality travel** experiences. Indeed, the French have a unique eye for quality that is not readily found in other countries. It's clearly expressed in the form and content of French architecture, hotels, restaurants, food, wine, music, entertainment, transportation, museums, clothes, and accessories. After all, the French continue to set world standards in many of these areas. Many French products, especially clothes and accessories, are envied throughout the world by those willing to pay high prices for top quality goods. In both Hong Kong and Paris, for example, Japanese tourists endure long lines and some abuse to acquire high priced French designer goods.

❑ France offers one of the best quality travel experiences anywhere in the world.

❑ The French have a unique eye for quality that is not readily found in other countries.

❑ France is a place where ideas germinate, where dreams are made, where romance comes true, and where the good life is easily understood and hopefully realized.

❑ France seems to be everyone's favorite country and Paris their favorite city.

Whatever you say about France, it definitely is not a make-shift, muddle-through country uncertain about where it is coming from or where it is going, although some Frenchmen may contest the latter. The proud French have a grand and sometimes infamous history, with many conquering heros immortalized in concrete, marble, and bronze statutes, museums, and tombs; a well articulated and distinctive culture; and a sense of who they are and where they are going. As you will quickly discover, there is a French way of doing things. Many people, including the French, think it's the right way. And often it is. Whether it's right or wrong, you can be assured it's done in style and with an eye toward quality. Even doggie do-do in many parts of Paris gets scooped up in style with green and white motorcycle-mounted municipal vacuum sweepers. Only in France!

FRANCE IN YOUR FUTURE

France is more than just another country to visit. Greater than the sum of its parts, France is a stand-out country that exudes a particular character which attracts millions of adoring visitors to its cities, villages, and beaches each year. For many people, visiting France is a dream come true. For others who decide to work or study here for several months, or even a few years, France is a place where ideas germinate, where dreams are made, where romance comes true, and where the good life is easily understood and hopefully realized. It's everything they ever wanted to see and do, and then much more.

Not surprising, many visitors quickly become chauvinistic

about this place: travel the world and you'll find no finer places than Paris and the French Riviera, or perhaps a few other places in France. Stay and travel in France a while and you'll understand what such chauvinism is all about. It's a charming sort of isolationism.

A UNIQUE, INSCRUTABLE PLACE

Above all, France is filled with unique treasures and pleasures that will forever enrich your life. Indeed, France seems to be everyone's favorite country and Paris their favorite city. It's a country of great beauty, history, glory, passion, and just plain good living. Think of France and you immediately think of grand style, taste, culture, and quality in everything from food and clothes to architecture, language, and contentious relationships. You also think of a complex country that defies most stereotypes. To be French is to be both different and difficult to understand, a kind of inscrutable people.

If this is your first visit to France, you'll go there with many expectations which may or may not be realized. Perhaps you've heard the French are unfriendly, they don't speak English, and the place is extremely expensive. But then you discover that many of the French are indeed friendly and accommodating, many speak English, and not everything need be expensive if you know how to travel and live this country right. Perhaps you're expecting to visit some of the world's greatest museums, sample fabulous cuisine, and stay in outstanding hotels. But then you discover the museums are interesting, the food is fine, and the hotels are okay, although extremely overpriced for what you get. Maybe there's more hype here than what you've been led to believe. But then, maybe it's true. You'll have to judge for yourself.

- ❑ There's a lot of truth to the old adage *"Once you've seen the lights of Paris, you can never go home."* While physically you'll return home, mentally you'll often find yourself in France.

- ❑ France's appeal goes far beyond the standard tourist attractions. It's all wrapped up in ambience, lifestyle, and character. There's something very seductive about this place.

- ❑ While our primary focus is on acquiring the treasures (shopping), we're into much more than just procurement and acquisitions.

THE ULTIMATE SEDUCTRESS

France is the ultimate seductress, a beauty that will captivate you and before long persuade you to return to continue enjoying her many treasures and pleasures. As many a traveler learned long ago, France is hard to resist. Indeed, Paris overflows with exiles, refugees, and a wide assortment of other types of expatriates who have decided to make France their temporary, if not permanent, home. There's a lot of truth to the old adage *"Once you've seen the lights of Paris, you can never go home."* While physically you'll return home, mentally you'll often find yourself in France. You'll probably acquire new standards by which to judge other places in the world, and you'll often have flashbacks of that terrific time you had in France. It's no accident that some of the world's great non-French revolutionary leaders (Lenin, Mao, Ho Chi Minh), writers (Hemingway), and artists (Picasso) developed new ideas and techniques in France. And many still do today. Perhaps some of those famous cafés at St-Germain-des-Prés along Blvd. St-Germain in Paris, which seem to draw a disproportionate number of tourists and wannabes, are now centers for new intellectual and political ideas that will come to the fore in the 21st century.

Don't go visit France before starting your first job or if you are between jobs. Once there, you'll probably acquire a bad case of wanderlust that may be detrimental to your long-term career development!

While France is a place of many myths, it yields some wonderful and satisfying travel experiences that will motivate you to return to this fascinating country again and again. Walk its streets and beaches, drive its roads, visit its perched hill towns and châteaus, climb its towers, sample its cafés, discover its markets, experience its light, and visit places that have made France the military, intellectual, artistic, and fashion envy of the world and you'll begin to understand France's magnetic and seductive character.

There's something about France and the French that is so appealing to outsiders who often rank France as their favorite destination and thereby use it as a standard to judge other countries, including their own! Could it be those museums, restaurants, and hotels? Probably not. France's appeal goes far beyond the standard tourist attractions. It's all wrapped up in ambience, lifestyle, and character. There's something very seductive about this place. France stimulates the senses. It's what writers and artists learned and expressed long ago—this is a place where you can live life to its fullest.

TRIPS FOR TREASURES

So where are we going and what will we be doing? We're going to explore the many treasures and pleasures of Paris, the French

Riviera, and Monaco. While our primarily focus is on acquiring some treasures (shopping), we're into much more than just procurement and acquisitions. There are a lot of great things to see and do here. We're going into the heart Paris, climb the Eiffel Tower and a few other major monuments, visit a few key museums without lingering too long, sample some of the best restaurants, stay at hotels offering good value, and shop 'til we drop in Paris' many shops, department stores, and markets. Most important of all, we're going to walk this fascinating city and enjoy its many outdoor pleasures, from sidewalk cafés to parks and markets. In the French Riviera and Monaco we shift gears somewhat by exploring several intriguing perched villages and hill towns offering unique shopping, sightseeing, and dining opportunities. What we outline here are numerous treasures and pleasures you can experience within an intense two to three week period.

PARIS AND THE FRENCH RIVIERA

Paris and the French Riviera simply brim with unique treasures and pleasures. Indeed, these are two of France's and Europe's most interesting and stimulating places to visit.

We've chosen to focus on Paris and the French Riviera because both places represent some the best of the best in French treasures and pleasures. While **Paris** may not be the "real" France—especially after you encounter all the tourists and expatriates—thank God it's a major part of France. This so-called City of Lights, renowned for its fantastic illumination at night, remains a beacon for many world travelers. Consisting of a series of quaint villages linked together by wide boulevards, narrow streets, and a winding river dissecting the city into the famous Right and Left banks, Paris is a big sprawling metropolis of low-rise buildings punctuated by grand architecture and numerous distinctive monuments and public buildings, from the Eiffel Tower and Notre Dame to the Arc de Triomphe and Sacré-Coeur.

Paris seems to be everyone's favorite big city, and for good reason. It's one of the most "user-friendly" cities in the world. While it boasts an excellent public transportation system (subway and buses), Paris is best approached and savored on foot. Uniquely designed, it invites you to walk its many interesting boulevards, streets, parks, and markets. Stroll along the banks of the Seine River, watch the world go by at a sidewalk café, get a bird's-eye view of the city from the Eiffel Tower or Sacré-Coeur, or have a spontaneous picnic of pastries or sandwiches on a park bench and you'll quickly fall in love with this place.

Paris has an electric quality that goes far beyond its attractive evening illumination. Except on Sunday, people are everywhere. Paris' grand yet low-level architecture testifies to the greatness of this city as well as demonstrates a fact of urban life àla the French—a big city can be exciting, beautiful, and livable. Many Parisians may escape to country homes on weekends, but few would think of abandoning this city forever. Paris is the heart and soul of France. It is a wonderful experience for the many millions of travelers who pass through this city again and again. As many a visitor has learned, home is never the same after experiencing Paris!

The **French Riviera**, also known as Côte d'Azur, encompasses some of France's prime beachfront real estate with such famous cities as Nice and Cannes in the southeast of France. Our French Riviera also includes the Principality of Monaco (Monte Carlo) because of its geographic proximity and its related French treasures and pleasures. A heavily touristed area from May to September, drawing visitors from all over the world, the French Riviera is France's and Europe's great playground for the rich and famous. Here's where wealthy politicians, royalty, businesspeople, sports figures, movie stars, Russia's new rich, crime figures, and a large assortment of wannabes come to see and be seen as well as indulge in the pleasures of gambling, dining, shopping, and sailing. It's the center for the world-famous film festival (Cannes), auto races (Monte Carlo), beaches (Nice), and conventions (Cannes). Aside from the great shopping, terrific restaurants, and fine hotels found in the major cities of Monte Carlo, Nice, and Cannes, you'll find attractive perched villages and hill towns offering a wide array of fine art and local crafts as well as exceptional museums exhibiting the art of some of the world's greatest artists. This is the area of such great artists as Picasso, Matisse, and Chagall and their museums. Here you will want to rent a car to explore the unique treasures and pleasures of this intriguing region. Unless you visit during high season and get stuck in the potentially horrendous traffic, the French Riviera and Monaco will not disappoint you. If you are a connoisseur of great art, you're likely to fall in love with this beautiful area!

 # THE TREASURES AND PLEASURES

The Treasures and Pleasures of Paris and the French Riviera is a different kind of travel book for a very special type of traveler.

Like other books in this series, this is not another smorgesboard of names, addresses, popular sites, sightseeing tours, or pretty pictures nor does it promote cheap travel or the latest travel fads. You'll find plenty of excellent travel guides—most of which are ostensibly revised annually—that already cover such travel experiences. We, on the other hand, primarily focus on quality shopping, dining, and accommodations as well as special tours for people who wish to experience the best of the best of what Paris and the French Riviera have to offer discriminating travelers.

The book is designed to provide you with the necessary information to enjoy this country's many treasures and pleasures. Going beyond popular sites, including major museums, churches, and monuments, we focus on the where, what, and how of acquiring France's many treasures by becoming an effective shopper. We especially designed the book with three major considerations in mind:

❏ In the French Riviera and Monaco we'll explore several intriguing perched villages and hill towns offering unique shopping, sightseeing, and dining opportunities.

❏ While Paris may not be the "real" France, thank God it's a major part of France.

❏ Paris is best approached and savored on foot. Uniquely designed, it invites you to walk its many interesting boulevards, streets, parks, and markets.

❏ The French Riviera is France's and Europe's great playground for the rich and famous. If you are a connoisseur of great art, you're likely to fall in love with this beautiful area!

- Learn a great deal about French society and culture by meeting its many talented artists, craftspeople, and shopkeepers and exploring its many cities, towns, and villages.

- Do quality shopping for items having good value.

- Discover unique items that can be integrated into your home and/or wardrobe.

As you will quickly discover, this is not a guide on how to find great bargains in inexpensive France, although we do show you where and how to find bargains on quality items. Nor are we preoccupied with shopping in France's famous markets for cheap goods—places you may find disappointing and, with a few exceptions, a waste of precious travel time. And we are not particularly interested in shopping for items imported from neighboring countries, such as Italy, Switzerland, Germany, or Belgium, which tend to be very expensive. Given such close proximity to these countries, we prefer visiting them on our own and thus buying directly at the source.

This is not to say we only focus on "Made in France" products. On the contrary. As you'll quickly discover, France is much larger than just its relatively modest geographic boundaries. While official colonialism has all but ended—except for a few Pacific Islands—it remains well and alive in France's many wonderful antique, arts, crafts, and home decorative shops! Indeed, on our most recent trip to France, we acquired a unique African ceremonial stool that originated in Benin, a beautiful carved stool from Borneo, a rice cutter from the Philippines, a Sudanese bowl, two Ethiopian shields, and a fabulous Vietnamese painting along with some wonderful quality "French" jewelry, clothes, and accessories. And these goods are by no means confined to Paris. Even shops in some of the small perched villages in southern France offer interesting international products from Africa, Asia, and the South Pacific. We love to venture into France's many antique, arts, crafts, and home decorative shops that offer unique items from Africa, Asia, and the South Pacific for two reasons: given France's long colonial tradition, it remains one of Europe's most international countries, drawing products from all over the world but with a French eye toward quality selections; and we have a personal interest in collecting such items from the same Third World countries represented in France's many shops. Paris in particular simply brims with attractive items from all over the world.

While you will find bargains in France, this book focuses on quality shopping for unique items that will retain their value. As such, although we are concerned with shopping to save money and to get bargains while shopping for unique products, we prefer finding the best of what there is available and selectively choose those items we both enjoy and can afford. Rather than purchase several pieces of fake jewelry, we prefer purchasing a single piece of exquisite jewelry that will last longer and be appreciated for many years to come. We learned long ago that while purchasing cheap items and tourist kitsch may seem appropriate at the time, such items quickly lose their value as well as our interest.

Our general shopping rule is this: A "good buy" is one that results in acquiring something that has good value; when in doubt, go for quality because quality items will hold their value and you will enjoy them much more in the long run.

Many French are good at practicing this rule especially when it comes to buying clothes. Rather than having a closet full of suits and coats—most of which are seldom worn—many French buy one or two good quality suits and coats that will last a long time in terms of fabrics, colors, and styling. While they may wear the same suit or coat over and over again, these people tend to remain stylish by accessorizing themselves and their clothes with attractive belts, scarves, hats, shoes, and jewelry. Many French do not spend a lot money on a lot of clothes. Rather, they buy a few very good quality garments that will give them repeated good use. For example, instead of buying five $200 coats that you may wear only a few times each or which may wear out quickly, why not invest in one $800 coat that you will wear repeatedly, and which will last and look stylish for years? In this sense, the high-quality and much used $800 coat becomes relatively inexpensive when compared to the supposedly inexpensive alternatives.

We also include many of the best hotels and restaurants in Paris and the Riviera. By "best" we mean places that offer excellent value, service, and product. Make no mistake about it, hotels and restaurants tend to be expensive in France compared to similar places back home. While many of the best hotels and restaurants also are extremely expensive (US$800+ per night for a hotel room or US$200 per person for dinner), we identify many other outstanding hotels and restaurants that are relatively inexpensive or moderately priced. In this sense, we've tried to provide a good range of hotels and restaurants that meet our criteria of "the best" and respond to the varied preferences of our readers. After all, you may be the type of traveler who seeks out the finest hotels and restaurants because you want to pamper yourself when traveling in France—you want everything to be better than back home! On the other hand, you might be the type of traveler who would rather spend your money on shopping and sightseeing; you only need a comfortable place to sleep and prefer finding inexpensive places to eat. We've attempted throughout this book to respond to the needs of both types of travelers. For both groups, we outline some of the best of the best hotels and restaurants.

Our selections for sightseeing tend to follow a similar pattern. While we survey many of the standard sights in Paris and the Riviera, especially museums and monuments, we're also aware that many of our readers are not great museum-goers, monument-climbers, or modern art-lovers. Although some may be embarrassed to admit it (*Others may think I'm uncultured!*), many of these people get bored after an hour or two at the great Louve Musuem. The same people also may get bored visiting more than two cathedrals. On the other hand, many of these people prefer walking the streets, observing people, exploring villages and neighborhoods, or taking a river cruise to "doing" museums and monuments. We understand these varied preferences. Accordingly, we show you how to do the Louve in one hour, visit two of the best cathedrals, and include a wide range of things to do in addition to the standard museums and monuments that France is so famous for.

BEWARE OF RECOMMENDED SHOPS

Throughout this book we concentrate on providing you with information on the best of the best of Paris' and the French Riviera's treasures and pleasures. We prefer not recommending and listing specific shops and services—even though we have favorite places when visiting France. We know the pitfalls of doing so. Shops that offered excellent products and service during one of our visits, for example, may change ownership, personnel, or policies from one year to another. In addition, our shopping preferences may not be the same as yours.

❑ We primarily focus on quality shopping, dining, and accommodations as well as special tours for people who wish to experience the best of the best of what Paris and the French Riviera have to offer discriminating travelers.

❑ While official colonialism has all but ended, it remains well and alive in France's many wonderful antique, arts, crafts, and home decorative shops!

❑ A "good buy" is one that results in acquiring something that has good value; when in doubt, go for quality because quality items will hold their value and you will enjoy them much more in the long run.

❑ By "best" we mean places that offer excellent value, service, and product.

Our major concern is to outline your shopping options in Paris and the Riviera, show you where to locate the best shopping areas, and share some useful shopping strategies that you can use anywhere in France. Armed with this knowledge and some basic shopping skills, you will be better prepared to locate your own shops and determine which ones offer the best products and service in relation to your own shopping and travel goals.

However, we also recognize the "need to know" when shopping in France. Therefore, throughout this book, we list the names and locations of various shops we have found to offer good quality products. In many cases we have purchased items in these shops and can also recommend them for service and reliability. But in most cases we surveyed shops to determine the type and quality of products offered without making purchases. To buy in every shop would be beyond our budget, as well as our home storage capabilities! When we do list specific shops, we do so only as reference points from which to start your shopping. We do not guarantee the quality of products or service. In many cases we have found our recommendations to be shops of exceptional quality, honesty, and service. We believe you should have the advantage of this information, but we also caution you to again evaluate the business by asking the necessary questions.

If you rely solely on our listings, you will miss out on one of the great adventures of shopping in France—discovering your own special shops that offer unique items, exceptional value, and excellent service.

Should you encounter problems with these recommendations, we would appreciate hearing about your experiences. We can be contacted in care of our publisher:

Ron and Caryl Krannich
IMPACT PUBLICATIONS
9104-N Manassas Drive
Manassas Park, VA 22111-5211
Fax 703/335-9486
E-mail: impactp@impactpublications.com

While we cannot solve your problems, future editions of this book will reflect the experiences—both positive and negative—of our readers. We appreciate your thoughtful observations and comments.

EXPECT A REWARDING ADVENTURE

Whatever you do, enjoy France's many treasures and pleasures as found in Paris and the French Riviera. These are very special areas that offer unique travel adventures.

So arrange your flights and accommodations, pack your credit cards and traveler's checks, take your sense of humor, and head for one of the world's great destinations. You should return home with much more than a set of photos and travel brochures and a weight gain attendant with new eating habits. You will acquire some wonderful products and accumulate many interesting travel tales that can be enjoyed and relived for a lifetime.

Experiencing the treasures and pleasures of Paris and the French Riviera only takes time, money, and a sense of adventure. Take the time, be willing to part with some of your money, and open yourself to a whole new world of treasures and pleasures. If you are like us, your adventure will introduce you to an exciting world of quality products, friendly people, and interesting places that you might have otherwise missed had you passed through these places only to eat, sleep, see sights, and take pictures. When you travel and shop in Paris and the French Riviera, you learn about some exciting places by way of the people, products, and places that define this country's many treasures and pleasures.

PART I

Traveling Smart

2

Know Before You Go

The more you know about Paris and the French Riviera before you depart on your adventure, the better prepared you should be to enjoy its many treasures and pleasures. Indeed, you should be aware of several myths as well as numerous practical realities, such as weather, documents, transportation, duties, customs, and recommended resources, as you prepare for your trip to France.

MYTHS AND REALITIES

The following myths prevent some travelers from truly enjoying Paris and the French Riviera:

MYTH #1: **The French are unfriendly and rude.**

REALITY: We generally find the French to be a friendly and accommodating people. Amongst themselves they can be very verbal, confrontational, contentious, and serious in demeanor. They definitely are not a spontaneous nor uninhibited people with strangers. The only seemingly unfriendly

French we found were money-changers at the railway station. Given the nature of their jobs, we understand why these may be the least friendly people you may encounter!

MYTH #2: **It's difficult to get around in France because the French refuse to speak English; I need to learn French before I go.**

REALITY: More and more French speak English and are willing do so when approached by non-French speaking visitors. English is widely spoken and understood in Paris and many places along the French Riviera. After all, these are very cosmopolitan and international cities. Indeed, Paris alone receives nearly 50 million visitors a year. Many restaurants offer menus in English, and waiters and waitresses often speak some English; if not, they will usually find someone who does speak English to assist you. You will seldom have difficulty getting around because of your lack of local language skills. The major problem with language is found outside the large cities where few people may speak or understand English. In these places you may need to use a combination of a phrase book and sign language to communicate your needs. Try to learn a few basic French words or phrases for approaching people. We have yet to hear of anyone who got lost or went hungry in France for more than a few minutes because they did not speak French!

MYTH #3: **Everything in France is expensive; I can't afford to go.**

REALITY: You can afford to go, and you should regardless of all the horror stories you've heard about the high cost of traveling in France. Yes, France can be a very expensive place to visit, especially if you confine your visit to the upper end of our destinations, Paris and the French Riviera. A quick reality check will be the first cup of coffee you order at a café. Once you discover that coffee costs US$5, it's really not that good, and you hate to leave any behind, such high prices could well ruin your trip. You'll have second thoughts about routinely ordering another potentially bad cup of coffee! Indeed, you know you're in an exceptionally expensive place that can quickly bleed your travel budget. But keep in mind some basic facts about traveling in this part of the world. The US dollar is weak against many major world currencies. Paris is a major international city on par with Tokyo, London, Hong Kong, and New York. When was the last time you visited these places and didn't complain about costs? The French Riviera is one of the world's major destinations for the rich and famous. You'll discover a very high standard of living in these places. Hotels and restaurants can be very expensive, and many of the best located shops tend to cater to the wealthy with their knock-your-socks-off jewelry, haute couture clothing, and exquisite arts and antiques. But like any other place you may have traveled to, you also can find relatively inexpensive places to stay and reasonably priced eateries. Rather than staying in a US$450 a night four-star hotel with all the amenities expected of top-flight business accommodations, you may opt to stay in a very nice, comfortable, and well located two- or three-star hotel for US$80 to US$150 a night. If you're traveling between Paris and the French Riviera, you can find a nice hotel or motel for less than US$40 a night, including breakfast. And if you want to beat the high cost of four-star restaurants, plan to dine in small neighborhood restaurants that locals frequent and occasionally organize a picnic from the local supermarket or grocery store. And if you really want to save money on everything from transportation to hotels and restaurants, consider visiting France on an all-inclusive packaged tour. Our point is that France is only as expensive as you let it be. What you find in France is a disproportionate number of expensive travel alternatives—the real high end for such travel basics as hotels and restaurants (you really do need to eat and sleep!). And it's these basics that quickly eat into travel budgets that you may wish to spend on other things, such as shopping and sightseeing. The best way to control those ostensibly expensive basics is to plan, plan, and plan your trip. Before arriving in France, identify hotels and restaurants that best fit into your budget. Make hotel reservations well in advance—two to three months ahead, if possible—to ensure you will get what you want. If you arrive in France without planning such basics, you may quickly find you are forced into a different budget category than you had originally planned. And such an experience can well ruin your trip as you constantly feel you are financially in the wrong place at the wrong time! The good news is that a few basics in Paris are very inexpensive, especially public transportation (buses and the metro).

MYTH #4: France is a safe place to travel.

REALITY: France is a relatively safe to travel in, depending on where you are used to traveling. While auto accidents and crime are not widespread, you still need to be very careful here. If you choose to rent a car and drive yourself, be sure to drive defensively. French drivers constantly speed; some may attempt to discipline you if you are in the wrong lane of a four-lane highway by cutting sharply in front of you. The roads are relatively safe, but novice drivers need to be very alert to others' driving habits. Also, watch your valuables. Purse snatchers and pick pockets are well and alive in France. Big cities, such as Paris, with lots of tourists congregating around major sites and metro stations, are their favorite territories. Always secure your valuables and anticipate the unanticipated. Unfortunately, Paris has recently experienced several terrorist bombings aimed at the popular and efficient underground Metro system. Indeed, during our last visit to Paris, our frequent Metro stop, St-Michel, was bombed just a few hours after we left the station, with several people seriously injured. The same station was bombed three months earlier, just after we had left Paris, and several people were killed and injured at that time. We quickly got the message and decided to curtail our use of the Metro and relearned the joys of walking in Paris. Our point is that you should expect the unexpected in France. Watch your valuables. Take normal precautions. And just be careful for your personal safety.

MYTH #5:   **The best food and greatest restaurants in the world are found in France.**

REALITY: Everything is relative, depending on where you come from and where you have traveled before. Restaurants in France are often overrated and overpriced for what you get—hyped by restaurant reviewers who should know better. Service is often slow, portions small, rooms smoke-filled and noisy, and the check shocking. Make no mistake about it; you can find some great restaurants in Paris and the French Riviera, and we identify these accordingly. Indeed, some of the best restaurants and dining experiences in the world can be found in France. But most restaurants are simply average and many are very disappointing. If you arrive with very high expectations for food and restaurants, you may be disappointed. We come from the Washington, DC area where we are used to great restaurants and good service—every coup d'etat worldwide gives us four new international restaurants—and we have some terrific French restaurants at half the price of our Parisian experiences. Consequently, we've not been overly-impressed with our French dining experiences and perhaps we are more critical than others. We certainly don't get great value for our dining francs in France!

MYTH#6:   **The traffic in Paris is the worst in the world!**

REALITY: The traffic in Paris looks and feels like traffic in most other large busy cities of the world. If you think it's the worst, then you haven't traveled much! In fact, the traffic in Paris is relatively orderly and sane compared to other places we've visited, including Los Angeles and Washington, DC. Even driving in Paris is not too bad, except for finding a parking place.

LOCATION AND AREA

Paris, the capital of France, is a city of over 10 million people occupying an area of 432 square miles. Situated in northern France, it is cut in two by the curving River Seine. The parts of the city on either side of the Seine are referred to as the left (the south) and the right (the north) bank. The 20 arrondissements (or districts) uncoil like a snail from around the 1st arrondissement which is comprised of the area around the Louvre on the right bank.

- ❑ Paris is a city of over 10 million people occupying an area of 432 square miles.

- ❑ Spring and fall are probably the nicest times to visit Paris.

- ❑ Crowds in the Riviera are the greatest during the summer months.

- ❑ Some resorts in the Riviera, especially in St. Tropez and Antibes, close in the winter in October and reopen in April.

- ❑ No visas are required for entry into France by US or Canadian visitors for visits of less than 3 months.

The Riviera is located on the southeast coast of France with the Mediterranean to the south and a wonderful array of hilltowns and perched villages forming a second tier to the Riviera to the north. The area is comprised of the coastline from Menton in the east (the first French town after leaving San Remo in Italy) and Bandol (east of Marseille) to the west.

This area, referred to as the Cote d'Azur by the French is more likely to be called the Riviera the nearer east one goes toward Italy as well as by Americans to whom the coastal cities and resorts of Toulon, St. Tropez, Cannes, Nice, and Monte Carlo in Monaco, conjure images of millionaires' Riviera villas, yachts at anchor in picturesque harbors and sun drenched throngs sunning on beaches. The lesser known second Riviera of artists and craftsworkers' villages of Biot, St-Paul-de-Vence, Vallauris, and the perfume capital of the world, Grasse, are nestled in the hills above the sunny Mediterranean.

CLIMATE, SEASONS, WHEN TO GO

Who hasn't dreamed of being in Paris in the springtime? In fact, spring and fall are probably the nicest times to visit Paris. The weather is mild, the throngs of tourists who come in June have not yet arrived or they have left the city at the end of August. The shops that are closed for most of August are open their usual hours. True, a spring or fall shower could inconvenience you for a day or two, but the odds are in your favor that you'll be able to enjoy shopping the streets of Paris or even a romantic stroll along the Seine.

July and August are the warmest months, though with average daytime temperatures of 66° degrees it is seldom uncomfortably hot. December through February average the coolest temperatures—though it rarely freezes in Paris. August rainfalls are the highest on average, so perhaps the Parisians know what they're doing when they close many shops and restaurants and leave the city in August—statistically the warmest and wettest month of the year.

Along the Riviera the summer months are the hottest, but with average temperatures in the eighties, that's no reason not to go. Of course, the crowds are also the greatest during the summer months. In fact some of the resorts, especially in St. Tropez and Antibes, close in October for the winter months. If your travels take you to the Riviera during the winter months you'll find the crowds have disappeared and there is still a lot of sunshine along the coast although it can get a bit nippy and even in late October we saw few people on the beach. It seldom rains during the summer with spring and autumn having the greatest likelihood of rainfall.

REQUIRED DOCUMENTS

There are no visas required for entry to France by citizens of the United States or Canada for visits of less than three months. A valid passport is all that is required, but since regulations do sometimes change, you are advised to check with the French Embassy or Consulate nearest you as you make preparations for your trip. Both U.S. and Canadian drivers' licenses are valid in France.

Non-EU (European Union) nationals can bring duty-free into France 200 cigarettes or 50 cigars or 250 grams of smoking tobacco (these amounts are doubled if you live outside of Europe); 2 liters of wine and either 1 liter of alcohol over 38.80 proof or 2 liters under 38.80 proof; 1.75 ounce of perfume. Items such as clothing and sporting equipment for personal use are admitted if they do not appear intended for sale.

GETTING THERE

AIR

Paris is served by nearly every international airline, and many airlines fly between the U.S. and France. The main French carrier, Air France, offers travel on the Concorde if speed is of the essence and money is no object as well as some low cost seats on regularly scheduled flights offered through Jet Vacations (800/538-0999). Air France also offers an Intra France Pass which allows you to fly within France for $85 each flight; however, the pass is sold only in conjunction with transatlantic travel purchased from Jet Vacations before you leave the U.S.

At the time this book went to press Jet Vacations was offering other specials such as Paris-Nice flights for $40 each way for off-peak travel or $70 during peak travel periods, as well as a package that included round-trip Air France airfare New York-Paris with passage from Paris to London via the Chunnel on the train and return from London to New York via Paris for $449.

□ Air France offers an Intra France Pass which allows you to fly within France for $85 for each flight.

□ Paris has two international airports. Orly is closer to the city center.

□ The train from London to Paris takes 3-3½ hours.

□ You get the best price on a car rental by booking the car and prepaying the fees before you leave home. Call the major car rental firms and compare prices.

United Airlines, American, Delta, Northwest, Continental, TWA and U.S. Air all offer flights between the U.S. and France and Air Canada flies between France and Canada.

Airfares are usually at their peak with any airline during the summer months—usually July through September—but it can vary with the airline, so it pays to check around. APEX fares (Advance Purchase Excursion) will generally save you money but penalties do apply if your plans change and there are usually required stays and limited days of the week that you can travel.

Keep in mind that there are two international airports in Paris—Charles De Gaulle and Orly. Orly is located a bit closer to the Paris city center, is somewhat smaller, and some people think an easier airport to navigate than Charles De Gaulle. In recent years our flights have always been out of De Gaulle and we have not experienced any problems.

TRAIN

If you are traveling to Paris from Europe, you may choose to arrive by train. With the opening of the Channel Tunnel, it is now possible to travel from London to Paris by train in 3-3½ hours, and trains are frequent from most other European cities. From Italy, we have taken the overnight train which leaves Rome at 7:30pm and arrives in Paris about 10:30am the next morning. Of course we missed some scenery while we slept, but we arrived fresh and saved the expense of a hotel for the night.

While the train fare was not cheap—about $250 per person for a private compartment for two; it was half the cost of flying between the two cities plus we saved the cost of one night in a hotel.

If you do decide to take an overnight train you will need to decide whether you want to book a private compartment or share a compartment with four other people—a couchette. If you do prefer the private compartment, make sure that is what you book. The couple ahead of us boarding the train were quite chagrined to find that what they thought was to be a private compartment was to be shared with strangers. Be careful of your personal belongings on the train. Make sure your compartment door is locked and you may even wish to position a suitcase inside so that it blocks access to your compartment. There have been some complaints of thievery aboard the night trains. The clever thieves pump gas to induce sleep into the unwary passengers' compartment. The next morning the unsuspecting traveler discovers he or she has been robbed.

Paris has six major train stations, so make sure you know where you will be arriving if you are hoping to make hotel reservations near your train station.

CAR

If you plan to travel to several European cities and have more luggage than you care to haul on and off trains or just wish to have maximum flexibility, you may decide to rent a car. Car rentals, like just about everything else in France, seems expensive compared to prices in the United States. You can get the best prices on a car rental by booking the car and prepaying the fees before you leave home. Call the major car rental firms and compare prices; the company that gave us the best deal when we called (Hertz) may not be offering the best prices when/where you want to travel.

- Hertz   800/654-3131
- Avis   800/331-1084
- National   800/477-6285
- Kenwel   800/678-0678

We picked up our prepaid car in Florence on the day we were leaving the city and headed toward Monaco and the French Riviera. With a car we had flexibility to alternate our time between the seaside towns and the perched villages in the hills above the Riviera. From Cannes we drove to Paris stopping at Versailles on the way. We stopped at our hotel long enough to drop off our luggage, then returned the car we had picked up in Italy at the Hertz office not far from the Arc de Triomphe and walked back to our hotel. While in Paris it is best to walk, take public transportation or taxis. You do not want to drive a car while in Paris; parking is difficult and traffic is dense. You will spend too much precious time finding parking for the car.

BUS

If you are already in Europe, the least expensive way to get to Paris is by bus. Eurolines is Europe's largest bus operator. At present, Eurolines does not have a U.S. based sales agent. But any travel agent in Europe can arrange a ticket for the bus.

VAT

The Value Added Tax (VAT)—commonly levied on goods purchased in EU countries—differs from the sales tax levied in the United States in that it is already added onto the price quoted for goods rather than added at the point of sale. In France the rate can add from 12-18% onto the cost of most items, with books, food and medicines exempted. There has been an even higher amount on many luxury items such as jewelry, but with the economic unification of Europe these taxes have been reduced dramatically for France to remain competitive. There is no VAT on antiques.

As a visitor, if you are making a large purchase—2000FF minimum (established by law) or more at one store—on an item you will take with you when you leave the country (or the final EU country you are visiting) you probably qualify for *detaxe*—a tax refund. But you must actively pursue your refund in order to get your money.

There are two ways *detaxe* works. Which way you will get *detaxe* depends upon the store in which you make your purchase. With the first method the store where you make your purchase will prepare two credit card receipts—one for the cost of the merchandise minus the VAT and a separate one for the amount of the VAT only. The charge for the merchandise is put through immediately and the store hold the sales receipt for the VAT. The store will give you a *detaxe* invoice which you must have stamped by customs officials before you leave France or the final EU country you are visiting. Be sure you have the goods with you at the airport or border—not in luggage you have already checked through to your destination—in case the custom official asks to see the item as proof you are taking it with you. Mail the officially stamped invoice back to the store in the envelope they provided for you. When the store receives the invoice stamped by customs they will destroy the separate credit card sales receipt for the VAT amount. This is the better system for you since you never actually pay the tax (only if you fail to have the invoice stamped by customs and mail it to the store will this amount be charged to your account) and you get the full VAT refund with no service charges deducted. We have made purchases this way and it has worked as claimed.

The second method is more commonly used by stores and not quite as beneficial for you works this way: you pay the full amount quoted as the sales price—the merchandise price with the VAT included. You get the completed *detaxe* invoice from the store where you make the purchase, have the form stamped by French customs as you leave the country and mail the form back in the envelope provided by the store. Your refund check will come to you in the mail—usually 6-12 weeks later. There is normally a service charge deducted from the check you receive for this service. We have always received our check though sometimes later than we expected.

In short, the procedure for utilizing the *detaxe* system:

- Always have your passport or passport number with you when you shop.

- If you are considering a purchase of at least 2000FF— ask what amount qualifies for *detaxe* in that store (although the minimum is set by law, a store may require a higher amount), whether one item or a combination of items qualify, and if you must make all the purchases at the same time. Some stores will allow the buyer to accumulate receipts for up to six months and pool them for *detaxe*.

- Get the *detaxe* form completed at the store where the purchases are made. Keep the form and envelope provided together.

- Have the *detaxe* forms stamped by French customs (or in final EU country you depart)—remember to have the items with you—and mail in the envelope provided by the store. If you leave the country or the EU by train let the conductor know you have *detaxe* forms that need to be stamped at the border. On an overnight train the conductor will usually handle this for you.

You must remember to ask about *detaxe* every time you are contemplating a large purchase. If the store doesn't volunteer or you don't ask—no *detaxe*!

IMMIGRATION AND CUSTOMS: ABROAD

If you have your necessary documents—a valid passport is all that is presently required of U.S. citizens—immigration should be relative fast whether you arrive by plane, train or car. If you arrive by plane from a country outside the EU you normally will proceed the immigration formalities quickly. If you enter France from another EU country, you may hardly be aware you have crossed a border. When we entered France on the overnight train from Rome to Paris, the conductor collected our passports prior to our retiring for the night; he took care of the formalities for us at the border and returned our passports to us in the morning before our arrival in Paris. On another trip when we drove from Italy to France we were simply waved through at the border. We were not asked to stop or show a passport.

Although visitors do have an allowance of what they can bring into France without paying duty, you would have to be bringing a lot of questionable items with you or be truly unlucky to even be checked. However, non EU nationals can take in duty-free 200 cigarettes or 50 cigars or 250 grams of smoking tobacco. This amount is doubled if you live outside Europe. You can also take in two liters of wine and one liter of alcohol over 22 proof and 2 liters of wine 22 proof or under. You can also take in 50 grams of perfume, a quarter liter of toilet water, 500 grams of coffee and 200 grams of tea. Those over 14 can take in 300 F (about $60) of other gods; for those under 15 the limit is 150F (about $30).

It is a good idea to carry prescription drugs in their properly identified containers and a copy of the prescription itself may be useful should you have trouble with customs either abroad or upon your return home. Although it is always possible to be given a thorough check as you move from one country to another, when traveling between the United States and France or between EU countries, it is most likely that you will move through the process quickly.

CUSTOMS: RETURNING HOME

It's always good to know U.S. Customs regulations before leaving home. If you are a U.S. citizen planning to travel abroad, the United States Customs Service provides several helpful publications which are available free of charge from your nearest U.S. Customs Office, or write P.O. Box 7407, Washington, D.C. 20044.

- *Know Before You Go* (Publication #512): outlines facts about exemptions, mailing gifts, duty-free articles, as well as prohibited and restricted articles.

- *Trademark Information For Travelers* (Publication #508): deals with unauthorized importation of trade-marked goods. Since you will find copies of trade-marked items in markets—ubiquitous "knock-offs"— this publication will alert you to potential problems with custom inspectors prior to returning home.

- *International Mail Imports:* answers many travelers' questions regarding mailing items back to the U.S. The U.S. Postal Service sends all packages to Customs for examination and assessment of duty before they are delivered to the addressee. Some items are free of duty and some are dutiable. Do check on this before you leave the U.S. so you won't be surprised after you make your purchases in France.

U.S. citizens may bring in U.S. $400 worth of goods free of U.S. taxes every 30 days; the next $1000 is subject to a flat 10% tax. Goods beyond $1400 are dutied at varying rates applied to different classes of goods. If you are in Paris and uncertain about U.S. duties on particular items, contact the U.S. Embassy and ask for local U.S. Customs assistance.

CURRENCY AND EXCHANGE RATES

The French monetary unit is the franc (F). The value of the franc relative to the dollar fluctuates; at the time this book went to press the franc was worth about 20¢. Coins are minted in units of 5, 10, 20 and 50 centimes and 1, 2, 5 and 10 francs. Bills are printed in denominations of 10, 20, 50 and 100 francs.

ELECTRICITY

Electricity in France, as well as most of Europe, is 220 volts AC. You will need a converter to change the foreign voltage to the lower voltage required by the appliances you normally use in the U.S. if your appliance is not dual voltage. You will also need an adapted plug so that you can plug into the different wall plugs—most are two pin (round) plugs—found in France.

You can readily find both adapter plugs and voltage converters in most Radio Shack stores, or if you have difficulty finding them locally you may wish to contact either of two mail order firms:

Magellan's
Box 5485
Santa Barbara, CA 93150
Phone 1-800-962-4943
Fax 1-805-568-5406

Franzus Company
P.O. Box 142
Beacon Falls, CT 06403
Phone 1-203-723-6664
Fax 1-203-723-6666

ANTICIPATED COSTS

Paris and the French Riviera could well become your most expensive trip ever if you don't plan your costs accordingly. Indeed, everything seems to be expensive here, from the US$5 cup of coffee to the US$400-800 a night hotel room. Expect to spend US$5 a gallon for gasoline and over US$100 per person for dinner at a nice restaurant. You can easily spend US$1000 a day on hotels, meals, and entertainment, not to mention a few thousand dollars more a day on shopping! If money is no object, go ahead and enjoy the many pricey treasures and pleasures Paris and the French Riviera readily offer.

The cost of travel in Paris and the French Riviera is high for several reasons. First, the US dollar is presently weak compared to the French franc. Second, the cost of French labor is very high and thus reflected in your cost of travel. Third, French taxes are high, especially the ubiquitous Value Added Tax (VAT) which is hidden in most prices. Indeed, one-third of a price could very well be taxes.

Your best travel deal will be a group tour. A seven-day tour for under US$2,000, including round-trip transportation, is a real steal compared to what the same trip might cost you if you attempted to do it on your own. Given the cost of independent travel in France, group tours can dramatically save you money on hotels, restaurants, and transportation. However, if you prefer doing this trip on your own and you wish to watch your costs, we strongly recommend that you do a great deal of pre-trip planning. With sufficient planning, you can significantly cut the costs of travel to Paris and the French Riviera. We recommend doing the following:

■ **Transportation:** Rent a car for exploring the French Riviera. While the cost of gasoline may be high, most cars get good gas mileage, and renting a car is the most convenient and inexpensive way of seeing this delightful area. Plan to visit the major cities of Monte Carlo, Nice, and Cannes as well as drive into the hills to enjoy the many art shops, restaurants, and sights of such delightful towns and villages as St. Paul, Biot, and Vallauris. But be careful how you go about arranging for your car rental. If you wait until you arrive in France to arrange a car rental, you could pay over US$100 a day for a car. You can rents a car for under US$35 a day if you reserve it before you arrive in France. Comparative shop for your car rental by calling several of the car rental firms identified on page 23. You may be surprised what you learn. A firm that offered the best price three months ago may now be the most expensive. You literally need to shop around for the best deal every time you plan to visit France. Hertz, Avis, Budget, and Europcar offer competitive prices—but be sure to compare prices and ask about special deals and discounts. We normally do such planning at least eight weeks before we arrive in France. If you plan to visit the French Riviera during the high season, arrange your car at least three months in advance. In Paris, use the relatively inexpensive public transportation system—buses and the underground Metro. Taxis in Paris can be expensive—US$10-$15 for short trips around the city. Except on Sundays, when the city is relatively deserted, you don't want to drive in Paris. The traffic is not really the major problem—it's the parking that seems nonexistent!

■ **Restaurants:** If you want to experience the best of the best restaurants available in the French Riviera, expect to pay a very high price for such an experience. Dinner at a top restaurant can easily cost US$150 per person. Assuming you may not be budgeted to dine at such rates on a daily basis, you should plan to seek less expensive alternatives. Our general rule of thumb is that most restaurants, including very basic ones, cost at least two to three time more than back home. If, for example, you are used to paying US$25 per person for dinner back home, expect to pay US$50 to US$75 for a comparable dinner. However, comparables may be difficult to find since portions tend to be smaller and meals tend to be served in courses. If you really want to cut the costs of dining in Paris and the French Riviera, consider doing the following:

- **Consult several books on inexpensive restaurants:** One of our favorite and most reliable guides to reasonably priced restaurants in Paris is Sandra Gustafson's popular *Cheap Eats in Paris* (Chronicle Books). Pick up her latest edition which is available in most bookstores that have a large travel section on France.

- **Seek alternatives to restaurants:** In addition to restaurants, eateries in France come in several different forms and cost levels: cafés, bistros, brasseries, tearooms, and wine bars. We'll also find pastry shops, street vendors serving a variety of fast foods, bargain ethnic restaurants (especially Greek), and international fast-food restaurants, such as McDonald's, Burger King, and Kentucky Fried Chicken. However, expect to pay twice as much for your McDonald's burger in France as you would pay back home.

- **Organize a picnic in a park or in your hotel room:** Small grocery stores and supermarkets are well stocked with wine, soft drinks, fruit juices, cheeses, meats, fruits, vegetables, and prepared deli foods. You can easily put together a wonderful and relatively inexpensive meal by organizing a meal in this manner. You also may want to purchase drinks here rather than use your hotel mini-bar. Take, for example, the relative costs of your basic can of Coke Cola. It may cost you US$9 in your hotel mini-bar, US$6 in a restaurant, US$3 from a street vendor, US$2 at a tiny market, or US$1 at a supermarket. We usually try to locate a supermarket near our hotel which results in saving a great deal of money on the high cost of soft drinks. Wine is surprising cheap if purchased at the right place. Given the over-production of French wines, the prices are incredibly cheap. You can get a good bottle of wine in a supermarket for under US$5. However, a similar bottle of wine may cost more than US$40 when ordered at a restaurant.

- **Entertainment:** Some of the cheapest and most satisfying entertainment in France is either free or almost free—just walking the streets (free), sitting at a sidewalk café (US$4-5 coffee), or visiting museums and monuments (usually admission fees). Other forms of organized entertainment can get very expensive. An evening at one of Paris' top cabarets, such as Le Crazy Horse, Les Folies Bergère, or Le

Mouline Rouge, can run more than US$135 per person. For really free entertainment, consult Beffart's *Paris For Free (or Extremely Cheap)* (Mustang Press).

- **Shopping:** This is a tough one to estimate. Shopping in Paris and the French Riviera can quickly deplete any semblance of a budget! First time visitors often become overwhelmed with the numerous shopping choices and the high prices of everything. However, you also quickly discover that shopping in France falls into a different category from shopping elsewhere, except perhaps Italy. The emphasis here is on quality, quality, and quality. Everything from art, antiques, and jewelry to clothes, accessories, and chocolates seems to scream quality. Add to this high rents, high taxes, and the high cost of labor and you have the perfect formula for high priced shopping. At the same time, you can find "bargains" and "deals" in France. You will find places where you can buy many of the designer label clothes and accessories at half price or better. In fact, the best deals in Paris are on high priced designer label clothes and accessories rather than on regular discounted clothes. A real deal is getting that gorgeous US$1,500 Christian Lacroix suit for US$600 rather than a US$300 jacket for US$200. The difference in styling, cut, colors, and overall quality is very evident. Once home, you'll love your US$600 quality bargain much more than the US$200 deal you got on what was really a cheap item to begin with. Ironically, your best buys will be on quality items that last and which you will admire for years to come. Indeed, you may become quickly addicted to French styling and quality. All it takes is money! At the same time, you will have fun exploring some of Paris' major markets which are filled with unique, and at times inexpensive, items.

FRENCH TOURISM OFFICES

You will find tourist offices in 3,400 cities, towns, and villages throughout France that can provide you with assistance. Known as "Offices de tourisme et Syndicats d'initiative," they provide information on accommodations, restaurants, transportation, and things to do and see. While many of these offices, especially the one in Paris, operate more like advertising centers for local businesses, they can be helpful. Most important of all, they have useful maps of their areas which will include major sites. The personnel will usually identify on the map where the best shopping will be found in the city, town, or village. Most of these offices have English-speaking personnel, although some offices in small towns and villages may not. We routinely stop at these offices to get a good map and basic orientation information, including recommendations on shopping, restaurants, and sightseeing. You can easily find these offices by asking at your hotel or looking for tourist office signs which are posted along the main streets. When you stop at the first office, ask for a copy of their directory to all 3,400 tourist offices. It's a small 56-page 4" x 6" booklet. It lists each office alphabetically by city, town, or village and includes the street address and phone number.

The tourist office in Monte Carlo leaves much to be desired. It seems to be overstaffed with personnel who socialize a lot amongst themselves rather than provide useful information to tourists. They do, however, provide a good map of the city.

Prepare For a
Unique Adventure

Preparation is the key to experiencing a successful and enjoyable adventure to Paris and the French Riviera. But it involves much more than just examining maps, reading travel literature, and making airline and hotel reservations. Preparation, at the very least, is a process of minimizing uncertainty by learning how to develop a shopping plan, manage your money, determine the value of products, handle Customs, and pack for the occasion. It involves knowing what products are good deals to buy in France in comparison to similar items back home. Preparation helps organize all the aspects of your trip.

DEVELOP AN ACTION PLAN

Time is money when traveling abroad. This is especially true in the case of Paris and the French Riviera. You will pay for spending an unnecessary extra day or two in the French Riviera in hotel and restaurant bills. The better you plan and use your time, the more time you will have to enjoy your trip. If you want to use your time wisely and literally hit the ground running, you should plan a detailed, yet tentative, schedule for each day. Most people visiting the Riviera will want to spend some time on the beach (except in cooler months), some time both sightseeing and shopping for crafts and art in and around the perched villages and hill towns above the beach areas as well as shopping the streets of the Riviera cities and seaside towns. List in order of priority the 10 things you most hope to accomplish in the time you have. At the end of each day **summarize** what you actually accomplished in relation to your 10 priorities and set your priorities for the following day.

Planning is fine but it will not ensure a successful trip. People who engage in excessive planning often overdo it and thus ruin their trip by accumulating a list of unfulfilled expectations. Planning needs to be adapted to good luck. You also should be open to unexpected events which may well become the major highlights of your travel and shopping experiences.

CONDUCT RESEARCH AND NETWORK

Do as much research as possible before you depart on your French adventure. A good starting place is the periodical section of your local library. Here you will find numerous magazine and newspaper articles on travel and shopping in Paris and the French Riviera. Indeed, these French destinations are some of the most popular subjects for travel writers. When you find references to shops, add these names to your growing list of places to visit.

You should also **network for information and advice**. You'll find many people, including relatives, friends, and acquaintances, who have traveled to Paris and the French Riviera. Many of these people are eager to talk about their trip as well as share their particular travel secrets with you. They may direct you to some great shops where they found arts, crafts, jewelry, clothes, and accessories of good quality or at exceptional prices. Everyone seems to have their favorite restaurant recommendations and tips on what to see and how long to stay in any one place. When organizing your shopping plan, ask basic who, what, where, why, and how questions:

- **What** shops did you particularly like?
- **What** do they sell?
- **Whom** should I talk to?
- **Where** is the shop located?
- **How** did you pack and ship large items?
- **When** were you last there?

This final question is particularly significant. Not only do shops change ownership or go out of business, but prices constantly change. Information gleaned from people's experiences over the past 2-3 years will be most relevant.

Be sure to record all the information that you receive in an orderly manner. Use, for example, an ordinary address book to list the names, addresses, telephone numbers, and products of shops; list them alphabetically by types of merchandise.

Don't neglect to contact the French Government Tourist Office nearest you. Ask for a map and any information on travel and shopping in Paris and the French Riviera that would assist you in planning your trip.

MANAGE YOUR MONEY WELL

It's best to carry traveler's checks, two or more major credit cards with sufficient credit limits, U.S. dollars, and a few personal checks. If you use ATMs, you might want to take your ATM card with you. Our basic money rule is to take enough money and sufficient credit limits so you don't run short. How much you take is entirely up to you, but it's better to have too much than not enough when you're shopping in France.

Credit cards are the most convenient means for managing your money in France. We prefer using credit cards to pay for major purchases as well as for those unanticipated expenses incurred when shopping. Most major hotels and stores honor MasterCard, Visa, American Express, and Diner's cards. It's a good idea to take one or two bank cards and an American Express card.

Take plenty of **traveler's checks** in U.S. denominations of $50 and $100. Smaller denominations are often more trouble than they are worth. In France you will usually receive a better exchange rate with traveler's checks than with cash. Most major banks, hotels, restaurants, and shops will also take traveler's checks, although some do add a small service charge for accepting them. Banks and money changers will give you the best exchange rates, but at times you'll find hotels to be more convenient because of their close proximity and better hours.

Personal checks can be used to obtain traveler's checks with an American Express card or to pay for goods to be shipped later—after your check has cleared your bank. Some shops will also accept personal checks. Remember to keep one personal check aside to pay Customs should you have dutiable goods when you return home, although Customs also accepts credit cards.

Use your own judgment concerning how much **cash** you should carry with you. Contrary to some fearful ads, cash is awfully nice to have in moderate amounts to supplement your traveler's checks and credit cards. Several US$1 bills are handy for tips when you first arrive. Consider carrying an "emergency cash reserve" primarily in $50 and $100 denominations, but also a few $20's. Cash can be used instead of your larger denomination traveler's checks when you want to change a small amount of money to local currency.

USE CREDIT CARDS WISELY

Credit cards can be a shopper's blessing if used in the right manner. They are your tickets to serendipity, convenience, good exchange rates, and a useful form of insurance. Widely accepted throughout France, they enable you to draw on credit reserves for purchasing many wonderful items you did not anticipate finding when you initially planned your adventure. In addition to being convenient, you usually will get good exchange rates once the local currency amount appearing on your credit slip is converted by the bank at the official rate into your home currency. Credit cards also allow you to float your expenses into the following month or two without paying interest charges and may even add miles to your frequent flyer account. Most important, should you have a problem with a purchase, your credit card company may assist you in recovering your money and returning the goods. Once you discover your problem, contact the credit card company with your complaint and refuse to pay the amount while the matter is in dispute.

❑ Use credit cards to pay for hotels and restaurants and for major purchases.

❑ Carry one or two bank cards and an American Express card.

❑ Consider requesting a higher credit limit on your bank cards.

❑ Take plenty of $50 and $100 traveler's checks.

❑ Keep one personal check aside to pay Customs should you have dutiable goods when you return home.

❑ Carry an "emergency cash reserve" primarily in $50 and $100 denominations.

❑ Keep a good record of all charges in local currency— and at official exchange rates.

Although your credit card company is not obligated to do so, many times they will assist you in resolving a problem. Businesses accepting these cards must maintain a certain standard of honesty and integrity. In this sense, credit cards may be an excellent and inexpensive form of insurance against possible fraud and damaged goods when shopping abroad. If you rely only on cash or traveler's checks, you have no such institutional recourse for recovering your money.

A few other tips on the use and abuse of credit cards may be useful in planning your trip. Use your credit cards for the things that will cost you the same amount no matter how you pay, such as lodging and meals in the better hotels and restaurants or purchases in most department stores. Consider requesting a higher credit limit on your bank cards if you think you will be charging more than your current limit allows.

Be extremely careful with your credit cards. Keep a good record of all charges in French francs—and at official exchange rates—so you don't have any surprises once you return home! Remember, when the French write "1" on your credit card slip, it looks like a "7". Remember this when you check your credit card slip against your credit card bill.

SECURE YOUR VALUABLES

Be sure to keep your traveler's checks, credit cards, and cash in a safe place along with your travel documents and other valuables. Consider wearing a money belt or a similar safety cache. While the money belt may be the safest approach, the typical 4" x 8" nylon belts can be uncomfortable in hot and humid weather. Women may want to make a money pouch which can fasten inside their clothing. Another approach for women is to carry money and documents in a leather shoulder bag which should be kept with you at all times, however inconvenient, even when passing through buffet lines. Choose a purse with a strap long enough to sling around your neck bandolier style. Secure the purse with a strong grip and always keep it between you and the person accompanying you. Purse snatchers can quickly ruin your vacation if you are not careful.

Men should carry their wallet in a front pocket. If you keep it in a rear pocket, as you may do at home, you invite pickpockets to demonstrate their varied talents in relieving you of your money, and possibly venting your trousers in the process. If your front pocket is an uncomfortable location, you probably need to clean out your wallet so it will fit better.

You may also want to use the free hotel safety deposit boxes for your cash and other valuables. If one is not provided in your room, ask the cashier to assign you a private box in their vault. Under no circumstances should you leave your money and valuables unattended in your hotel room, at restaurant tables, or in dressing rooms. Remember, there are many talented and highly motivated thieves who prey upon what they see as unsuspecting rich tourists. You may want to leave your expensive jewelry at home so as not to be as likely a target of theft. If you get robbed, chances are it will be in part your own fault, because you invited someone to take advantage of your weaknesses by not being more cautious in securing your valuables. In our many years of traveling we have not been robbed. But we try to be careful not to encourage someone to take advantage of us. We know people who have had problems, but invariably they were easy and predictable targets, because they failed to take elementary precautions against thieves.

TAKE KEY SHOPPING INFORMATION

Depending on what you plan to buy, you should take all the necessary information you need to make informed shopping decisions. After all, you don't want to end up purchasing a Hermes scarf in Paris for US$300 and then discover you can get the same item back home for US$200, or even purchase it on your flight back home for only US$180! Put this information in a separate envelope. If you are looking for home furnishings, along with your "wish list" you should include room measurements to help you determine if particular items will fit into your home. You might take photographs with you of particular rooms you hope to furnish. Be sure to include measurements of dining tables and beds just in case you find some wonderful table linens and bedspreads in France.

❑ Take with you measurements and photographs of rooms that could become candidates for home decorative items.

❑ Be sure to take information on any particular clothes, accessories, or jewelry (sizes, colors, comparative prices) you with to look for or have made when in France.

❑ Do comparative shopping before arriving in France.

If you plan to shop for clothes, your homework should include taking an inventory of your closets and identifying particular colors, fabrics, and designs you wish to acquire to complement and enlarge your present wardrobe. Keep in mind that good quality clothes and accessories in France can be very expensive. But you will most likely be buying top quality designer-label clothes, purses, and belts which are also very expensive back home. If you are from the U.S., you should look at comparable selections found at the top department stores, such as Saks Fifth Avenue, Neiman Marcus, Macy's, and Nordstrom. This means visiting their designer-label and couture sections for comparable quality and prices.

DO COMPARATIVE SHOPPING

You should do comparison shopping before you leave home. Once you arrive in France, the only comparisons you can make are between various shops you encounter in Paris and the French Riviera. You'll never know if you are getting a good deal unless you have done your homework before hand.

Unless you know the comparable value of goods back home, you won't recognize a bargain when it stares you in the face. Since few things are bargains in France, chances are you will be looking for unique items that are not readily available elsewhere. This is especially true in the cases of clothes, accessories, and jewelry. French design and styling is unique, and you will quickly recognize it once you begin surveying shops in France. Take, for example, women's belts. The French are especially good at designing chic leather belts that nicely accessorize outfits. Chances are you won't find the large variety of such belts back home because they are uniquely French. They also are very expensive, ranging from US$80 to US$300 each. But you many quickly fall in love with such belts and decide to spend the money on something you simply can't get back home and for something you decided you really can't live without. Or better yet, visit some of the shops selling the prior seasons couture clothing and accessories at 40-60% discount. So much for comparative shopping! At least you know you can't find such items back home at any price.

The first step in doing comparative shopping is determining exactly what you want and need. Make lists. As you compile your list, spend some time "window" shopping in the local stores, examining catalogs, and telephoning for information.

KEEP TRACK OF RECEIPTS

It's important to keep track of all of your purchases for making an accurate Customs declaration. Since it's so easy to misplace receipts, you might want to organize your receipts using a form similar to the example on page 40. Staple a sheet or two of notebook or accountant's paper to the front of a large manila envelope and number down the left side of the page. Draw one or two vertical columns down the right side. Each evening sort through that day's purchases, write a description including style and color of the purchase on the accompanying receipt, and enter that item on your receipt record. Record the receipt so later you'll know exactly which item belongs to the receipt. Put the receipts in the manila envelope and pack the purchases

Customs Declaration Record Form

	RECEIPT #	ITEM	PRICE (Francs)	PRICE (US$)
1.	1433613	YSL belt	576	$120.00
2.				
3.				
4.				

Put the receipts in the manila envelope and pack the purchases away. If you're missing a receipt, make a note of it beside the appropriate entry.

PACK RIGHT FOR FRANCE

Packing is one of the great travel challenges for many people. Trying to get everything you think you need into one or two bags can be frustrating, especially if you are visiting two or more countries which have different climates. You'll either take too much, and carry more than is necessary, or you'll take too little, thinking you'll buy what you need there, only to find that just the right items are ever so elusive.

We've learned over the years to err on the side of taking too little. If we start with less, we'll have room for more. Our ultimate goal is to make do with three changes of very versatile outfits, loosely packed into the lightest and largest carry-on bag the airlines will allow. Good hotels provide efficient laundry and dry-cleaning services, and you can always hand wash your "undies" yourself if you choose. Since inexpensive luggage is readily available (try the markets or the vendors in front of department stores), there's really no need to take extra luggage for purchases you may make along the way. However, if you know you're going to buy a lot, you might decide to take a second empty suitcase with you. We have done this by nesting one inside the other with our trip clothing packed in the inside piece of luggage as well as by stuffing a second piece of luggage with bubble wrap and other packing materials we will need to protect our purchases. While softsided luggage is lighter weight, it may not provide as much protection as a good hardsided piece for either your clothing or your shopping treasures.

Your goal should be to avoid lugging extensive wardrobe, cosmetics, library, and household goods around the world! Why not adopt our guiding principle for packing: "When in doubt, leave it out."

Above all, you want to return home loaded down with wonderful new purchases without paying extra weight charges. Hence, pack for the future rather than load yourself down with the past.

TAKE COMFORTABLE SHOES

Paris is definitely a walking city which requires good walking shoes to navigate many miles of very hard concrete sidewalks. Please don't buy new shoes for your trip unless you have several weeks to break them in. We prefer to clean up and polish two very comfortable pair of shoes which we've worn for a year or more.

We recommend taking at least one pair of comfortable walking shoes and one pair of dress shoes. Several major manufacturers of sport shoes make attractive shoes designed just for walking. Take only essential shoes which will coordinate with all of your outfits.

PART II

Paris

Welcome to Paris

Paris is everything you ever dreamt of and much much more. Truly one of the world's most beautiful, romantic, and livable cities, Paris is filled with exciting sights, interesting people, intriguing places, and plenty of things to see, do, and eat. The accolades seem to go on and on for this unique city of lights, life, and livability. It seems to be everyone's favorite first or second city for enjoying life's many treasures and pleasures.

If you enjoy big cities, you'll love this one. It literally defies most "big city" stereotypes. For many seasoned travelers and tested urban dwellers, this is what a truly great city should be. Just bring a sense of adventure, and lots of money! Even the locals find Paris to be excessively expensive. While it's hard to get bored here, it's easy to exceed your budget on all kinds of unexpected expenses. Indeed, you can quickly go broke in Paris on oh-so-wonderful shopping treasures, dining pleasures, and accommodations. It's a very expensive city if you seek the best of the best in hotels, restaurants, and shopping.

But there are a lot of other things to see and do here that are free or relatively inexpensive. In fact, some of the best things in Paris are free or almost free. The cheapest pleasure of all is just walking the streets. And you can even find haute couture bargain shopping on the streets of Paris.

GETTING TO KNOW YOU

If this is your first visit to Paris, you need to hit the ground running because there is much to see and do here. You don't want to waste your time trying to figure out where you are and where you need to go. Here are some basic geographic tips that should help speed up the process of getting to know Paris.

Paris is structured like no other city we have ever encountered. It's a combination of French art, grandeur, and bureaucracy all rolled up into one marvelous entity. Best of all, this unique structure makes perfect sense when it comes to understanding maps, finding addresses, and navigating Paris' many streets, Métro lines, districts, and neighborhoods.

Over 10 million people live within the confines of this 432 square mile city. Dissected by the charming yet working Seine River, the city is conveniently divided into the Right Bank (north) and the Left Bank (south). These two sides are, in turn, stitched together by 32 bridges, 15 of which center on the city's two famous islands, Ile de la Cité and Ile St-Louis, where Paris began several centuries ago.

Each bank has its own distinctive character. Within a day or two you will probably identify yourself as either a Left Bank or a Right Bank person.

We often think we're Left Bank people, but we've also become Right Bank people the more we explore both sides of the Seine River.

The good news is that the treasures and pleasures of Paris are widely distributed throughout both the Left and Right Banks. The bad news may be your sore feet—you'll be doing an incredible amount of walking. Make sure you have a comfortable pair of walking shoes because you'll need them every day.

- ❑ Paris is a very expensive city if you seek the best of the best in hotels, restaurants, and shopping.

- ❑ Some of the best things in Paris are free or almost free.

- ❑ Paris is structured like no other city—a combination of French art, grandeur, and bureaucracy all rolled up into one marvelous entity.

- ❑ The treasures and pleasures of Paris are widely distributed throughout both the Left and Right Banks.

- ❑ The Left Bank is Paris' traditional educational, intellectual, and political center. Shopping here too!

- ❑ The Right Bank is where you will discover Paris' famous streets, monuments, museums, hotels, restaurants, and shopping areas.

THE LEFT BANK

The appealing Left Bank is Paris' traditional educational, intellectual, and political center. Here you find the famous and festive Latin Quarter best symbolized in the area surrounding

St-Germain-des-Prés with its famous outdoor cafés, students, bookstores, art shops, narrow streets as well as the imposing Pantheon, the popular Orsay Museum (Musée d'Orsay), the grand Eiffel Tower, and the powerful Invalides with its adjacent Army Museum and Dome Church (Napoleon's tomb). For many people, the Left Bank is the soul of Paris, if not France. This is a fun, people-oriented area where you will want to just leisurely wander, people watch, visit a few museums and monuments, and shop for chic clothes, attractive jewelry, and unique arts, antiques, and crafts. You may quickly find yourself drawn to its many sidewalk cafés and ethnic restaurants. Many visitors prefer staying at the less expensive and often charming hotels found throughout major sections of the Left Bank. We usually stay and dine here as well as do some of our major shopping in this area.

THE RIGHT BANK

The Right Bank also has a very different character. Much of what symbolizes France is found in this area. Crossing the great divide, the Seine River, you enter into the heart of Paris. Here's where you will discover Paris' famous streets, monuments, museums, hotels, restaurants, and shopping areas. Aside from the Left Bank's Eiffel Tower, the most powerful symbol of Paris is found along the Right Bank's main boulevard, the famous Champs-Élysées which connects the Arc de Triomphe to the Place de la Concorde. Rich in history and architecture, the Right Bank also boasts the world-famous Louvre Museum, George Pompidou Centre, Palais Royal, Place Vendôme, Opera-Garnier, Sacré-Cœur Basilica, and Ritz Hotel. Here's where you will find the major department stores (Printemps, Galeries Lafayette), chic shops (also rue du Faubourg-St-Honoré and av. Matignon), jewelers (at Place Vendôme), and Paris' famous flea market and antique stalls at Porte de Clignancourt (called Marché des Puces de Paris-Saint Ouen). You can literally overdose on the many museums and shops found within only a few minutes walk of crossing the river and entering the Right Bank.

THE TWO ISLANDS

Between these two banks lie Paris' two famous islands which remain rich with history and imposing historical monuments: Notre-Dame Cathedral, Saint-Chapelle, Conciergerie, and the Palais de Justice. Administratively part of a Right Bank district (the 4th arrondissement), the islands have their own distinct

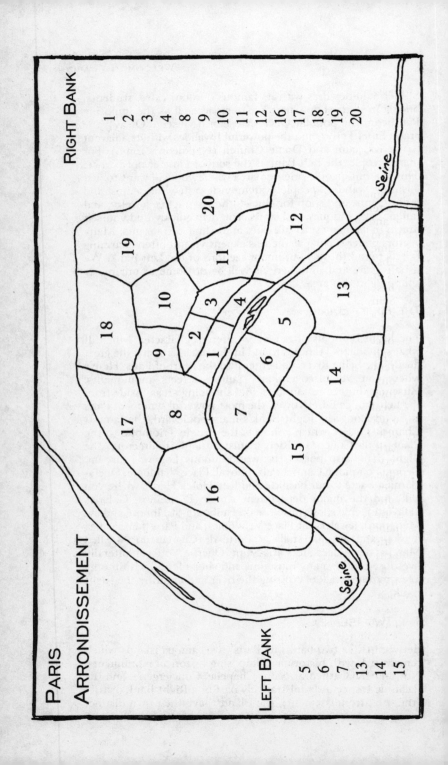

character separate from both the Left and Right Banks. On a nice day, this is one of the most charming areas of Paris to just stroll, watch people, have a picnic, and enjoy the sights of the river and city.

A CITY OF CLEAN VILLAGES

What surprises many first-time visitors to Paris is its small town character wrapped into such a sprawling metropolitan area. A large and bustling, yet compact, metropolis distinctive for its 18th and 19th century architecture and monuments, Paris is noted for its relative absence of high-rise buildings and for its grand boulevards, gardens, park benches, narrow streets, and the charming Seine River. In fact, administratively Paris is organized as a series of villages, each with its own mayor, council, police force, post offices, and taxing and spending authority that delivers different levels of service. The poor sections of the city, for example, tend to provide fewer quality services than the wealthier parts of the city, especially when it comes to street and sidewalk cleaning services.

❑ Paris is organized as a series of villages, each with its own mayor, council, police force, post offices, and taxing and spending authority.

❑ Paris is an unusually clean city with one of every 8 municipal employees deployed as street cleaners.

❑ With trash picked up daily and mail delivered three times a day, Parisians expect a certain quality of life that is reflected in their high taxes and costly standard of living.

❑ The first thing you need to understand is the structure and character of Paris' 20 *arrondissements* (municipal wards).

Paris is an unusually clean city. One of every eight municipal employees, for example, is deployed as part of an army of street cleaners. Dressed in bright green uniforms, and armed with green brooms or vacuum-mounted motorbikes to eliminate litter, trash, and animal droppings, these workers are in charge of maintaining Paris' 800 miles of streets.

Parisians enjoy of level of city services unparalleled for most large cities. With trash picked up daily and mail delivered three times a day, Parisians expect a certain quality of urban life—much of it aimed at maintaining the glory and grandeur of Paris —which is clearly reflected in their high taxes and cost of living. Streets are well petrolled, and crime is much lower here than in comparable cities in the U.S. It's relatively safe to walk streets alone at night in many areas of the city.

The political and administrative organization of Paris is clearly reflected in how individuals orient themselves to the city, be it via a map, riding the underground Métro, or just walking the streets. Paris is divided into distinct areas, or 20 *arrondissements* (municipal wards), each with its own boundaries and political and administrative organization. If you want to efficiently and effectively navigate the streets of Paris, you need to first understand as well as approach the city by means of this key organizational principle. If not, you may quickly become confused and lost as place names and addresses make little sense to you.

So, the first thing you need to do is to understand the structure and character of these arrondissements. As you plan to visit various places in Paris, you'll be venturing into the villages of this "mother" of all cities.

THE 20 VILLAGES CALLED "PARIS"

You need to approach Paris like everyone else does—think of the city as being divided into 20 different areas or arrondissements. These are the "villages" of Paris with their own leadership, bureaucracy, and special set of municipal challenges. You especially need to understand this structure because most addresses and directions are usually given in these terms.

Each arrondissement, abbreviated as "arr.", is numbered and has its own distinctive character. While they are by no means of equal interest to visitors, let's quickly survey the 20 and then focus on the ones that yield Paris' best treasures and pleasures.

❑ **1st Arrondissement:** Right Bank. A *"must visit again and again"* area. This is one of Paris' best known areas and one of the first and last stops for many visitors. Bounded on the south by the Seine River, the west by Place de la Concorde, the east by Boulevard de Sebastopol, and the north by rue Etienne Marcel, this area encompasses the popular museum, the **Louvre**; the beautiful gardens of **Jardin des Tulieries**; the elegant **Place Vendôme** surrounded by fabulous jewelry stores and the **Ritz Hotel**; the **Palais Royal**; the elegant designer shops lining **Rue St. Honoré** and **Rue de Rivoli**; and the popular but somewhat confusing shopping, entertainment, and culture complex called the **Forum Les Halles**. Except for the more middle-class and sometimes seedy Forum Les Halles (Paris' red light district of prostitutes and peep shows is located around the corner along Rue St. Denis), this area shouts history, wealth, elegance, and grand architecture. You can spend hours, indeed days, exploring the many treasures and pleasures found throughout this area. Visit a few exquisite jewelry shops in and around the magnificent Place Vendôme, such as the Italian jeweler Giamaria Buccellati or Boucheron, and you'll quickly recognize what quality is all about. Unfortunately, you'll probably discover you didn't bring enough money with you to Paris! Well, there's always another time for Paris, and these shops will most likely continue as long-term Parisian institutions. Just bring more money the next time!

❑ **2nd Arrondissement:** Right Bank. Immediately north of the 1st arrondissement, this area houses Paris' famous stock exchange, **Bourse des Valeurs** (4 Place de la Bourse). You can join a free guided tour given twice each afternoon and see French capitalism working at its most chaotic pace. The eastern section of this area (Sentier) is Paris' wholesale garment district. You also will find one of Paris' most famous bars here—Willi's Wine Bar (13 Rue des Petits-Champs). Overall, there is not much of interest in this area compared to other nearby arrondissements.

❑ **3rd Arrondissement:** Right Bank. Rich in history and once (17th century) Paris' most elegant district, this somewhat seedy area is once again going through a transformation. Located directly east of the 2nd arrondissement, part of the area is known as the **Marias** (the marsh or swamp) Along **Temple Street** (R. Vieille du Temple) you will find several clothing wholesalers and factory outlets offering discounted clothes and accessories. Nothing shouts quality or speaks to us as worth another trip up this somewhat depressing street. The best thing going in this district is the **Picasso Museum** (Musée Picasso) housed at the Hôtel Salé (5 Rue de Thorigny). This fine collection of 203 paintings, 1,500 drawings, and 30 sketchbooks was "given" to the city in exchange for "forgiving" horrendous taxes owed by the Picasso estate— a wonderful example of doing good by paying up!

❑ **4th Arrondissement:** Right Bank. This is another one of those *"must visit"* areas of Paris. Bordered on the south by the Seine River and to the east by a canal and the Bastille, this area is rich in history and architecture. It is one of the most pleasant areas to walk. It includes the two islands from which Paris originated, the touristy Ile de la Cité and the more residential Ile St-Louis. Here you can visit such classic medieval sites as the church and flying buttresses of **Notre-Dame Cathedral**; the two stained glass chapels of the impressive **Sainte-Chapelle**, and the **Conciergerie** where Marie Antoinette spent her final days before loosing her head at the guillotine. But there's much more to this district. You'll want to cross several of the 15 bridges linking the islands to the Right Bank, walk Rue Saint-Paul, visit the antique shops at the **Village Saint-Paul**, and continue on to **Place Des Vesges**, the oldest and unquestionably the most beautiful and architecturally contiguous residential and commercial squares in Paris. Major streets such as **Rue de Rivoli** and **Rue des Francs Bourguois** are lined with shops offering everything from clothes to antiques. If you like museums and you're into modern art (post-1905) and unusual exhibits, visit the **George Pompidou Centre**, home of the National Museum of Modern Art as well as art libraries and an industrial design center. You can't miss it—its exterior looks like a ugly boiler system (some call it art, but others know better). Now the third most popular tourist attraction in Paris, the Centre continues to be controversial, and ugly.

- ❑ The 1st arrondissement shouts history, wealth, elegance, and grand architecture.

- ❑ The Picasso Museum in the 3rd arrondissement is a wonderful example of doing good by paying up!

- ❑ Now the third most popular tourist attraction, the George Pompidou Centre in the 4th arrondissement continues to be controversial, and ugly.

- ❑ The 6th arrondissement is famous for its students, artists, musicians, actors, intellectuals, and tourists in search of the "real" Paris.

- ❑ The Musée d'Orsay (7th arrondissement) is the favorite museum for those who prefer 19th century French art to the offerings of the Louvre (pre-19th century) and the George Pompidou Centre (20th century).

- ❑ **5th Arrondissement:** Left Bank. Located immediately south of the Isle de la Cité and Isle St. Louis and east of Boulevard St-Michel, this is Paris' famous Latin Quarter (Quartier Latin) of bohemian fame, revolutionary fervor, political unrest, and ethnic diversity. In 1871 the Paris Commune operated from this area, as did the student uprisings of May 1968. A very old and constantly changing section of Paris, this is where the University of Paris is located along with the **Sorbonne** and other related educational institutions. More than just a college town within a city, the Latin Quarter is extremely rich in history and celebrities, the stomping grounds of many leading intellectuals and writers, from Descartes to Hemingway. The student, intellectual, and artistic atmosphere of this area is reflected in the numerous bookstores, cafés, movie theaters, night clubs, and publishing houses that dot this area, especially along Boulevard St-Michel. A very ethnically diverse area, due to recent immigrants moving into this area, expect to find numerous Vietnamese, Chinese, Greek, Moroccan, and American Tex-Mex restaurants alongside some of Paris' best restaurants (La Tour d'Argent), clothing stores, fine antique, designer/decorative, and ethnographic arts and crafts shops. The famous and imposing **Panthéon**, noted for housing the remains of such luminaries as Voltaire, Rousseau, Victor Hugo, Emile Zola, and Jean Moulin, lies at the heart of this district. You'll also find some of Paris' most interesting churches here—**St-Séverin**, **St-Julien-le-Pauvre**, and **St-Etienne-du-Mont**—as well as the **Musée de Cluny** with its terrific collection of medieval art. The eastern section of this district is more residential and upscale but it also includes such noted places as the Arab Institute (**Institut du Monde Arabe**), a zoo (**Ménagerie**), the Old Roman Arena (**Arènes de Lutèce**), and the Natural History Museum (**Muséum National d'Histoire Naturelle**).

❑ **6th Arrondissement:** Left Bank. This is another one of those *"must visit"* sections of Paris, a district with real character and yielding a bounty of treasures and pleasures. Bounded in the north by the Seine River, the east by Boulevard St-Michel, the south by Boulevard du Montparnasse, and the west by Rue de Sévres and R. Des Saints Pères, this vibrant and diverse district is famous for its students, artists, musicians, actors, intellectuals, and tourists in search of the "real" Paris. This is the center for Paris' famous fine arts school, the Ecole Nationale Supérieure des Beaux-Arts. During the past five decades this area has become a major intellectual center in Paris. Famous writers, artists, actors, musicians, philosophers, and a host of wannabes have hung out in the many cafés, bars, brasseries, and nightspots that have made this area so famous. Indeed, Les Deux Magots, Café de Flore, and Brasserie Lipp, across from St-Germain-des-Prés, still draw the crowds. Indeed, among the many famous patrons of these and other cafés, bars, restaurants, and jazz clubs—where supposedly ideas germinated and relationships solidified—have been such American writers as Ernest Hemingway and F. Scott Fitzgerald, Russian revolutionaries Lenin and Trotsky, Surrealists Salvador Dali and Jean Cocteau, and philosophers Jean-Paul Sartre and Albert Camus. The most famous streets here are Boulevard Saint Germain and Boulevard du Montparnasse, which are lined with outdoor cafés, restaurants, bookstores, and clothing stores. The most famous area within this district centers on **St-Germain-des-Prés**, the oldest church in Paris. You'll enjoy exploring the many narrow streets with their small hotels, restaurants, and shops that give this area such a unique character. Several narrow streets near St-Germain-des-Prés yield some of Paris' best shops for clothes, accessories, arts, and antiques. Indeed you can easily spend two to three days shopping this delightful area. Some of the best shopping in all of Paris for clothes and accessories is found just south of Boulevard Saint Germain along such streets as Rue Bonaparte, Rue de Rennes, Rue du Dragon, Rue du Cherche Midi, R. De Grenelle, and R. De Sevres. For arts and antiques, head north of Boulevard Saint Germain, just behind St-Germain-des-Prés, to Rue de Seine, R. Des Beaux Arts, and Rue Bonaparte. Other drawing cards in this district include **Musée Eugène Delacroix**, **Palais Abbatial**, and the **Luxembourg Gardens**. This district remains one of our very favorite in all of Paris. It's also our first choice for accommodations.

❑ **7th Arrondissement:** Left Bank. Here's another *"must visit"* area; we're sure you will make this district one of your first stops in Paris. After all, it's the center for three of Paris' major tourist attractions—the Eiffel Tower, d'Orsay Museum, and Invalides. Located directly east of the 6th arrondissement, this district is bounded on the north by the Seine River, on the east by R. Des Saints Pères, on the southwest by Avenue de Suffren, and in the southeast by Rue de Sèvres. If there is one symbol of Paris and France, it's the **Eiffel Tower**. Do it. You'll get a magnificent view of the city from the top and learn a little bit about the history of both the building of the Eiffel Tower and the evolution of Paris. If you don't mind paying US$140 per person for dinner, dine at one of Paris' best restaurants, Jules Verne, which is located on the first level of the Eiffel Tower and gives you a marvelous view of the "city of lights" at night. Be sure to make reservations far in advance (two weeks or more) since the restaurant tends to be fully booked. The **Musée d'Orsay**, located in a beautiful converted train station overlooking the Seine River, is one of France's very best museums. It's the favorite museum of many visitors who prefer 19th century French art to the offerings of the Louvre (pre-19th century) and the George Pompidou Centre (20th century). You also should visit **Invalides** with its Arms Museum (Musée de l'Armée) and Dôme Church. The museum is one of Paris's best, a true tour de force on French military history. The Dôme Church is where Napolean is interned along with other famous French military leaders, such as Vauban and Marshal Foch, each with their own uniquely designed sarcophaguses. This is one of the world's most beautiful and memorable crypts—a real tribute to 17th century French architecture and to the glory of France's great, and often controversial, military leaders. This area also yields some excellent shopping, especially along Rue de Grenelle, Boulevard Raspall, Rue de Babylone, Boulevard Saint Germain, and Rue de Varenne.

❑ **8th Arrondissement:** Right Bank. This is another *"must visit"* district brimming with all kinds of treasures and pleasures. Bounded on the south by the Seine River, on the east by Rue Royale and Rue d'Amsterdam, on the north by Boulevard de Courcellés and Boulevard des Batignolles, and on the west by Avenue Marceau and the Arc de Triomphe, this district offers some of Paris' finest monuments, boulevards, squares, buildings, restaurants, hotels, shops, and entertainment. This also is one of the most touristed areas of Paris. Many first-time visitors head directly to the grand **Avenue des Champs Elysées**, France's most famous boulevard, and the **Arc de Triomphe**, a symbol of Paris on par with the Eiffel Tower. Take the elevator to the top of the Arc and you'll be rewarded with a panoramic view of the city and the twelve streets that radiate from the Arc. Within a block of the Arc, along with main avenue, is the local tourist office which dispenses literature and information on Paris. The Avenue is lined with shops, small shopping arcades, cafés, restaurants, fast-food outlets, and theaters, few of any particular note. Locals and returning visitors lament the "declining" nature of this famous street, with the invasion of McDonald's and now Planet Hollywood. Although the city has attempted to revive this area to its former grandness, with wider sidewalks and more trees, you'll have to explore nearby streets to discover the real treasures and pleasures of this area. Walk to the end of Champs-Elysées and you come to **Place de la Concorde**, one of the most important squares in 19th century French history, its

3,300 year old Obelisk of Luxor. Nearby is the architecturally magnificent glass-domed **Grand Palais** as well as the **Petit Palais, Madeleine,** and the **Palais de l'Élysée.** The streets in this district yield Paris' top quality shopping, rivaling anything Milan, London, New York, or Rodeo Drive in Hollywood have to offer. Just stroll down the exclusive **Rue du Faubourg St. Honoré** or **Avenue Montaigne** and you'll know you've just encountered the world's top haute couture and designer shops. The selections and quality are fabulous but the prices may seem astronomical. In some shops the cheapest blouses start at US$700! And the signature Hermès scarves start at US$280. You'll also find haute couture and designer discount shops offering 30-60% off last season's designs, many of which appeared on the catwalks of fashion shows. Some of Paris' finest art and antique shops are found along Avenue Matignon and a few adjacent streets. The whole area boasts great restaurants (Taillevent), hotels (The Crillon), and nightclubs (Crazy Horse Saloon). This is one of the most intense yet pleasant areas of Paris to walk, window shop, and immerse yourself in French history and architecture. This is the one area you can easily blow your budget on irresistable French fashions accessories, art, and antiques.

❑ **9th Arrondissement:** Right Bank. Located just north of the 2nd arrondissement, bounded in the south by Boulevard Haussmann and Boulevard des Italiens, on the west by Rue d'Amsterdam, on the east by Rue Poissonniere, and on the north by Rue de Clichy and Boulevard de Rochechouart, the area is best noted for the **Opéra Garnier** (Paris Opera House) and Paris' two major department stores, **Galeries Lafayette** and **Printemps,** located adjacent to each other on Boulevard Haussmann; **Marks & Spencer** is located just across the street. The famous **Folies Bergère** is also located here as is Paris' most incredible food shop, **Fauchon.** You'll find numerous shops in this area, including Paris' best English language bookstore, **Brentano's** (37, Avenue de l'Opéra), along with most major airline offices and banks. The area also boasts chic shops in the Place de l'Opera and the popular **Café de la Paix** and **Harry's Bar.** Many noted writers, actors, singers, and artists have passed through this area.

❑ **10th Arrondissement:** Right Bank. Located directly east of the 9th arrondissement and north of the 3rd arrondissement, this area is of little interest to most visitors. Aside from two train stations (Gare du Nord and Gare de L'Est) and a few good restaurants, this area has a disproportionate number of run down commercial buildings and porno shops.

❑ **11th Arrondissement:** Right Bank. Located east of the 3rd arrondissement, there is little here of interest to visitors. This is one of the poorer and more run down sections of Paris. The southwest corner of this area shares the **Place de la Bastille** and **Opéra de Paris Bastille** with the 12th arrondissement, an area experiencing redevelopment.

❑ **12th Arrondissement:** Right Bank. Located south of the 11th arrondissement, this area is undergoing urban renewal with new shops, restaurants, and housing complexes. Much of this new development starts at the **Opéra de la Bastille** and run several blocks southeast along Avenue Daumesnil. A new shopping complex, **Galerie Daumesnil**, has just opened in this area. An interesting Asian, African, and Oceanic art museum, the **Musée des Arts Africains et Océaniens** (293 Avenue Daumesnil), is found in the southeast section of this area. This is actually France's old colonial museum. Just beyond the museum, to the east, is one of Paris' largest and most popular parks, the **Bois de Vincennes**, with its zoos, museums, lakes, and lovely gardens. One of the major train stations, Gare de Lyon, also is located here.

❑ Take the elevator to the top of the Arc de Triomphe and you'll be rewarded with a panoramic view of the city and the twelve streets radiating from the Arc.

❑ Although the city has tried to revive the Champs Elysées to its former grandness, with wider sidewalks and more trees, you'll have to explore nearby streets to discover the real treasures and pleasures of this area.

❑ The 8th arrondissement is the one area you can easily blow your budget on irresistable French fashions, accessories, art, and antiques.

❑ The Basilica of Sacré-Cœur and the Marché aux Puces de Clignancourt (flea market) in the 18th arrondissement should be on your "Top 10" list of things to see and do in Paris.

❑ **13th Arrondissement:** Left Bank. Located in the southeast corner of the city along the Seine River, this district has little to offer visitors other than **La Manufacture des Gobelins** (42 Ave des Gobelins), the famous tapestry factories dating from the 17th century which originally supplied tapestries for the Palace of Versailles; today its world-famous weavers continue to use traditional weaving techniques in producing tapestries using the modern designs of Picasso, Miró, and Matisse. You can tour the factories from 2-3pm, Tuesday through Thursday. This experience alone may make a trip to this district worth while.

❑ **14th Arrondissement:** Left Bank. Located just south of the 5th and 6th arrondissements, this area is famous for its **literary cafés** (La Coupole, La Rotonde, Le Select, and La Dôme) at the corner of Boulevard du Montparnasse and Boulevard Raspail. These were the favorite haunts of such famous figures as Ernest Hemingway, Scott Fitzgerald, Henry Miller, Josephine Baker, James Joyce, Matisse, Jean-Paul Sartre, and Roman Polanski. Toward the southern section of this district, along **Rue d'Alésia**, you'll find numerous factory outlet shops selling discounted clothing and accessories. However, the quality and prices are not sufficient to warrant a special trip here—unless you have lots of time to kill in Paris!

❑ **15th Arrondissement:** Left Bank. Located south of the Eiffel Tower (7th arrondissement), this is one of Paris' wealthiest areas and home to many of its politicians. But you will find few attractions to warrant venturing very far into this district, which is the largest of any district in Paris. The most noteworthy places to visit are the antique shops at the **Village Suisse** (Avenue de Suffren, which is adjacent to the Eiffel Tower) and the **Institut Pasteur** (25 Rue du Docteur Roux), France's leading medical research center and the place where HIV virus was discovered in 1983.

❑ **16th Arrondissement:** Right Bank. Located opposite the Eiffel Tower on the western side of the city, this is one of Paris' weathier areas. Various times during its history this areas has been home to Benjamin Franklin, Prince Rainier of Monaco, the Shah of Iran, and Charles Debussy. This area is noted for its numerous museums, galleries, gardens, architecture, boulevards, and shop. Museum goers will enjoy the **Musée de Balzac, Musée Guimet** (Asian art), **Musée Arménien, Musée d'Art Moderne de la Ville de Paris, Musée de la Mode et du Costume Palais Galliera, Musée de la Contrefaçon, Musée de Radio-France,** and **Musée National d'Ennery.** Others will enjoy the beautiful **Jardin du Trocadéro** (gardens) and the **Cimetière de Passy**. The monumental and colonnaded **Palais de Chaillot**, with its four museums, theater, Cinémathèque, and Trocadéro fountains, dominates the entrance into this area via the Eiffel Tower. One of the best shopping streets in Paris is also located here, the avenue Victor Hugo, with its upscale designer shops. Paris' largest boulevard also is found here, Avenue Foch.

❑ **17th Arrondissement:** Right Bank. Located north of the 8th arrondissement and west of the 18th arrondissement, this is essentially a conservative bourgeois residential area of little interest to most visitors. The southwestern section of this district borders the **Arc de Triomphe** and includes the **Palais des Congrès de Paris**. The area also includes some of Paris' best restaurants (Guy Savoy and Michel Rostang).

❑ **18th Arrondissement:** Right Bank. Located in the far northern section of the city, north of both the 9th and 10th arrondissement, and east of the 17th and west of the 19th, this is one of Paris' most famous historical districts that remains popular today. A mixed area for treasures and pleasures, it's still well worth a visit. The steep hill area of Montmartre, a somewhat exhausting climb to the top, lies at the center of this district and yields its major attractions. Montmartre used to be the home of Renoir and Toulouse-Lautrec, and favorite haunt for many of Paris' famous artists, writers, and poets who frequented the area's many popular cabarets, bordellos, bars, and restaurants. The area has long had a reputation for sleaze alongside many worthwhile treasures. Prostitutes still ply their trade in Place Blanche. Today, parts of this area still have a bohemian character but much of it is somewhat rundown with a combination of souvenir shops, restaurants, bars, and sidewalk vendors, few of any particular note worth visiting. This is still home for the famous **Moulin Rouge** (82 Blvd. De Clichy) and the **Place du Tertre**, the popular old village square noted for its portrait artists (watch the prices and con artists!), colorful restaurants, souvenir shops, and the highest point in Paris. It includes a few of Paris' major attractions which make this a *"must visit"* area: **Basilica of Sacré-Cœur** (great view of the city from the top), **Marché aux Puces de Clignancourt** (Paris' biggest and best flea market loaded with antique treasures—open Saturday, Sunday and Monday), and several museums and galleries (**Espace**

Montremartre Salvador Dali, Musée de Montmartre, Musée d'Art Naïf Max Fourny, Musée de l'Art Juif). Indeed, Sacré-Cœur and the flea market should be on your "Top 10" list of things to see and do in Paris.

❑ **19th Arrondissement:** Right Bank. Located immediately east of the 18th arrondissement and north of the 20th arrondisement, this northeast district is one of Paris' most ethnically diverse areas, attracting immigrants from many of France's former colonies. It is primarily residential and relatively poor. Offering few attractions, it is home for the impressive **Cité des Sciences et de l'Industrie** (science and industry museum) and the **Parc des Buttes Chaumont** (a popular park for children, complete with donkey rides and puppet shows).

❑ **20th Arrondissement:** Right Bank. Located south of the 19th arrondisement, east of the 11th arrondisement, and north of the 12th arrondisement, this is another ethnically diverse (Muslims, Jews, and North Africans) and relatively poor area offering few attractions for most visitors. Its most noted attraction is Paris' largest and most celebrated cemetery, **Cimetière Père-Lachaise**. Here lie such famous musicians, writers, artists, and actors as Chopin, Oscar Wilde, Marcel Proust, Simone Signoret, Yves Montand, Edith Piaf, Gertrude Stein, Colette, Isadora Duncan, and the celebrated rock star Jim Morrison (you'll need a map, obtained at the entrance, to navigate this rather disorienting cemetery).

JUST BEYOND PARIS

Metropolitan Paris includes a few other areas offering worthwhile attractions. These areas are located to the east, west, and south of Paris' 20 arrondissements. Most can be easily reached within 30 minutes to one hour by the underground Métro or train. If you have extra time, you might want to visit some of these attractions, the latter three of which literally turn into full-day trips:

❑ **La Defénse:** If you ever wondered why Paris lacks highrise commercial buildings, look no further; city planners decided to confine them to one area on the outskirts of Paris. Located immediately west of the 17th arrondissement where Av. Charles de Gaulle meets the Seine

River (aligned with the Arc de Triomphe, Champs-Elysée, and the Louvre), this is Paris' architectural showcase for modern high-rise commercial buildings. Numerous multinational companies operate from this city of concrete and glass. If you enjoy bold contemporary architecture, be sure to visit this area. Here you will find the giant open concrete cube, the **Grande Arche de La Défense**, that dominates the Plaza de la Défense, along with the **Musée de l'Automobile** and the **Imax Cinema**. Many visitors with an extra day in Paris enjoy visiting this area.

❑ **Palace of Versailles:** Located about 15 kilometers southwest of Paris, this is France's most famous palace, attracting over 4 million visitors a year. Extravagant and ostentatious, it's a good example of 17th century royal excesses. It once served as King Louis XIV's, XV's, and XVI's private city boasting nearly 20,000 residents. It also explains why the French treasury was always broke. Frequently crowded with long lines, it's best to go directly to the office on the left to get a ticket for an English-language tour of the palace. By doing this you will by-pass the long lines which may take more than an hour to gain entry into the palace. The highlights of the main palace include the Hall of Mirrors (**Galerie des Glaces**), the royal apartments (**petis appartements**), and the opera house (**Opéra Royal**). Be sure to leave time to walk parts of the 250-acre grounds with their beautifully manicured lawns, gardens, and shrubs as well as grandiose fountains, statues, stairways, and lakes. You may also want to visit two other buildings on the ground, **Petit Trianon** and **Grand Trianon**. Overall, this is one of those "grand" experiences you will probably either love or hate—few are neutral. You should plan to spend the whole day visiting Versailles. And do so only if you have first done everything you wanted to do in Paris. You can get to Versailles by **train** (take the RER line C5 at the Gare d'Austerlitz, St-Michel, Musée d'Orsay, Invalides, Pont de l'Alma, Champ-de-Mars, or Javel station to the Versailles Rive Gauche station and then switch to a shuttle bus), **Métro** (exit at Pont de Sèvres and take bus 171 to château), or **car** (N10 highway). Expect to take 45 minutes to one hour to get there from Paris. The palace is open every day except Monday and a few holidays from 9am to 6pm, between May 3 and September 30, and from 9am to 5pm, from October 1 to April 31. The park and gardens are open every day from dawn to dusk. You can see special fountain displays every Sunday between May 8 and September 30 from 3:30pm to 5:00pm. For more information, call 30-84-74-00. The cost of admissions varies (US$8 to US$18) depending on which areas you plan to visit. Admission fees for adults are reduced on Sundays.

❑ **Palace of Fontainebleau:** Located approximately 40 miles south of Paris, this attractive resort and hunting lodge of French kings and favorite retreat of Napoléon I is an impressive example of 16th century Renaissance architecture. It also houses lots of 16th, 17th, 18th, and 19th century French history. You'll want to tour the château, visit the gardens and carp pond, and view the beautiful forest surrounding the property. The most convenient way to get to Fontainebleau from Paris is to take the train from Gare de Lyon for a 35 minute to one hour trip. Get off of the train at Avon and take a bus to the château, which runs every 15 minutes for the two-mile trip. Open daily, except Tuesday, from 9:30am to 12:00pm and from 2:00pm to 5:00pm. Cost of admissions is 31F; children under 18 enter free. For more information, call 60-71-50-70.

❑ **Disneyland Paris:** Originally called Euro Disney and located 20 miles east of Paris, this 1,500 acre entertainment resort complex was initially opened in 1992 to great fanfare and controversy. After a few troubled years and a name change, it appears to be a qualified success. Like its American and Japanese counterparts, Disneyland Paris is loaded with theme parks, attractions, entertainment, restaurants, hotels, and shopping. Major attractions include Adventureland, Frontierland, Fastasyland, Discovery land, Space Mountain, and Indiana Jones and the Temple of Doom. Trains from Paris to Disneyland Paris, which take nearly 40 minutes, depart every 10-20 minutes from the following RER-A stations: Charles de Gaulle-Etoile, Auber, Château-Les Halles, Gare de Lyon, and Nation. Roundtrip fare is 70F. Open mid-June to mid-September, 9:00am to 10:00pm and mid-September to mid-June from 10:00am to 6:00pm and from 10:00am to 9:00pm during December and spring school holidays. Prices vary with seasons, ranging from 150-195F for adults and 120-150F for children under 12.

MAJOR STREETS AND SQUARES

Paris has a few major streets and squares that crosscut the 20 arrondissements and are *"must visit"* places for many visitors. Some of the most popular such streets for discovering Paris' many treasures and pleasures include:

❑ **Champs Elysées**: Right Bank, 8th arr. This is France's most famous boulevard that links the Louvre to the Arc de Triomphe. Recently rehabilitated to its former glory, it's once again a broad tree-lined boulevard plied by hordes of pedestrians. However, except for the Arc de Triomphe and the tourist office, there's nothing here that's particularly elegant and there's not much to see or do other than observe the tourists. With the exception of a few small shopping arcades, the shops in this area tend to be very touristy, the restaurants and fast-food outlets are not particularly noteworthy, and movie theaters seem to be the most popular pastime for locals. Nonetheless, the street still has a mystique about it that continues to draw large crowds of visitors. Perhaps the recent addition of Planet Hollywood has given new meaning, if not vitality, to this street!

❑ **Rue du Faubourg-Saint-Honoré**: Right Bank, 8th arr. This is one of Paris' most upscale streets for fashions and accessories. The landmark shop here is the fabulous Hermès (24, Rue du Faubourg-St-Honoré) with its chic and exquisitely designed scarves, leather accessories, jewelry, and clothes offered at high prices. Other top name clothing and accessory shops line this upscale street: Lanvin, Lagerfeld, Façonnable, Gucci, Givenchy, Guy Laroche, Yves Saint Laurent, Jaeger, Trussardi, Revillon, Leonard, Chloé, Ungano, Etro, Sonia Rykiel, Louis Féraud, and Pierre Cardin. It also includes some major jewelers, such as Poiray, Cartier, Pomellato, and Arfan, as well as a branch of Burma, one of Paris' best shops for reproduction jewelry. The street simply dazzles visitors with quality products and high prices.

❑ **Avenue Montaigne**: Right Bank, 8th arr. This is another one of Paris' most upscale shopping streets. The elegant shops here represent Paris' major designers and haute couture houses: Christian Dior, Nina Ricci, Valentino, Emanuel Ungaro, and Chanel. The famous Plaza Athénée hotel is located in the heart of this area. The adjacent Avenue George-V includes additional shops and restaurants catering to the tastes of the wealthy clientele frequenting this area.

❑ **Place de la Madeleine:** Right Bank. 8th arr. This is one of Paris' famous squares dominated by the Madeleine Church and surrounded by many fine shops. Fauchon, which is located on the square, is Paris' famous and expensive supermarket. It stocks over 20,000 food items, from the exotic to the mundane. Numerous colorful cafés, restaurants, bakeries, clothing stores, and decorating shops dominate this area.

❑ **Place Vendôme:** Right Bank. 1st arr. This is Paris' most elegant and upscale square. The beautiful yet simple architecture dominating this square is home to some of the world's most famous jewelers (Boucheron, Van Cleef & Arpels, Mauboissin, Paget, Chaumet, Mikimoto, Repossi, Gianmaria Buccellati, Chanel, Cartier, Alexandre Raza), the Ritz Hotel, and Giorgio Armani and Emporio Armani for men's and women's clothing. Just around the corner, along Rue Saint-Honoré, are some of Paris' best estate jewelry shops (G. Linde and Albuquerque). Just north of the square, along Rue de la Paix, are three fine jewelry shops—Poiray, Corum, and H. Stern—and an excellent fabric shop, Henri Maupiou.

❑ **Ave de Matignon:** Right Bank. 8th arr. Located northeast of Rond-Point (Champs-Elysées), this street is lined with numerous art galleries, antique shops, and one of Paris' best haute couture discount shops, Anna Lowe (55, Avenue Matignon). If you go a little further and turn right onto Rue de Penthièvre, you'll find additional discount clothing stores. Another right puts you onto the narrow Rue de Miromesnil where you will find additional art and antique shops.

❑ **Boulevard Haussmann:** Right Bank. 8th and 9th arr. This is one of Paris' most famous boulevards named after the 19th century architect of a newly designed Paris of broad streets and boulevards. The most interesting part of this street is near the Opéra Garnier. Here you will find two of France's major department stores, Printemps and Galeries Lafayette, as well as the British department store, Marks and Spencer. There's not much else to recommend along this street other than these stores.

❑ **Rue de Rivoli:** Right Bank. 1st and 4th arr. This street cuts through the heart of Paris' most popular treasures and pleasures. Extending near the beautiful Place des Vosges in the east past the Lourve and ending at the Place de la Concorde in the west, this street is lined with numerous shops, department stores, restaurants, and cafés. The section across from the Lourve offers some of the most interesting shops, especially the expansive Louvre des Atiquaires (2 Place du Palais Royal), an upmarket antique center with 250 shops. Some of Paris' best hotels are located along this or adjacent streets: Hôtel Crillon, Hôtel Meurice, and the Inter-Continental.

❑ **Avenue Victor Hugo:** Right Bank. 16th arr. This is another one of Paris' elegant shopping streets. The street runs southwest of the Arc de Triomphe into the heart of the 16th arrondissement. The best quality shops are found from the Arc de Triomphe section of the street to where Rue Paul Valery crosses Avenue Victor Hugo. Here you will find such noted shops as Celine, Francesco Ferri, Guy Laroche, Ophee, Nina Ricci, Emmanuel K., Cerruti 1881, Yves Saint Laurant, O.J. Perrin, and Francois Pinet.

❑ **Boulevard Saint Germain:** Left Bank. 6th and 7th arr. This is one of Paris' most lively and noteworthy streets. Running through large sections of the 6th and 7th arrondissements, the most interesting section of this street is between Rue de Bac and Boulevard Saint Michel. The real center of activity is around St. Germain des Pres. Here you will find the famous cafés and numerous restaurants and shops lining this busy street of students, artists, and tourists.

❑ **Rue de Grenelle:** Left Bank. 7th arr. This is one of the most elegant shopping streets on the Left Bank. Very narrow, the street is lined with fine French, Italian, and Japanese boutiques offering the latest is fashions and accessories along with antique and small pastry shops. The best of this shopping is found between Boulevard Raspil and Rue du Dragon, and especially at the intersection of Rue de Grenelle and Rue des Saints Péres. Here you will find Kenzo, Cerruti 1881, Barbara Bui, Roberto Verino, Montana, Robert Merlox, Dona Anna, Sergio Rossi, Stephane Kélian, Salvatore Ferragamo, Prada, Yves

Saint Laurant, Lisa Frey, Sonia Rykiel, Inscription Rykiel, Sonya Rykiel Enfant, and Revillon.

❑ **Rue de Seine:** Left Bank. 7th arr. Here's one of the most concentrated areas for art, antique, and ethnographic shops. This area runs the length of Rue de Seine as well as includes all of Rue des Beaux Arts and parts of Rue Bonaparte. Located within five minutes walk northeast of St. Germain des Pres, you'll find everything from shops offering modern French paintings to those offering pre-Columbian artifacts, African art, and South Pacific artifacts. Art lovers will have a field day here!

❑ **Rue du Dragon:** Left Bank. 7th arr. This street is really an extension of the fine shops found along Rue de Grenelle and Rue des Saints Péres. It's lined with numerous shoe stores that are popular with both locals and tourists in search of good value.

❑ **Rue de Université:** Left Bank. 7th arr. Running from St. Germain des Pres to the Eiffel Tower, this street has numerous antique shops, especially in the section between St. Germain des Pres and Boulevard Saint Germain.

UNDERSTANDING ADDRESSES

Once you understand this basic arrondissement structure of Paris, navigating the streets of Paris becomes relatively easy. Take, for example, Parisian addresses. The last two digits of the postage code for each address indicates the particular arrondissement for that address. A hotel with the postal code 75006 means it's in the 6th (06) arrondissement. An address with the postal code 75016 would be located in the 16th arrondissement. Most street addresses are numbered consecutively, with odd numbers on one side of the street and even numbers on the other side of the street.

ACQUIRE A GOOD MAP

It's essential to explore Paris with the help of a good map. Most hotels and Métro stations will give you a small fold-out map of the city which includes the major streets, sights, and Métro stops. While this general map is useful for getting an overview of the city, it leaves much to be desired if you are looking for specific places and addresses.

We normally navigate the streets of Paris with two different maps published by Michelin. *Paris Tourism* is a useful fold-out map that clearly delineates each of the arrondissements and includes all major streets, sites, Métro stations, taxi stands, post offices, pharmacies, and after-theater dining spots. It also includes a Metro map and useful summaries of major sights, shopping, museums, parks, gardens, addresses, and transportation alternatives. This is our working overview map. It constantly answers many questions about Paris. It's available in many shops for 10F (US$2.40).

Our second map is actually a mini-atlas of the city, *Paris Plan*. Also published by Michelin and widely available in small shops and bookstores for 45F (US$11.00), this easy to carry pocket-size atlas runs 130 pages and provides 60 detailed maps which cover every section of the city. It includes streets normally absent on the small fold-out maps. Best of all, it includes a street locator index for finding any address in Paris. This immensely useful atlas should be one of your very first purchases on Paris. It will quickly pay for

❑ The last two digits of the postage code for each address indicates the particular arrondissement for that address.

❑ We normally navigate the streets of Paris with two different maps published by Michelin—a fold-out (*Paris Tourism*) and a mini-atlas (*Paris Plan*). You'll find it's virtually impossible to find a specific address unless you have a street locator index as found in *Paris Plan*.

❑ If you have very limited time in Paris, perhaps two or three days, we recommend heading for the 1st, 4th, 6th, 7th, and 8th arrondissements.

❑ Most shops are closed on Monday, a good day to focus on non-shopping types of activities, and the flea market.

❑ The streets of Paris are best approached and savored on foot.

itself by saving you time in finding places. If you attempt to navigate the streets of Paris by only using a fold-out map, you will constantly become frustrated with the lack of details for finding particular places. You'll find it's virtually impossible to find a specific address unless you have a street locator index as found in *Paris Plan*.

Both of these maps are available in major travel bookstores in the U.S. such as **Travel Books and Language Center** (4931 Cordell Avenue, Bethesda, MD, Tel. 800/220-2665), **Book Passage** (1 Tamal Vista Boulevard, Corte Madera, CA (Tel. 800/321-9785), **Traveller's Bookstore** (22 W. 52 St., New York, NY 10019, Tel. 212/664-0995), **MapLink** (25 E. Mason St., Santa Barbara, CA 93101, Tel. 805/965-4402), and most **Rand McNally** travel bookstores nationwide (Tel. 800/333-0136 for the location nearest you). Most of these stores also have catalogs which include numerous resources on Paris. You may want to get copies of these maps before departing for Paris.

SCHEDULING RIGHT, STARTING OUT RIGHT

While each of Paris' districts has something to offer visitors, the city's major treasures and pleasures—shops, hotels, restaurants, museums, galleries, monuments, churches, gardens, and other attractions—are found in seven arrondissements of the Left and Right Banks:

> **Left Bank:** 6th and 7th
> **Right Bank:** 1st, 4th, 8th, 16th, and 18th

You will want to plan most of your activities around these arrondissements. However, if you have very limited time in Paris, perhaps two or three days, we recommend heading for the many treasures and pleasures concentrated in the 1st, 4th, 6th, 7th, and 8th arrondissements.

Where you start your Paris adventure really depends on your particular interests. If this is your first visit to Paris and you love the sights, you may want to immediately head for some of the major monuments and museums that are so closely associated with the major images of Paris—the **Eiffel Tower, Arc de Triumphe, Avenue des Champs Elysèes, Notre-Dame Cathedral, Sacré-Cœur Basilica, The Louvre, Place de la Concorde,** or **Invalides**. If you want three of the best views of sprawling Paris, climb to the top of the Eiffel Tower, Arc de Triumphe, and Sacré-Cœur Basilica. If you love shopping for fashion and jewelry, drop your bags and head directly for **Place Vendome** (1st), **Rue du Faubourg St. Honoré** (8th), **Av. Montaigne** (8th), **Avenue Victor Hugo** (16th), and **Rue de Grenelle** (7th). If your shopping interests primarily focus on arts and antiques, head for **Rue de Seine** (6th), **Rue de l'Université** (7th), **Av. Matignon** (8th), **Village Suisse** (15th), or the many antique markets found within the huge flea market, **Marché aux Puces de Clignancourt** (18th—open Saturday, Sunday and Monday). If you are a "people" and "atmosphere" type of person, go directly to the **Latin Quarter**, especially to **Saint-Germain-des-Prés** (6th) as well as the **Montparnasee** (6th) and **Montmartre** (18th) areas. Do keep in mind that most shops are closed on Monday, a good day to focus on non-shopping types of activities, except for the flea market in the 18th.

All of our seven major arrondissements, except the 18th, are located adjacent to the Seine River and thus can be easily

explored on foot. However, the far northern 18th arrondissement is most conveniently reached by the underground Métro.
If you plan to visit one or two adjacent arrondissements each
day, you can quickly and conveniently cover most of Paris'
attractions within five or six days, although seven or eight days
would be ideal. You'll probably want to devote a separate day
to the 18th arrondissement, preferably Saturday, Sunday, or
Monday, because of the popular flea market in this area
(Marché aux Puces de Clignancourt). Monday is probably the
best day to go there since most shops elsewhere in Paris are
closed on Monday.

If you are a museum-goer, chances are you may spend a
half-day or full-day exploring each of Paris' three major
museums: The Louvre (1st), George Pompidou Centre (3rd),
and Musée d'Orsay (7th). You may also want to explore many
of Paris' other museums. If you are not into museums, but still
feel a need to visit these places, you can easily cover all three
museums in one day—two hours per museum may be just
enough "culture" for you!

GETTING AROUND WITH EASE

The streets of Paris are best approached and savored on foot.
It's one of the most inviting cities to explore on foot. Indeed,
our preference for walking has been recently reinforced by
major disruptions in what was ostensibly the world's finest
public transportation system. As we go to press, Paris remains
paralyzed due to political unrest that has effectively shut down
all of its public transportation systems. Paris' public transportation system is great, when it functions. When it becomes
disrupted by public employee strikes, which occur frequently,
or terrorist activities, which increasingly occur, walking is a
great alternative. If you are unfortunate enough to be in Paris
during such shutdowns, take to the streets on foot. You'll
probably see, do, and enjoy Paris much more on foot.

We always prefer walking this city rather than taking public
transportation. In fact, during our most recent trip we managed
to take the Métro only twice and a taxi three times. We did the
rest of Paris on foot.

Armed with a good map, you should be able to easily cover
each arrondissement on foot. Occasionally you may need to
take public transportation to go from one district to another.
And at times you may want to rent a bicycle. Here are your
major transportation alternatives:

❑ **Rent-a-car:** You really don't want the headache of driving a car in Paris. Except on Sunday, the traffic is horrendous and the parking is especially problematic. If you want to drive in Paris, do so on Sunday when the city is relatively quiet. If you plan to rent a car, do so for making excursions outside Paris. It's best to arrange your rental car before arriving in France. Rates are much cheaper and you'll be assured of the type of car you need. Our last rental car (Hertz), which we arranged in the U.S., cost us US$35 per day. Had we rented it in Paris, it would have cost us nearly US$100 a day. Be sure to shop around for the best rates. In this highly competitive business, many car rental firms will match the rates of other firms and even bargain with you over the phone!

❑ **Subway:** Paris boasts one of the world's most efficient and convenient underground subway systems, the Métro. If you've not used such a system, Paris is a great place to learn. You may experience some initial confusion, but within 15 minutes you'll probably figure out what you need to do in order to get where you want to go. Stations and lines are well marked and conveniently located in reference to major places in Paris which also are well marked on most maps. Once you locate your destination on a station map, follow the signs to the correct platform. Since maps are generously displayed overhead in each car and the names of stations are clearly marked, you should have little difficulty getting on and off at the right stations. If you need to transfer to another line, follow the orange signs at the transfer stations (*correspondences*) to the proper line. Few trips require more than one transfer. The cost of using the Métro within the 20 arrondissements and into several nearby suburbs is a flat 7F ($1.35). If you plan to use the Métro often, you may want to take advantage of the bulk ticket rate—purchase tickets in groups of 10 (*carnet*) for 41F ($7.80). Keep in mind two different signs you'll see at each station: the white SORTIE sign which means EXIT; and the bright orange CORRESPONDENCE sign that refers to the transfer

❑ It's best to arrange your rental car before arriving in France. Rates are much cheaper this way.

❑ Paris is a great place to learn how to use the subway. You may experience some initial confusion, but within 15 minutes you'll probably figure out what you need to do in order to get where you want to go.

❑ You can hail a cab alongside the street as long as you are not within 165 feet of a taxi stand.

❑ Paris is a bicycle-friendly city with lots of parks, gardens, bicycle lanes, and bike racks.

station. If you're transferring, make sure you follow the orange sign rather than exit. Be sure to hold on to your ticket since inspectors occasionally check them. The Métro runs from 5:30am to 1:15am. While it is relatively safe, do beware of pickpockets. We've also become less enthusiastic about using this system because of recent bombings. During 1995, for example, the Métro become a favorite target for terrorist bombings, especially at the St-Michel station, killing and injuring many people. While we enjoy using the Métro, we're also a bit gun-shy about using the system these days. And we're hesitant to recommend it when we know it is potentially dangerous. For example, during our most recent trip, a bomb exploded between two stations we used just nine hours earlier. While no one was killed this time, 27 people were injured and some had to have limbs amputated. For us, the message was loud and clear: avoid the Métro. There is no compelling reason why we should use it. We now tend to walk a lot more or use other forms of transportation. It will be a long time before we venture underground again. For information on the Métro, call 43-46-14-14.

❑ **Buses:** While less convenient and much slower than the Métro, buses do service most areas of Paris, and you can see the city from the windows. Bus routes run north to south or east to west, and they are clearly marked at bus stops and on buses. To catch a bus, just queue at the bus stop (marked on most maps) and motion for the bus to stop. Bus and Métro fares are the same and buses accept the *carnet* tickets. Buses operate daily from 7:00am to 8:30pm (a few operate earlier and run until 12:30am), except on Sunday and holidays when service is limited.

❑ **Taxis:** While just over 14,000 taxis ply the streets of Paris—not a particularly large number for over 10 million people—they are often difficult to find and they can be expensive. It's virtually impossible to get a taxi during rush hour. You'll find taxi stands or racks throughout the city where taxis ostensibly wait for passengers; most are found a busy intersections, at the major metro and REF stations, and at hospitals, train stations, and airports. These stands are marked on many maps of Paris. Alternatively, you can hail a cab alongside the street as long as you are not within 165 feet of a taxi stand. Taxis are vacant and available when the white taxi sign on the roof of the cab is lighted. If you plan to take a taxi to the airport or train station, it's best to reserve a taxi the day before. Taxis are metered (make sure it's engaged), but some drivers may try to overcharge you, especially when they drop you off at the airport (the fare mysteriously gets inflated by 40F!); don't be intimidated by such rip-off artists, and don't tip them. If you have difficulty finding a taxi, you may want to call a radio cab: 42-41-50-50, 42-70-41-41, 49-36-10-10, or 47-39-47-39. They may cost you twice as much as other cabs because they engage their meters from the point of dispatch rather than from the point of pickup. Expect most taxis rides within Paris to cost between 30F (US$7) and 90F (US$20), depending on your destination and traffic waiting time. The initial flag charge is 12F ($2.30) with each kilometer costing 5.20F ($1.10). In the evening this goes up to 7F per kilometer. Large pieces of luggage are charged at the rate of 6F per bag. Taxi drivers appreciate receiving 10-15% tips. We use taxis when we're in a hurry, when we're exhausted from walking, or when we're carrying large items.

❑ **Boat:** Most boats plying the Seine River are either working boats or sightseeing boats. However, one category of boats, the BatOBus, functions as a shuttle service along the river, operating from the Eiffel Tower (Port de la Bourdonnais)to Notre-Dame (Quai Montebello), making five stops along the way (Port de la Bourdannais, Port de Solferino, Quai Malaquais, Quai Montebello, Quai de l'Hotel de Ville). The complete trip takes nearly one hour and costs 60F for adults and 25F for children. However, you can get off at any stop and resume the route at some later time the same day. This is both a convenient and pleasant way of avoiding the street and sidewalk traffic and stopping at the major sites in this congested area.

❑ **Bicycles:** Paris is a bicycle-friendly city with lots of parks, gardens, bicycle lanes, and bike racks. One of the major bike rental companies is Bicy-Club (8 place de la Porte-de-Champerret, 17e, Tel. 47-66-55-92) which has several rental outlets in Paris. Bikes normally rent for 28F ($5.40) an hour or 100F ($21) per day. Call for details on locations and hours.

❑ **Discount passes:** Many visitors to Paris take advantage of the special discounted public transportation pass, the Paris-Visite pass. Good for three or five days on any of the public transportation systems (the Métro, buses, RER, and the funicular to the top of Montmartre), the pass costs 95F ($18.50) for three days of 150F ($29.00) for five days. You can purchase this pass at the main Métro stations, tourist offices, and the RATP (Régie Autonome des Transports Parisiens). One and two-day discount passes (*Formule 1*) also are available at the Métro stations: 28F ($5.40) for one day and 38F ($7.35) for two days.

You'll discover lots of other marvelous streets in Paris as you go to and from the arrondissements and streets we've identified thus far. Consider these to be the first of many streets you'll encounter on your way to uncovering the many wonderful treasures and pleasures of Paris.

BUSINESS HOURS

Most stores open between 9:30 and 10:00am and close at 7 or 7:30pm, although some stay open later. Many stores are closed on Sunday and part of Monday. Some shops close for two weeks during the month of August. Don't be surprised if some shops keep irregular hours, closing unexpectedly with a "Back in 5 Minutes" sign posted on the door.

5

Best Hotels and Accommodations

Paris abounds with fine and not so fine hotels and accommodations. You'll discover some of the world's most luxurious and memorable hotels in Paris (The Ritz, Crillon, Plaza Athénée) along with some truly dreadful places you'll want to quickly forget. In between these two extremes are some wonderful medium-range hotels offering good value, location, and amenities as well as oozing with charm and character.

As you will quickly discover, "value" is a relative concept when visiting Paris. Compared to the fabulous hotels we're used to staying in during our annual visits to Hong Kong, Thailand, and Singapore, hotels in Paris are often disappointing; they seem so overpriced for what you get. But we're probably spoiled in Asia. And we're further reminded that Paris is simply a very very expensive city for everything. So let's compare Parisian hotels to each other and accept the fact that we will not be getting as much value for our hotel franc or dollar compared to hotels in many other cities of the world.

 ## ANTICIPATED COSTS

Be forewarned that the cost of sleeping in Paris can be very high. A top hotel, for example, may charge from US$500 to

US$900 a night for a basic double room. Add this cost to the high cost of restaurants (Chapter 6), and you may be pushing nearly US$1000 a day in Paris—and that's before you start engaging on one of Paris' major pleasures, shopping! Many so-called budget hotels charge more than US$100 a night for a double room. And what you get for your money is often disappointing—tiny rooms, very noisy streets, limited service, and few amenities normally associated with hotels charging such prices.

❑ The cost of sleeping in Paris can be very high—US$500 to US$900 a night, with many so-called budget hotels charging over US$100 a night!

Therefore, it's important that you carefully examine the Paris hotel scene and make choices that best fit your travel needs. If money is no object and you enjoy staying in fabulous hotels, go ahead and splurge on one of Paris' truly fine hotels at US$600+ per night. Most of these hotels will be centrally located in the 1st or 8th arrondissements, and they will be near some of Paris' best restaurants and shops. On the other hand, if you're on a limited budget, if you plan to spend little time in your hotel, or if you prefer spending most of your money on things other than sleeping, you might want to find a nicely located budget or medium-range hotel for under US$200, or even under US$100, a night. Small and often charming hotels with lots of history and character, these one to three-star hotels are disproportionately found on the Left Bank, especially in the 5th, 6th, and 7th arrondissements.

❑ One to three-star hotels, often small, charming, and offering good value, are disproportionately found on the Left Bank, especially in the 5th, 6th, and 7th arrondissements.

❑ Paris has an estimated 2,000 hotels offering nearly 80,000 rooms.

❑ Most hotels are small operations with fewer than 50 rooms.

❑ Be sure to make reservations well in advance since many hotels run 90-100 percent occupancy most days of the year.

THE HOTEL SCENE

Paris has an estimated 2,000 hotels offering 80,000 rooms. While most hotels are small operations with fewer than 50 rooms, others are large properties with more than 200 rooms.

Even with this large number of hotels and rooms, you may have difficulty finding a room in Paris during certain times of the year. Remember, Paris must sleep nearly 20 million visitors a year, which translates into fully booked hotels for nearly 80 percent of the year. Many hotels run 90-100 percent occupancy most days of the year. The best time to find a room will be July and August when much of the city shuts down for the annual

French vacation.

The government grades hotels on a four-star system. Four-star hotels (★★★★)tend to be the best, offering a full-range of amenities normally expected from deluxe hotels found elsewhere in the world. You can expect to pay US$250-500 a night or more for a double at these properties. Two- (★★) and three-star hotels (★★★) have fewer amenities and, in many respects, offer some of Paris' best hotel buys. You can expect to pay US$120-240 a night for a double in these places. One-star hotels (★) offer very basic amenities and usually charge less than US$120 per night for a double. No star places may charge less than US$60 a day; many of them are your very basic run-down hotel.

❏ The first floor of a hotel is the ground floor. The second level is called the first floor.

❏ The streets of Paris tend to be very noisy, from early morning until late at night. If a hotel does not sound-proof its rooms, ask for a quieter room at the rear of the hotel or one facing the courtyard.

❏ The cost of using a mini-bar and having laundry done through your hotel can be extremely high. Indeed, it may cost more to launder socks than to buy them new!

❏ Many hotels include the price of a very basic but expensive breakfast in their rates. If you prefer to skip this breakfast, ask if the hotel will deduct the breakfast charge from your bill.

❏ Be prepared for hotels that do not have shower curtains in their bathtub/shower combinations. You may flood the floor!

UNIQUE QUALITIES AND CHOICES

Parisian hotels have their own distinct character that reflects both the structure of the city and the French way of traveling. Most hotels, including many large ones, architecturally tend to blend into neighborhoods. Indeed, you can walk down a street that has ten different hotels but never notice their existence. Most hotels put out a small sign with their name and designated stars. Even such top hotels as the Bristol, noted for its understated elegance, blends nicely into a major commercial street; you can easily miss it. Make sure you have the street number of your hotel so you can locate it by a specific address. Don't expect to see a big sign or front entrance announcing the existence of the hotel from a distance.

Many Parisian hotels are old properties that have undergone numerous renovations. As a result, elevators may be nonexistent or extremely small (just you and your bag will fit), hallways narrow, buildings noisy, and rooms small and irregular in size. Heating systems will be retrofitted and air-conditioning systems nonexistent. Small older hotels with 30 rooms may indeed have 30 rooms in 30 different shapes and sizes. Inexpensive hotels may only have a few rooms with private baths—places best used for sleeping.

Keep in mind that the first floor of a hotel is the ground floor. The second level is called the first floor.

Do inspect your room before accepting it. You may discover your room is much smaller than expected and it's in a noisy location. In fact, one of the major complaints of visitors to Paris is their small and noisy hotel rooms. After a sleepless and uncomfortable first night, many want to immediately move to a much quieter hotel with larger rooms.

The streets of Paris tend to be very noisy, from early morning until late at night. While many hotels sound-proof windows and walls, many others do not. Inspecting your room will give you a good idea if you will be exposed to a great deal of noise. Rooms toward the rear of the hotel, or those facing an inner courtyard, will be the quietest ones.

While all hotels must clearly post their rates, do ask about any extra charges, such as phone calls.

The cost of using a mini-bar and having laundry done through your hotel can be extremely high. Consider shopping at a nearby grocery store to stock your own drinks (the 4F grocery store Coca Cola may cost 30F from your mini-bar). Check the price of laundry service so you won't be shocked when you check out. Yes, it may cost more to launder socks than to buy them new!

If you need to take a taxi to the airport or train station, it's a good idea to have the front desk reserve a cab for a specific time at least 24 hours in advance. It's often difficult to get a cab at your hotel unless you make such prior arrangements.

CHOOSING YOUR BEST PLACE TO STAY

When surveying your hotel options in Paris, keep in mind the following selection criteria:

❑ **Amenities:** Do you prefer a modern new hotel to an older property? What amenities do you need? For example, do you require full business services, a concierge, health facility, tennis courts, swimming pool, large well-appointed room, bath tub and shower, mini-bar, cable TV, and outstanding restaurants? Or can you get by without a business center concierge, exercise facility, restaurants, and minibar as well as tolerate a small room without a television? What services are you likely to be paying for but which you do not need nor will you use?

❑ **Budget:** Do you prefer spending US$400-900 a night for a room in one of Paris' top deluxe hotels or do you want less expensive alternatives which offer fewer amenities? Do you want the price of breakfast included in your hotel bill or do you prefer other breakfast alternatives outside your hotel?

❑ **Character:** Do you want to stay in a place with lots of grand history and character, where many rich and famous celebrities stay, or do you prefer a small, quaint, and friendly hotel? Are architecture, decorating, terraces, and gardens important to you?

❑ **Convenience:** How important is an elevator or will you be content walking two or three flights of stairs? Will a tiny room with hardly any space to open your suitcase be okay or do you need a much larger room to spread out? Since many hotels do not include a shower curtain in a bathtub/shower, will you be able to take a shower without flooding the bathroom floor and still be happy with your hotel? Do you have a television with English-language international programming? Will you need handicap access? Does the hotel designate some rooms as nonsmoking? Does the hotel permit pets in the room?

❑ **Location:** What do you want to be close to? Museums? Shops? Restaurants and cafés? Are you a Right Bank or Left Bank person in terms of budget and/or lifestyle? Do you prefer being located within a few minutes of a Métro station and restaurants or will you be satisfied walking some distance to these places?

❑ **Parking:** If you plan to drive into Paris, where will you park? Does the hotel have its own garage or do they make other parking arrangements? How much can you expect to pay for parking each day? Have you made parking reservations along with your hotel reservations?

❑ **Peace and quiet:** Do you prefer being on busy thoroughfares where the action is or do you like smaller and quieter back streets? Are rooms relatively quiet or do they have paper-thin walls?

❑ **Views of the city:** Would you like to have a fabulous view of the city, viewing the Eiffel Tower or Notre Dame Cathedral from your window?

In general, most hotels in Paris are very clean although many are old and worn. Others may have smoke and pet odors. Given the close proximity to busy streets, many hotel rooms can be very noisy unless they are properly sound-proofed. When making a reservation, ask for a quiet room which may face the back of the hotel rather than a noisy street. Other hotels may have paper-thin walls—you'll quickly get acquainted with noisy neighbors and their bedtime habits!

Many hotels include the price of a very basic but expensive breakfast in their rates. Consisting of coffee, hot chocolate, fruit juice, bread, and a croissant often served in a charming breakfast room, this breakfast may add from 40F to 110F per person (US$10 to $25) to your hotel bill. If you prefer to skip the breakfast, ask if you can book the room without breakfast ahead of time and reconfirm the room without breakfast rate when you check in. Most hotels will deduct the amount, but only if you ask in advance. You may prefer doing what many Parisians do for breakfast—stop at their favorite corner café for coffee and a croissant for about half the price you will pay in most hotel breakfast rooms. On the other hand, you may prefer breakfast in a charming hotel dining room.

- ❏ Be sure to book your hotel well in advance.

- ❏ If you arrive in Paris without reservations, contact the Paris Tourist Office for assistance.

- ❏ You can cut the high costs of hotels in Paris by 20-50% by using hotel discounters, travel clubs, and travel agencies participating in discounted hotel plans.

- ❏ If you book your hotel through a travel agent, ask to see the agency's current preferred-rate directory which lists hotels offering special discounts.

- ❏ Some of the best buys in Parisian accommodations will be medium-range hotels (2 and 3 star properties).

- ❏ The 1st and 8th arrondissements are home to most of Paris elegant luxury hotels.

All "extras" cost when it comes to accommodations. Hotels offering full amenities, from business centers to tennis courts, will cost two to four times more than hotels offering basic a- menities. If you drive into Paris and will need your car later, the cost of hotel parking can be expensive—US$25-50 a day.

And be prepared for hotels that do not have shower curtains in their bathtub/shower combinations. If there is one major irritant for Americans traveling in Europe, it's the absence of a basic shower curtain that would help keep the bathroom floor dry. If you are not used to bathing in this manner, you are likely to flood the bathroom floor which then becomes danger- ously slippery. We are still baffled why so many hotels in Paris, as well as elsewhere in France and Europe, cannot provide what seems to be such a basic and rational bathroom provision. Obviously Europeans must be more adept at bathing under these circumstances than Americans!

BOOKINGS

If you are traveling independently, you can book many hotels through your travel agent or you can contact them directly by fax, phone, or mail. Do book your hotel well in advance. Since many popular hotels become fully booked several weeks in advance, and many small properties only have a few rooms, it's important to have confirmed reservations a few weeks before you arrive in Paris.

However, should you arrive in Paris without a hotel reservation, you can contact the **Paris Tourist Office** for assistance: 127 Avenue des Champs Elysées, Tel. 49-52-53-54. Open from 9:00am to 8:00pm, this office has information on hotels and will assist you in finding a hotel. This office also has branches at all train stations except Gare St-Lazare.

CUTTING THE RACK RATE

You can cut the high costs of accommodations in Paris by using hotel discounters, travel clubs, and travel agencies participating in discounted hotel plans. Several of these groups work with certain hotels that will extend a 20-50 percent discount off the published rack rate on certain rooms during certain times of the year (peak season may not qualify). You might try directly contacting a few of these companies:

❑ **Hotel Reservations Network:** 8140 Walnut Hill Lane, Suite 203, Dallas, TX 75231, Tel. 800/964-6835 or Fax 214/361-7299. Offers preferred-rate and last-minute discounts on mid-range hotels.

❑ **Room Exchange:** 450 7th Avenue, New York, NY 10123. Tel. 800/846-7000 or Fax 212/760-1013. Offers discounted rates on major hotels.

Various travel clubs also offer a few hotels in Paris at discount rates. **Encore** (800-/638-0930), for example, includes the fabulous George-V hotel at a 30 percent discount, a saving well worth the yearly membership fee ($49). Other groups, such as **Carte Royale** (800/847-3592), **Privilege Card** (800/359-0066), and the **International Airline Passengers Association** (800/527-5888), also include discounted hotels in Paris. Remember, you will need to join these clubs by paying an annual membership fee before you can take advantage of their discount arrangements and reservation systems.

You may discover there is little advantage booking your own discounted hotels since most travel agencies can do the same for you at no additional cost. In addition, they have access to several computerized reservation systems that include discounted rates. The trick is to find the right travel agency and to ask the right questions.

If you book your hotel through a travel agent, ask to see the agency's current **preferred-rate directory**. Hotels listed in this directory offer discounts which are available directly through travel agents. Most of the listings are for mid-range to expensive hotels heavily patronized by business travelers. If your agent does not belong to program (some small independent agents do not), contact another agent who is a member.

Your travel agent also should have computer access to the two major independent networks that offer preferred rates. If not, call them for the name of the agent nearest you: **ABC Corporate Services** (800/722-5179) and **Thor 24** (800/862-2111).

You also can purchase a copy of Travelgraphics' directory that lists hotels participating in their preferred-rate program: **Travelgraphics**, 6320 McDonough Drive, Suite A, Norcross, GA 30093, Tel. 800/633-7918. You can contact the hotels directly or have an agency make the discounted reservation for you.

Other groups to contact for information on travel agencies nearest you that participate in their discounted hotel programs include: **American Express** (800/872-8357 for Gold cardholders and 800/443-7672 for Platinum cardholders, **American Express Vacations** (check your local phone directory), **Carlson Travel Network** (800/337-5766), and **Uniglobe Travel International** (604/662-3800, ask about Key Cities Program), and **US Travel** (800/999-2471).

Keep in mind that only certain hotels participate in these discounted plans. Some of the best hotels, such as the Ritz, do not offer discounts through these groups. Since they tend to be fully booked most of the time, they have no incentive to join such discount programs. Therefore, expect to pay full rack rate at such hotels.

If you arrive in Paris without a reservation and it's not peak season, you can always ask for a discount. Hotels with vacant rooms will often extend discounts, if you ask them. After all, an unused room generates no revenue whereas a discounted room generates some money. In general, however, hotels in Paris are reluctant to do major discounting or participate in hotel discount plans.

BEST OF THE BEST

Pricing information (530-770F) indicates the lowest and highest cost for a double room. Our recommendations first start with annotated listings of the **best of the best** hotels which also tend to the the most expensive in Paris. As you will quickly discover, hotels in this category are found in only a few districts, especially the 1st and 8th arrondissements. Additional listings include some of the best hotels we've found for different budget categories which, in turn, reflect different levels of amenities and location.

Some of the best buys in Parisian accommodations will be **medium-range** hotels (two and three-star properties), such as the Le Notre-Dame Hôtel in the 5th arrondissement, the Hôtel Ferrandi in the 6th arrondisement, and Hôtel la Bourdonnais in the 7th arrondissement. While these hotels are by no means cheap by world standards (US$150-200 per night for a double), they are good values compared to the overall costs of accommodations in Paris. Many of these hotels are small and extremely charming; they are preferred by many visitors who feel they best represent the real Paris. These hotels are disproportionately found in the 4th, 5th, 6th, and 7th arrondissements. We've included many of the "best of the best" for this category of accommodations. For an excellent examination of these properties, including detailed annotations on the particulars of each property, we highly recommend Sandra Gustafson's latest edition of *Cheap Sleeps in Paris* (San Francisco: Chronicle Books), which is widely available in most major bookstores. It's very reliable and can save you hundreds of dollars by helping you select the right hotel. Most of our **inexpensive** hotels also are very small properties with lots of character.

Our **cheap cheaps** category includes the best of the mess—most are nothing to write home about; many are at best "cultural experiences"; but most are clean and safe. While we no longer stay in such places at our age (they are for the younger and more adventuresome crowd), the ones we identify are some of the "best of the best" for this category of accommodation. Compared to other hotels in Paris, they are amazingly cheap!

1ST ARRONDISSEMENT (RIGHT BANK)

The 1st arrondissement is home to some of Paris' finest hotels. Generally reflecting the upscale nature of this district, hotels in this district exhude class and elegance. If you want to stay at one of Paris' finest addresses, try one of the "best of the best" hotels here. At the same time, this area also has some very nice medium-range and budget hotels.

Overall, the 1st arrondissement is an excellent location from which to shop and see the sights of Paris. It is the most central location in Paris. You will be within short walking distance from The Louvre, Place Vendome, Palais Royal, and Jardin des Tuleries as well as all the treasures and pleasures of the exciting 4th, 6th, 7th, and 8th arrondissements.

❑ **Ritz:** 15 Place Vendôme, Tel. 43-16-30-30, Fax 43-16-31-78. 142 rooms located on the classiest and most exclusive square in Paris. Includes the Espadon Restaurant, one of Paris' very best. It doesn't get much more expensive than this at 2870-4170F. Very, very expensive ($$$$$$).

❑ **Meurice:** 228 Rue Rivoli, Tel. 44-58-10-10, Fax 44-58-10-15. 134 rooms. Lots of history in this well established property offering plush rooms and period decorating. An Italian CIGA hotel with impeccable service. Includes the famous Le Maurice restaurant. 2550-2950F. Very expensive ($$$$$).

❑ **Inter-Continental:** 3 Rue Catiglione, Tel. 44-77-11-11, fax 44-77-14-60. 410 rooms. Elegant architecture in one of the city's largest deluxe hotels. Spacious rooms overlooking a lovely courtyards. 2400-2600F. Very expensive ($$$$$).

VERY EXPENSIVE (★★★★): US$300-700

Castille	89 rooms
37 Rue Cambon	1690-2650F
Tel. 44-58-44-58	Fax 44-58-44-00
du Louvre	198 rooms
Place A. Malraux	1500-2000F
Tel. 44-58-38-38	Fax 44-58-38-01
Lotti	121 rooms
7 Rue Castiglione	1700-3300F
Tel. 42-60-37-34	Fax 40-15-93-56

EXPENSIVE (★★★): US$200-300

Mayfair	53 rooms
3 Rue Rouget-de-Lisle	950-1750F
Tel. 42-60-38-14	Fax 40-15-04-78
Royal St-Honoré	65 rooms
221 Rue St-Honoré	1220-1520F
Tel. 42-60-32-79	Fax 42-60-47-44

MEDIUM-RANGE (★★ to ★★★): US$120-200

Britannique	40 rooms
20 Avenue Victoria	600-830F
Tel. 42-33-74-59	Fax 42-33-82-65
de Londres et de Stockholm	20 rooms
21 R. des Prêtres Satin Germ. 'Auxerrois	690-800F
Tel. 42-33-78-68	Fax 42-33-09-95
Grand Hôtel de Champagne	40 rooms
17 Rue Jean-Lantier	721-812F
Tel. 42-36-60-00	Fax 45-08-43-33
Louvre St-Honoré	40 rooms
141 Rue St-Honoré	735-945F
Tel. 42-96-23-23	Fax 42-96-21-61
Mansart	57 rooms
5 Rue Capucines	606-875F
Tel. 42-61-50-28	Fax 49-27-94-44
Molière	29 rooms
21 Rue Molière	450-700F
Tel. 42-96-22-01	Fax 42-60-48-68
Novotel Les Halles	280 rooms
8 Place M.-de-Navarre	840-915F
Tel. 42-21-31-31	Fax 40-26-05-79

CHEAP CHEAPS (0 to ★): under US$75

Hotel du Palais	19 rooms
2 Quai de la Mégisserie	245-480F
Tel. 42-36-98-25	Fax 42-21-41-67

Hôtel Lille
8 Rue du Pelican
Tel. 42-33-3342

14 rooms
200-270F

2ND ARRONDISSEMENT (RIGHT BANK)

Hotels in this area are within easy walking distance of the major
sights and shopping of the 1st and 8th arrondissements. You
will find many good medium-range hotels in this area.

VERY EXPENSIVE (★★★★): US$300-700

Westminister
13 Rue Paix
Tel. 42-61-57-46

83 rooms
1250-2000F
Fax 42-60-30-66

Stendhal
22 Rue D. Casanova
Tel. 44-58-52-52

20 rooms
1501-1910F
Fax 44-58-52-00

EXPENSIVE (★★★): US$200-300

Édouard VII et rest. Le Delmonico
39 Avenue Opéra
Tel. 42-61-56-90

65 rooms
1150-1300F
Fax 42-61-47-73

L'Horset Opéra
18 Rue D'Antin
Tel. 44-71-87-00

54 rooms
970-1350F
Fax 42-66-55-54

MEDIUM-RANGE (★★ to ★★★): US$120-200

de Noailles
9 Rue Michodière
Tel. 47-42-92-90

58 rooms
680-850F
Fax 49-24-92-71

Favart
5 Rue Marivaux
Tel. 42-97-59-83

37 rooms
600-760F
Fax 40-15-95-58

Lautrec Opéra
8 Rue d'Amboise
Tel. 42-96-67-90

30 rooms
700-800F
Fax 42-96-06-83

INEXPENSIVE/BUDGET (★ to ★★): US$75-120

Baudelaire Opéra
61 Rue Ste Anne
Tel. 42-97-50-62

24 rooms
470-640F
Fax 42-86-85-85

CHEAP CHEAPS (0 to ★): under US$75

Vivienne
40 Rue Vivienne
Tel. 42-33-1326

44 rooms
290-460F
Fax 40-41-98-19

3RD ARRONDISSEMENT (RIGHT BANK)

This is a very mixed area for hotels. While you will be close to the Picasso Museum, you will be some distance from other major attractions and shops. Nonetheless, some good medium-range and budget accommodations can be found in this area. Plan to take the Metro from this area to other major districts or expect some long but pleasant walks to get to other areas on both the Right and Left Banks.

VERY EXPENSIVE (★★★★): US$300-700

Pavillon de la Reine
28 place Vosges
Tel. 42-77-96-40

32 rooms
1300-1700F
Fax 42-77-63-06

MEDIUM-RANGE (★★ to ★★★): US$120-200

des Chevalier
30 Rue de Tureene
Tel. 42-72-73-47

24 rooms
590-650F
Fax 42-72-5410

Meslay République
3 Rue Meslay
Tel. 42-72-79-79

39 rooms
550-660F
Fax 42-72-76-94

INEXPENSIVE/BUDGET (★ to ★★): US$75-120

Vieux Saule
6 Rue Picardie
Tel. 42-72-01-14

31 rooms
370-510F
Fax 40-27-88-21

4TH ARRONDISSEMENT (RIGHT BANK)

This is one of the nicest areas for accommodations, especially since it includes the two islands in the Seine which are home to Notre Dame Cathedral and Ste. Chapelle. Many visitors love staying at charming hotels on the Ile St. Louis. From here you have easy access to the 5th, 6th, and 7th arrondissements of the Left Bank and the many attractions of the 1st arrondissement are not far away.

EXPENSIVE (★★★): US$200-300

Jeu de Paume
54 Rue St-Louis-en-L'Ile
Tel. 43-26-14-18

32 rooms
895-1250F
Fax 40-46-02-76

MEDIUM-RANGE (★★ to ★★★): US$120-200

Bretonnerie
2 Rue Ste-Croix-de-la-Bretonnerie
Tel. 48-87-77-63

28 rooms
690-825F
Fax 42-77-26-78

Deux Iles
59 Rue St-Louis-en-I'Ile
Tel. 43-26-13-35

17 rooms
710-820F
Fax 43-29-60-25

Lutèce
65 Rue St.-Louis-en-I'Ile
Tel. 43-26-23-52

23 rooms
820-840F
Fax 43-29-60-25

INEXPENSIVE/BUDGET (★ to ★★): US$75-120

Beaubourg
11 Rue S. Le France
Tel. 42-74-34-24

28 rooms
490-850F
Fax 42-78-68-11

Castex Hôtel
5 Rue Castex
Tel. 42-72-31-52

27 rooms
290-380F
Fax 42-72-57-91

Place des Vosges
12 Rue Birague
Tel. 42-72-60-46

16 rooms
325-450F
Fax 42-72-02-64

CHEAP CHEAPS (0 to ★): under US$75

Practic	24 rooms
9 Rue d'Ormesson	250-375F
Tel. 48-87-80-47	Fax 48-87-40-04

5TH ARRONDISSEMENT (LEFT BANK)

If you prefer staying on the Left Bank, you'll find some excellent medium-range hotels here. One of our favorites, Le Notre Dame Hôtel, has great views of Notre Dame Cathedral.

EXPENSIVE (★★★): US$200-300

Colbert	36 rooms
7 Rue de l'Hôtel-Colbert	1,000F
Tel. 43-25-85-65	Fax 43-25-80-19
Royal St-Michel	39 rooms
3 Boulevard St-Michel	740-1120F
Tel. 44-07-06-06	Fax 44-07-36-25

MEDIUM-RANGE (★★ to ★★★): US$120-200

Grands Hommes	32 rooms
17 Place du Panthéon	725-775F
Tel. 46-34-19-60	Fax 43-26-67-32
Le Notre-Dame	23 rooms
1 Quai St-Michel	590-790F
Tel. 43-54-20-43	Fax 43-26-61-75
Panthéon	34 rooms
19 Place Panthéon	775-790F
Tel. 43-54-32-95	Fax 43-26-64-65
Parc Saint-Séverin	27 rooms
22 Rue de la Parcheminerie	610-1100F
Tel. 43-54-32-17	Fax 43-54-70-71
Résidence Henri IV	9 rooms
50 Rue Bernardins	700-900F
Tel. 44-41-31-81	Fax 46-33-93-22

Select   67 rooms
1 Place Sorbonne   650-890F
Tel. 46-34-14-80   Fax 46-34-51-79

INEXPENSIVE/BUDGET (★ to ★★): US$75-120

La Sorbonne   37 rooms
6 Rue Victor cousin   410-480F
Tel. 43-54-58-08   Fax 40-51-05-18

CHEAP CHEAPS (0 to ★): under US$75

Port-Royal Hôtel   48 Rooms
8 Boulevard Port-Royal   185-275F
Tel. 43-31-70-06

6TH ARRONDISSEMENT (LEFT BANK)

If you love staying in the Left Bank, then don't look any further
than the numerous charming hotels in this district.

VERY EXPENSIVE (★★★★): US$300-700

Lutétia   270 rooms
45 Boulevard Raspail   1650F
Tel. 49-54-46-46   Fax 49-54-46-00

Relais Christine   36 rooms
3 Rue Christine   1580-1650F
Tel. 43-26-71-80   Fax 43-26-89-38

EXPENSIVE (★★★): US$200-300

Left Bank   31 rooms
9 Rue de l'Ancienne Comédie   1,100F
Tel. 43-54-01-70 (US 800-528-1234)   Fax 43-26-17-14

L'Hôtel   24 rooms
13 Rue des Beaux-Arts   1050-1300F
Tel. 43-25-27-22   Fax 43-25-64-81

L'Odéon   29 rooms
13 Rue Saint-Sulpice   890-950F
Tel. 43-25-70-11   Fax 43-29-97-34

MEDIUM-RANGE (★★ to ★★★): US$120-200

Ferrandi
92 Rue de Cherche-Midi
Tel. 42-22-97-40

42 rooms
610-1000F
Fax 45-44-89-97

Latitudes St-Germain
7-11 Rue Saint-Benoît
Tel. 42-61-53-53

117 rooms
650-975F
Fax 49-27-09-33

Régent
61 Rue Dauphine
Tel. 46-34-59-80

25 rooms
775-975F
Fax 40-51-05-07

Saint-Germain-des-Prés
37 Rue Bonaparte
Tel. 42-26-00-19

30 rooms
800-1,050F
Fax 40-46-83-63

Saint-Grégoire
43 Rue de l'Abbé Grégoire
Tel. 45-48-23-23

20 rooms
775-900F
Fax 45-48-33-94

INEXPENSIVE/BUDGET (★ to ★★): US$75-120

Aviatic
105 Rue de Vaugirard
Tel. 44-44-38-21

43 rooms
490-670F
Fax 45-49-35-83

Dragon
36 Rue du Dragon
Tel. 45-48-51-05

28 rooms
390-450F
Fax 42-22-51-62

CHEAP CHEAPS (0 to ★): under US$75

Académies
15 Rue de la Grande Chaumiére
Tel. 43-16-66-44

21 rooms
245-300F

7TH ARRONDISSEMENT (LEFT BANK)

This is a choice location for Left Bank hotels. It's another good area for finding medium-range and budget accommodations. You'll be close to the Eiffel Tower and Invalides and have relatively easy access to the 1st, 6th, 8th, and 16th arrondissements. This is one of our favorite locations.

VERY EXPENSIVE (★★★★): US$300-700

Montalembert
3 Rue Montalembert
Tel. 45-48-68-11

51 rooms
1625-2080F
Fax 42-22-58-19

EXPENSIVE (★★★): US$200-300

Duc de Saint-Simon
14 Rue St-Simon
Tel. 44-39-20-20

29 rooms
1065-1465F
Fax 45-48-68-25

Le Tourville
16 Av. Tourville
Tel. 47-05-62-62

30 rooms
760-1390F
Fax 47-05-43-90

MEDIUM-RANGE (★★ to ★★★): US$120-200

La Bourdannais
111 Av. La Bourdonnais
Tel. 47-05-45-42

57 rooms
471-662F
Fax 45-55-75-54

Lenox Saint-Germain
9 Rue Université
Tel. 42-96-10-95

32 rooms
590-830F
Fax 42-61-52-83

Les Jardins D'Eiffel
8 Rue Amélie
Tel. 47-05-46-21

80 rooms
700-860F
Fax 45-55-28-08

Sèvres Vaneau
86 Rue Vaneau
Tel. 45-48-73-11

39 rooms
760-815F
Fax 45-49-27-74

Splendid
29 Av. Tourville
Tel. 45-51-24-77

48 rooms
680/990F
Fax 44-18-94-60

INEXPENSIVE/BUDGET (★ to ★★): US$75-120

Palais Bourbon
49 Rue de Bourgogne
Tel. 45-51-63-32

49 rooms
340-580F
Fax 45-55-20-21

CHEAP CHEAPS (0 to ★): under US$75

Grand Hôtel Lévêque　　　　　　50 rooms
29 Rue Cler　　　　　　　　　　　200-375F
Tel. 47-05-49-15　　　　　　　　　Fax 45-50-49-36

8TH ARRONDISSEMENT (RIGHT BANK)

This arrondissement has Paris' largest concentration of luxury hotels at budget-busting prices. Staying here puts you at the center of Paris' finest restaurants and shopping and within easy walking distance of its major attractions. Staying at one of the super-luxury hotels gives you an extremely prestigious Parisian address: you're probably a very important person or someone with lots of money and class!

❑ **Crillon:** 10 Place Concorde, 75008 Paris, Tel. 44-71-15-00, Fax 44-71-15-02. 120 rooms, 43 suites. It doesn't get much better, except arguably with the Plaza Athénée or the Ritz hotels, Paris' three most prestigious addresses. Located on the beautiful world-famous plaza, Place de la Concorde, this is the hotel of choice for the rich and famous. Richly decorated in 18th century style. Includes the all-star Les Ambassadeurs restaurant. 2800-4000F. Very, very expensive ($$$$$$).

❑ **Plaza Athénée:** 23-27 Avenue Montaigne, 75008 Paris, Tel. 47-23-78-33, Fax 47-20-20-70. 170 rooms, 41 suites. Located in heart of Paris' most exclusive shopping district, this is the hotel of the infamous Mata Hari and to many of today's international celebrities. Gorgeous property. Fabulously elegant hotel. 2400-3150F. Very, very expensive ($$$$$$).

❑ **Bristol:** 112 Rue du Faubourg St. Honoré, 75008 Paris, Tel. 42-66-91-45, Fax 42-66-68-68. 154 rooms, 41 suites. This well-appointed, elegant hotel is located along one of Paris' major shopping streets. Spacious rooms decorated with period furniture. Understated elegance. Includes an enclosed rooftop pool. 2500-4400F. Very, very expensive ($$$$$$).

❑ **George V:** 31 Avenue George-V, Tel. 47-23-54-00, Fax 47-20-40-00. 221 rooms, 39 suites. This lavish art deco hotel is another major address for the visiting rich and famous, including many American movie celebrities. 1800-3900F. Very expensive ($$$$$).

❏ **Royal Monceau:** 47 Avenue Hoche, Tel. 42-99-88-00, Fax 42-99-89-90. 180 rooms, 39 suites. Centrally located with a view of the Arc de Triomphe, this elegant hotel has hosted many world famous leaders. Large rooms. 2100-3200F. Very expensive ($$$$$).

❏ **Prince de Galles:** 33 Avenue George-V, Tel. 47-23-55-11, Fax 46-20-96-92. Located near the center of Paris' most exclusive shopping district. Elegantly furnished rooms. 2500-3300F. Very expensive ($$$$$).

VERY EXPENSIVE (★★★★): US$300-700

Balzac 6 Rue Balzac Tel. 45-61-97-22	56 rooms 1650-2200F Fax 42-25-24-82
Concorde St-Lazare 108 Rue St-Lazare Tel. 40-08-44-44	295 rooms 1260-1460F Fax 42-93-01-20
de Vigny 9 Rue Balzac Tel. 40-75-04-39	25 rooms 1900-2200F Fax 44-31-85-69
Golden Tulip St. Honoré 220 Rue du Faubourg St. Honoré Tel. 49-53-03-03	54 rooms 1500-1700F Fax 40-75-02-00
La Trémoille 14 Rue La Trémoille Tel. 47-23-34-20	94 rooms 1950-2930F Fax 40-70-01-08
Lancaster 7 Rue Berri Tel. 40-76-40-76	52 rooms 1950-2650F Fax 40-76-40-00
San Régis 12 Rue Jean-Goujon Tel. 44-95-16-16	34 rooms 1600-2750F Fax 45-61-05-48

Vernet	54 rooms
25 Rue Vernet	1550-2250F
Tel. 44-31-98-00	Fax 44-31-85-69

Warwick	142 rooms
5 Rue Berri	2090-2650F
Tel. 45-63-14-11	Fax 45-63-75-81

EXPENSIVE (★★★): US$200-300

Beau Manoir	29 rooms
5 Rue de l'Arcade	995-1155F
Tel. 420-66-03-07	Fax 42-68-03-00

Claridge Bellman	42 rooms
37 Rue Francois	1150-1350F
Tel. 47-23-54-42	Fax 46-23-08-84

Paris St-Honoré	104 rooms
15 Rue Boissy d'Anglas	800-1055F
Tel. 44-94-14-14	Fax 44-94-14-28

Powers	53 rooms
52 Rue François	800-1250F
Tel. 47-23-91-05	Fax 49-52-04-63

MEDIUM-RANGE (★★ to ★★★): US$120-200

Atlantic	88 rooms
44 Rue Londres	490-750F
Tel. 43-87-45-40	Fax 42-93-06-26

Flèche d'Or	61 rooms
29 Rue Amsterdam	550-750F
Tel. 48-74-06-86	Fax 48-74-06-04

Lido	32 rooms
4 Passage de la Madeleine	800-930F
Tel. 42-66-27-37	Fax 42-66-61-23

Lord Byron	31 rooms
5 Rue Chateaubriand	660-970F
Tel. 43-59-89-98	Fax 42-89-46-04

Ministère 31 Rue Surène Tel. 42-6621-43	28 rooms 410-660F Fax 42-66-96-04
Opal 19 Rue Tronchet Tel. 42-65-77-97	36 rooms 470-580F Fax 49-24-06-58
Queen Mary 9 Rue Greffulhe Tel. 42-66-40-50	36 rooms 710-890F Fax 42-66-94-92

INEXPENSIVE/BUDGET (★ to ★★): US$75-120

New Orient 16 Rue Constantinople Tel. 45-22-21-64	30 rooms 380-480F Fax 42-93-83-23

9TH ARRONDISSEMENT (RIGHT BANK)

You will find several good hotels in this district, from luxury to budget. This also is a good location because of the close proximity to the shopping and attractions of the 1st and 8th arrondissements. The best locations are near the Opéra Garnier and Madeleine.

❑ **Grand Hôtel Inter-Continental:** 2 Rue Scribe, Tel. 40-07-32-32, Fax 42-66-12-51. 478 rooms, 15 suites. This is Paris' largest luxury hotel and the ultimate business hotel. Built in 1862, it boasts large rooms and full amenities. 2300-2500. Very expensive ($$$$$).

VERY EXPENSIVE (★★★★): US$300-700

Ambassador 16 Boulevard Haussmann Tel. 44-83-40-40	298 rooms 1410-1710F Fax 42-46-19-84
Commodore 12 Boulevard Haussmann Tel. 42-46-72-82	162 rooms 1100-2050F Fax 47-70-23-81
Scribe 1 Rue Scribe Tel. 44-71-24-24	206 rooms 1750-2200F Fax 42-65-39-97

EXPENSIVE (★★★): US$200-300

Opéra Cadet	82 rooms
24 Rue Cadet	710-990F
Tel. 48-24-05-26	Fax 42-46-68-09

MEDIUM-RANGE (★★ to ★★★): US$120-200

Axel	38 rooms
15 Rue Montyon	490-750
Tel. 47-70-92-70	Fax 47-70-43-37

Blanche Fontaine	45 rooms
34 Rue Fontaine	507-509F
Tel. 45-26-72-32	Fax 42-81-05-52

du Pré	40 rooms
10 Rue Pierre-Sémard	630-740F
Tel. 42-81-37-11	Fax 40-23-98-28

Franklin	68 rooms
19 Rue Buffault	760-815F
Tel. 42-80-27-27	Fax 48-78-13-04

La Tour d'Auvergne	25 rooms
10 Rue de La Tour d'Auvergne	450-650F
Tel. 48-78-61-60	Fax 49-95-99-00

Léman	24 rooms
20 Rue de Tréman	390-730F
Tel. 42-46-50-66	Fax 48-24-27-59

St-Pétersbourg	100 rooms
33 Rue Caumartin	540-1020F
Tel. 42-66-60-38	Fax 42-66-53-54

INEXPENSIVE/BUDGET (★ to ★★): US$75-120

des Arts	26 rooms
7 Cité Bergère	390-420F
Tel. 42-46-73-30	Fax 48-00-94-42

Riboutté-La Fayette	24 rooms
5 Rue Riboutté	370-450F
Tel. 46-60-62-36	Fax 48-00-91-50

I 0TH ARRONDISSEMENT (RIGHT BANK)

While you can find some medium-range to inexpensive hotels in this area, most visitors do not stay here because it is inconveniently located in reference to the city's major attractions.

MEDIUM-RANGE (★★ to ★★★): US$120-200

L'Horset Pavillon
38 Rue Échiquier
Tel. 42-46-92-75

92 rooms
830-930F
Fax 42-47-03-97

Paix République
2 Bis Boulevard St-Martin
Tel. 42-08-96-95

45 rooms
560-950F
Fax 42-06-36-30

INEXPENSIVE/BUDGET (★ to ★★): US$75-120

Résidence Magenta
35 Rue Yves-Toudic
Tel. 42-40-17-72

32 rooms
320-390F
Fax 42-02-59-66

I 1TH ARRONDISSEMENT (RIGHT BANK)

Somewhat outside the city center, this area is beginning to be revived around the Bastille and the Opéra de Paris Bastille in the southwest corner of this district. You'll find several medium-range and budget hotels in this up and coming area.

MEDIUM-RANGE (★★ to ★★★): US$120-200

Méridional
36 Boulevard Richard-Lenoir
Tel. 48-05-75-00

36 rooms
600F
Fax 43-57-42-85

INEXPENSIVE/BUDGET (★ to ★★): US$75-120

Atlantide République
114 Boulevard Richard-Lenoir
Tel. 43-38-29-29

27 rooms
390-530F
Fax 43-38-03-18

Bel Air
5 Rue Rampon
Tel. 47-00-41-57

48 rooms
450-560F
Fax 47-00-21-56

Verlain
97 Rue St-Maur
Tel. 43-57-44-88

38 rooms
500-535F
Fax 43-57-32-06

CHEAP CHEAPS (0 to ★): under US$75

Nord et Est
49 Rue Malte
Tel. 47-00-71-70

45 rooms
320-360F
Fax 43-57-51-16

❙ 2TH ARRONDISSEMENT (RIGHT BANK)

Similar to the 11th arrondissement, this area is not particularly popular with visitors. Nonetheless, you will find some good budget accommodations here. The best location is near the newly developing section around the Opéra de Paris Bastille.

MEDIUM-RANGE (★★ to ★★★): US$120-200

Novotel Bercy
85 Rue Bercy
Tel. 43-42-30-00

129 rooms
710-760F
Fax 43-45-30-60

Pavillon Bastille
65 Rue Lyon
Tel. 43-43-65-65

24 rooms
955F
Fax 43-43-96-52

INEXPENSIVE/BUDGET (★ to ★★): US$75-120

Ibis Bercy
77 Rue Bercy
Tel. 43-42-91-91

368 rooms
450-455F
Fax 43-42-34-79

❙ 3TH ARRONDISSEMENT (LEFT BANK)

Not much here to recommend for accommodations. This is not a particularly attractive area for visitors. Nonetheless, you'll find some well priced budget accommodations here.

MEDIUM-RANGE (★★ to ★★★): US$120-200

Mercure Place d'Italie
178 Boulevard Vincent Auriol
Tel. 44-24-01-01

70 rooms
680-785F
Fax 44-24-07-07

INEXPENSIVE/BUDGET (★ to ★★): US$75-120

Média   19 rooms
22 Rue Reine Blanche   395-450F
Tel. 45-35-72-72   Fax 43-31-43-31

CHEAP CHEAPS (0 to ★): under US$75

Arts   37 rooms
8 Rue Coypel   275-360F
Tel. 47-07-76-32   Fax 43-31-18-09

14TH ARRONDISSEMENT (LEFT BANK)

The northern section of this arrondissement, at Montparnasse, is a good location for access into the popular 6th and 7th arrondissements.

VERY EXPENSIVE (★★★★): US$300-700

Méridien Montparnasse   914 rooms
19 Rue Cdt Mouchotte   1700-1900F
Tel. 44-36-44-36   Fax 44-36-49-00

MEDIUM-RANGE (★★ to ★★★): US$120-200

L'Aiglon   38 rooms
232 Boulevard Raspail   480-710F
Tel. 43-20-82-42   Fax 43-20-98-72

Mercure Montparnasse   178 rooms
20 Rue Gaîté   820F
Tel. 43-35-28-28   Fax 43-27-98-64

INEXPENSIVE/BUDGET (★ to ★★): US$75-120

Orléans Palace   92 rooms
185 Boulevard Brune   510-570F
Tel. 45-39-68-50   Fax 45-43-65-64

CHEAP CHEAPS (0 to ★): under US$75

Châtillon   31 rooms
11 Square Châtillon   320-350F
Tel. 45-42-31-17   Fax 45-42-72-09

15TH ARRONDISSEMENT (LEFT BANK)

The northern section of this arrondissement, along Avenue Suffren and Quai Grenelle, is well located in reference to the 9th arrondissement and the Eiffel Tower. This area offers a good range of hotels, from deluxe to budget. Breakfast at the Hilton is delightful!

VERY EXPENSIVE (★★★★): US$300-700

Hilton   429 rooms
18 Avenue Suffren   1860-2065F
Tel. 42-73-92-00   Fax 47-83-62-66

Nikko   761 rooms
61 Quai Grenelle   1480-2180F
Tel. 40-58-20-00   Fax 45-75-42-35

EXPENSIVE (★★★): US$200-300

Mercure Porte de Versailles   91 rooms
69 Boulevard Victor   884-1064F
Tel. 44-19-03-03   Fax 48-28-22-11

Sofitel Porte de Sèvres   523 rooms
8 Rue Louis-Armand   1280F
Tel. 40-60-30-30   Fax 45-57-04-22

MEDIUM-RANGE (★★ to ★★★): US$120-200

Mercure Tour Eiffel   64 rooms
64 Boulevard Grenelle   900F
Tel. 45-78-90-90   Fax 45-78-95-55

INEXPENSIVE/BUDGET (★ to ★★): US$75-120

Alizé Grenelle   50 rooms
87 Avenue Emile-Zola   410-490F
Tel. 45-78-08-22   Fax 40-59-03-06

CHEAP CHEAPS (0 to ★): under US$75

Tourisme   60 rooms
66 Avenue La Motte-Picquet   280-410F
Tel. 47-34-28-01   Fax 47-83-66-54

16TH ARRONDISSEMENT (RIGHT BANK)

This is one of the Paris' upscale districts, especially along Avenue Victor Hugo, Avenue Kléber, and Rue Longchamp. A good location for access to the popular 8th arrondissement.

VERY EXPENSIVE (★★★★): US$300-700

Baltimore
88 Bis Avenue Kléber
Tel. 44-34-54-54

104 rooms
1690-2950F
Fax 44-34-54-44

Le Parc Victor Hugo
55 Avenue Raymond-Poincaré
Tel. 44-05-66-66

107 rooms
1690-2300F
Fax 44-05-66-00

Raphaël
17 Avenue Kléber
Tel. 44-28-00-28

64 rooms
1950-2950F
Fax 45-01-21-50

St-James Paris
43 Avenue Bugeaud
Tel. 44-05-81-81

20 rooms
2100-3000F
Fax 44-05-81-82

EXPENSIVE (★★★): US$200-300

Alexander
102 Avenue Victor Hugo
Tel. 45-53-64-65

62 rooms
830-1300F
Fax 45-53-12-51

Rond-Point de Longchamp
86 Rue Longchamp
Tel. 45-05-13-63

57 rooms
730-1000F
Fax 47-55-12-80

MEDIUM-RANGE (★★ to ★★★): US$120-200

Étoile-Maillot
10 Rue de Bois de Boulogne
Tel. 45-00-42-60

28 rooms
660-800F
Fax 45-00-55-89

Gavarni
5 Rue Gavarni
Tel. 45-24-52-82

30 rooms
550-570F
Fax 40-50-16-95

Massenet
5 Bis Rue Massenet
Tel. 45-24-43-03

41 rooms
500-760F
Fax 45-24-41-39

Regina de Passy
6 Rue de la Tour
Tel. 45-24-43-64

64 rooms
630-900F
Fax 40-50-70-62

17TH ARRONDISSEMENT (RIGHT BANK)

While this is primarily a residential area, the southern section of this district borders on the Arc de Triomphe. It includes several very nice hotels, ranging from deluxe to medium-range. A good location for access to the 8th arrondissement.

VERY EXPENSIVE (★★★★): US$300-700

Concorde La Fayette
3 Place Général-Koenig
Tel. 40-68-50-68

943 rooms
1420-1820F
Fax 40-68-50-43

Méridien
81 Boulevard Gouvion St. Cyr
Tel. 40-68-34-34

1007 rooms
1450-1850F
Fax 40-68-31-31

EXPENSIVE (★★★): US$200-300

Splendid Etoile
1 Bis Avenue Carnot
Tel. 45-72-72-00

57 rooms
890-1650F
Fax 45-72-72-01

MEDIUM-RANGE (★★ to ★★★): US$120-200

Balmoral
5 Rue Général-Lanrezac
Tel. 43-80-30-50

57 rooms
500-700F
Fax 43-80-51-56

Magellan
17 Rue Jean-Baptiste-Dumas
Tel. 45-72-44-51

75 rooms
407-594F
Fax 40-68-90-36

Quality Inn Pierre
25 Rue Théodore-de-Banville
Tel. 47-63-76-69

50 rooms
790-870F
Fax 43-80-63-96

Regent's Garden
6 Rue Pierre-Demours
Tel. 45-74-07-30

39 rooms
640-930F
Fax 40-55-01-42

INEXPENSIVE/BUDGET (★ to ★★): US$75-120

Palma
46 Rue Brunel
Tel. 45-74-74-51

37 rooms
380-460F
Fax 45-74-40-90

18TH ARRONDISSEMENT (Right Bank)

This is the area of Paris' largest flea market and the popular Sacré-Cœur Basilica. There's not much to recommend here for accommodations. The area is inconveniently located in reference to other major districts. Most people prefer coming to this area via the Metro rather than stay here and then commute to other districts.

EXPENSIVE (★★★): US$200-300

Terrass
12 Rue Joseph-de-Maistre
Tel. 46-06-72-85

88 rooms
930-1230F
Fax 42-52-2911

MEDIUM-RANGE (★★ to ★★★): US$120-200

Mercure Montmartre
1 Rue Caulaincourt
Tel. 44-69-70-70

308 rooms
710-770F
Fax 44-69-71-72

INEXPENSIVE/BUDGET (★ to ★★): US$75-120

Roma Sacré Cœur
101 Rue Caulaincourt
Tel. 42-62-02-02

57 rooms
410-430F
Fax 42-54-34-92

19TH ARRONDISSEMENT (Right Bank)

Not much here to recommend. Visitors normally avoid this relatively poor area.

CHEAP CHEAPS (0 to ★): under US$75

Hôtel Le Laumiè	54 rooms
4 Rue Petit	255-370F
Tel. 42-06-10-77	Fax 42-06-72-50

20TH ARRONDISSEMENT (RIGHT BANK)

Similar to the 19th arrondissement, this is a relatively poor area where few visitors venture. Most noted for its cemetery, Cimetière du Père Lachaise, where major celebrities are buried.

INEXPENSIVE/BUDGET (★ to ★★): US$75-120

Palma	32 rooms
77 Avenue Gambetta	340-395F
Tel. 46-36-13-65	Fax 46-36-03-27

CHEAP CHEAPS (0 to ★): under US$75

Super Hôtel	32 rooms
208 Rue Pyrénées	280-500F
Tel. 46-36-97-48	Fax 46-36-26-10

162 SHINING AND ASPIRING STARS

We've reclassified our hotels into quality and cost categories for ease of review and decision-making. The abbreviations in the third column indicate the location of each hotel by arrondissement (1st, 7th 16th) and whether it's located in the Right Bank (RB) or Left Bank (LB).

Our ten five-star hotels represent the very "best of the best" in Parisian accommodations. These are the ultimate in luxury—price-is-no-object properties. Our four-star hotels normally cost between US$300 and US$700 per night for a double. The three-star hotels will cost US$200-300 per night. The medium-range two- and three-star hotels cost US$120-200 per night. Our one and two-star hotels go for US$75-120 per night. Anything else goes for less than US$75 a night.

If you select a hotel based on this listing, please refer to the previous section which includes brief information on the property, especially the address and fax and telephone numbers.

★★★★★	Bristol	8th/RB	$$$$$
	Crillon	8th/RB	$$$$$
	George V	8th/RB	$$$$
	Grand Hôtel		
	Inter-Continental	9th/RB	$$$$
	Inter-Continental	1st/RB	$$$$
	Meurice	1st/RB	$$$$
	Plaza Athénée	8th/RB	$$$$$
	Prince de Galles	8th/RB	$$$$
	Ritz	1st/RB	$$$$$
	Royal Monceau	8th/RB	$$$$
★★★★	Ambassador	9th/RB	$$$$
	Baltimore	16th/RB	$$$$
	Balzac	8th/RB	$$$$
	Castille	1st/RB	$$$$
	Commodore	9th/RB	$$$$
	Concorde La Fayette	17th/RB	$$$$
	Concorde St-Lazare	8th/RB	$$$$
	de Louvre	1st/RB	$$$$
	de Vigny	8th/RB	$$$$
	Golden Tulip St. Honoré	8th/RB	$$$$
	Hilton	15th/LB	$$$$
	Le Parc Victor Hugo	16th/RB	$$$$
	La Trémoille	8th/RB	$$$$
	Lancaster	8th/RB	$$$$
	Lotti	1st/RB	$$$$
	Lutétia	6th/LB	$$$$
	Méridien	17th/RB	$$$$
	Méridien Montparnasse	14th/LB	$$$$
	Montalembert	7th/LB	$$$$
	Nikko	15th/LB	$$$$
	Pavillon de la Reine	3rd/RB	$$$$
	Raphaël	16th/RB	$$$$½
	Relais Christine	6th/LB	$$$$
	San Régis	8th/RB	$$$$
	Scribe	9th/RB	$$$$
	Stendhal	2nd/RB	$$$$
	St-James Paris	16th/RB	$$$$½
	Vernet	8th/RB	$$$$
	Warwick	8th/RB	$$$$½
	Westminister	2nd/RB	$$$$
★★★	Alexander	16th/RB	$$$
	Beau Manoir	8th/RB	$$$
	Claridge Bellman	8th/RB	$$$½

	Colbert	6th/LB	$$$
	Duc de Saint-Simon	7th/LB	$$$½
	Édouard VII et rest.		
	Le Delmonico	2nd/RB	$$$
	Jeu de Paume	4th/RB	$$$
	Le Tourville	7th/LB	$$$
	Left Bank	6th/LB	$$$
	L'Horset Opéra	2nd/RB	$$$
	L'Hôtel	6th/LB	$$$
	L'Odéon	6th/LB	$$$
	Mayfair	1st/RB	$$$
	Mercure Porte de Varsailles	15th/LB	$$$
	Opéra Cadet	9th/RB	$$$½
	Paris St-Honoré	8th/RB	$$$
	Powers	8th/RB	$$$
	Rond-Point de Longchamp	16th/RB	$$$
	Royal St-Honoré	1st/RB	$$$½
	Royal St-Michel	6th/LB	$$$
	Sofitel Porte de Sèvres	15th/LB	$$$½
	Splendid Etoile	17th/RB	$$$½
	Terrass	18th/RB	$$$½
★★–★★★	Atlantic	8th/RB	$$
	Axel	9th/RB	$$
	Belmoral	17th/RB	$$
	Blanche Fontaine	9th/RB	$$
	Bretonnerie	4th/RB	$$½
	Britannique	1st/RB	$$½
	de Noailles	2nd/RB	$$½
	de Londres et		
	De Stockholm	1st/RB	$$½
	des Chevalier	3rd/RB	$$
	Deux Illes	4th/RB	$$½
	du Pré	9th/RB	$$
	Étoile-Maillot	16th/RB	$$½
	Favart	2nd/RB	$$
	Ferrandi	6th/LB	$$
	Flèche d'Or	8th/RB	$$
	Franklin	9th/RB	$$½
	Gavarni	16th/RB	$$
	Grand Hôtel de		
	Champagne	1st/RB	$$½
	Grands Hommes	5th/LB	$$½
	La Bourdannais	7th/LB	$$
	La Tour d'Auvergne	9th/RB	$$
	L'Aiglon	14th/LB	$$

Latitudes St-Germain	6th/LB	$$
Lautrec Opéra	2nd/RB	$$½
Léman	9th/RB	$$
Lenox Saint-Germain	7th/LB	$$½
Les Jardins D'Eiffel	7th/LB	$$½
L'Horset Pavillon	10th/RB	$$½
Lido	8th/RB	$$½
Lord Byron	8th/RB	$$
Louvre St-Honoré	1st/RB	$$½
Lutèce	4th/RB	$$½
Magellan	17th/RB	$$
Mansart	1st/RB	$$½
Massenet	16th/RB	$$
Mercure Montparnasse	14th/LB	$$½
Mercure Montparnasse	18th/RB	$$½
Mercure Place d'Italie	13th/LB	$$½
Mercure Tour Eiffel	14th/LB	$$$
Méridional	11th/RB	$$½
Meslay République	3rd/RB	$$
Ministère	8th/RB	$$
Molière	1st/RB	$$
Notre Dame	5th/LB	$$
Novotel Bercy	12th/RB	$$½
Novotel Les Halles	1st/RB	$$½
Opal	8th/RB	$$
Paix République	10th/RB	$$
Panthéon	5th/LB	$$½
Parc Saint-Séverin	5th/LB	$$½
Pavillon Bastille	12th/RB	$$$
Quality Inn Pierre	17th/RB	$$½
Queen Mary	8th/RB	$$½
Régent	6th/LB	$$½
Regent's Garden	17th/RB	$$
Regina de Passy	16th/RB	$$
Résidence Henri IV	5th/LB	$$½
Saint-Germain-des-Prés	6th/LB	$$½
Saint-Grégoire	6th/LB	$$½
Select	5th/LB	$$½
Sèvres Vaneau	7th/LB	$$½
Splendid	7th/LB	$$½
St-Péterbourg	9th/RB	$$
★–★★ Alizé Grenelle	15th/LB	$
Atlantide République	11th/RB	$½
Aviatic	6th/LB	$½
Baudelaire Opéra	2nd/RB	$

	Beaubourg	4th/RB	$$
	Bel Air	11th/RB	$½
	Castex Hôtel	4th/RB	$
	des Arts	9th/RB	$
	Dragon	6th/LB	$½
	Ibis Bercy	12th/RB	$
	La Sorbonne	5th/LB	$½
	Média	13th/LB	$
	New Orient	8th/RB	$½
	Orléans Palace	14th/LB	$½
	Palais Bourbon	7th/LB	$½
	Palma	17th/RB	$
	Palma	20th/RB	$
	Place des Vosges	4th/RB	$
	Résidence Magenta	10th/RB	$
	Riboutté-La Fayette	9th/RB	$
	Roma Sacré Cœur	18th/RB	$
	Verlain	11th/RB	$
	Vieux Saule	3rd/RB	$½
0–★	Académies	6th/LB	½
	Arts	13th/LB	½
	Châtillon	14th/LB	½
	Grand Hôtel Lévêque	7th/LB	½
	Hôtel du Palais	1st/RB	½
	Hôtel Le Laumiè	19th/RB	½
	Hôtel Lille	1st/RB	½
	Nord et Est	11th/RB	½
	Port-Royal Hôtel	5th/LB	½
	Practic	4th/RB	½
	Super Hôtel	20th/RB	½
	Tourisme	15th/LB	½
	Vivienne	2nd/RB	½

13 GOOD VALUE HOTELS

If you're looking for good value and you don't want to spend a fortune on a hotel room, we highly recommend staying at some of Paris' best two and three-star hotels. For between US$100 and US$200 a night, you can be centrally located in a small but very charming hotel that is clean, comfortable, and quiet. In fact, many of these hotels become one of the most enjoyable aspects of visiting Paris. They often become pleasant cultural experiences that don't bust the budget.

Three of our favorite such hotels are conveniently located in the Left Bank. We've stayed in these places and would be happy to return to each at some future date.

❑ **Le Notre-Dame Hôtel:** 1 Quai St-Michel, 75005 (5th arr.), Tel. 43-54-20-43, Fax 43-26-61-75. 26 rooms. A real gem. The location and view doesn't get much better than from this small and charming hotel located across the street from the Seine and with gorgeous views of Notre-Dame Cathedral. Rooms are sound-proofed so you can watch the noisy traffic pass in front of the Cathedral without having to hear it. Be sure to request a corner room with a view (#22 and 32). You'll have to walk one flight of stairs from the ground floor to the reception area on the first floor. Rooms are small but all have a bath with tub and/or shower. Excellent and helpful service. Metro stop is just across the street, restaurants are everywhere, and you're basically in the 6th arrondissement. Book well in advance (2-3 months) because this has become a very popular hotel (featured recently in *Condé Nast Traveler* as one of their "Room With a View" selections). We would even book further in advance to guarantee one of the few corner rooms facing the Cathedral. Single 550F (no view) or 760F (view); double 650F (no view) and 870F (view); duplex 1250F (view). 45F extra per person for breakfast.

❑ **Hôtel Ferrandi:** 92 Rue de Cherche-Midi, 75006 (6th arr.), Tel. 42-22-97-40, Fax 45-44-89-97. 42 rooms. Located along a relatively quiet street but with easy access to major streets (Montparnasse, Sèvres, Raspail). This well managed property includes several nice size rooms (some are very small) that are well furnished and comfortable. Helpful front desk. Has a charming sitting area, with fireplace, and a delightful breakfast area. Close to several small restaurants and discount shops. Includes a parking garage—space in garage should be requested when reservation is made (125F per day). Single 480F; double 610-1000F; triple 1000F; apartment 1100F. Breakfast is 60F extra per person.

❑ **Hôtel la Bourdonnais:** 111 Avenue de la Bourdonnais, 75007 (7th arr.), Tel. 47-05-45-42, Fax 45-55-75-54. 60 rooms. Centrally located between the Eiffel Tower and Invalides, this older property offers clean, well-furnished, and quiet rooms in a charming residential neighborhood. While the well worn doors could be upgraded, the rooms are very comfortable and some include spacious bath-rooms. Includes a nice sitting area on the ground floor and a sunny breakfast area. The hotel is near several restaurants and a supermarket which are found just around the corner. It's also adjacent to one of Paris' top 20 restaurants, La Bourdannais. If you want to try a top restaurant that's just outside your hotel door, it doesn't get much more convenient than staying at this hotel! Single 490F; double 570-630F; triple 680F; quad 740F; suite 975F. Breakfast is 35F extra per person.

Other medium-range hotels receiving high marks from seasoned travelers to Paris include the following:

- ❑ Colbert (5th arr.)
- ❑ Latitudes St-Germain (6th arr.)
- ❑ Left Bank Hôtel (6th arr.)
- ❑ Massenet (16th arr.)
- ❑ Molière (1st arr.)
- ❑ Parc Saint-Séverin (5th arr.)
- ❑ Regina de Passy (16th arr.)
- ❑ Saint-Grégoire (6th arr.)
- ❑ Saint-Germain-des-Prés (6th arr.)

If you're looking for an inexpensive one-star hotel, you can't do much better than the **Port-Royal Hôtel** (8 Boulevard Port-Royal, 75005, Tel. 43-31-70-06) in the 5th arrondissement. It out-performs some two and three-star hotels for an unbelievable price of 185-275F for a double (add 15F for a room with a shower)!

Since all of these hotels are very popular with travelers, be sure to make your reservations well in advance. We highly recommend faxing or telephoning the hotels to ensure proper reservations.

6

Restaurants and Food Galore!

S o, you've got to eat, whether you want to or not. For some travelers, eating is one of those activities that must be done, and done with as little expensive as possible; even a picnic in the park or in one's hotel room will do. For others, dining becomes one of the great pleasures of travel, and especially one of the highlights of visiting Paris, the reputed culinary capital of the world! They want to experience the best of the best in dining, expecting to sample exceptional culinary talent. And for still others, learning about French cuisine is a great way to better understand the French people and culture.

A MOVEABLE FEAST, A CULTURAL EXPERIENCE

Ernest Hemingway referred to Paris as "a moveable feast." Indeed it is when it comes to Paris' many food markets and its thousands of eating establishments. Food is everywhere, be it in restaurants, cafés, bistros, brasseries, wine bars, tea rooms, supermarkets, gourmet shops, street markets, corner vendors, pastry shops, or bakeries. It overwhelms the visitor who has so much to choose from but so little knowledge of where to start what may well turn into an incredible culinary adventure.

Whatever your preferences, you'll find numerous dining alternatives in Paris, from the all-star gastronomic temples serving haute cuisine at more than US$200 per person to the more mundane budget restaurant, fast food outlet, or friendly small neighborhood grocery store. You won't go hungry in the famous culinary capital, but you can easily wreck havoc on your travel budget if you don't plan the "what" and "where" of dining in Paris. In fact, it's not difficult to spend over $300 a day per person on food—US$40 for breakfast, US$75 for lunch, and US$200 for dinner. On the other hand, you can eat well in Paris for under $40 a day.

Whatever your dining preferences and budget, you have indeed come to the world's most incredible food mecca. If you become intrigued with French cuisine and Paris' numerous ethnic eateries, you may want to spend much of your time discovering Paris' many dining pleasures. If you plan well, Paris will surely satisfy your appetite and you'll learn a great deal about French lifestyle and culture. You may even think the French are what they eat!

- ❑ You won't go hungry in Paris, but you can easily wreck havoc on your travel budget if you don't plan the "what" and "where" of dining in Paris.

- ❑ It's not difficult to spend over $300 a day per person on food, but you can also eat well in Paris for under $40.

- ❑ Dining in Paris is serious business with more than 20,000 eateries to choose from.

- ❑ You may pay three to five times more in Paris for comparable cuisine than you might pay back home. The reason for such high prices is that Paris is simply very expensive!

BEWILDERING CHOICES

For first-time visitors, dining in Paris appears to be no simple matter. Dining here is serious business with more than 20,000 eateries to choose from and numerous colorful food markets to visit. **Rungis**, the huge 625 acre wholesale food market, with nearly 2,000 sellers on the southern outskirts of Paris, is where it all begins. Here, early in the morning, Paris' restauranteurs compete with other wholesale buyers for the very finest in meats, fish, poultry, game, fruits, vegetables, dairy produce, and cut flowers transported here from all over France. While visitors can't buy at Rungis—only professional buyers—you can at least observe the fascinating activity that eventually results in some of the world's finest cuisine being served in some of the world's very best restaurants.

The structure of French dining alternatives can be daunting to many newcomers who would just as soon go on a diet, look for an inexpensive fast-food outlet, stay close to their hotel restaurant, or hang out at the local grocery store or pastry shop than enter a restaurant, café, brasserie, tea room, or wine bar where the menus look truly foreign!

Never fear. Your dining choices in Paris are both plentiful and appropriate to all types of tastes and budgets. Best of all, many menus are in English and, when not, waiters and waitresses are often happy to help you translate the menu as well as recommend appropriate menu choices. How well you will dine in Paris is another matter altogether. In Paris you'll discover great haute cuisine restaurants serving the world's most outstanding and innovative dishes, but you may also end up in places that are very mediocre and frankly disappointing.

If you want to dine Paris right and discover its many unique gastronomic treasures and pleasures, you'll need some assistance in finding places that meet your goals and expectations. Perhaps you want to sample the work of Paris' greatest chefs (**Joël Robuchon, Alain Senderens, Alain Passard**); dine at truly fine restaurants with million dollar views of the City of Lights at night (**Jules-Verne** or **Tour d'Argent**); bask in some of the most beautiful restaurants in the world (**Grand Véfour, Lapérouse, Maxim's**); or simply dine at some of the world's finest gastronomic temples (**Joël Robuchon, Taillevent, Ambroisie, Laurent, Lasserre, Lucas-Carton**). Or perhaps you want to sample some of Paris' most famous cafés (**Les Deux Magots, Café de Flore, Fouquet's**), ethnic restaurants (**Yugaraj, l'Atlas, Kim-Anh**), or inexpensive restaurants that offer good food and atmosphere (**Parraudin, La Marlotte, Bristot Le P'Tit Troquet**) most of which are found in the 5th, 6th, and 7th arrondissements of the Left Bank. Why not experience a fascinating cultural dimension of French food by visiting one of Paris' incredible food emporiums or colorful street markets? Or maybe you would like an educational experience—join a French cooking school for a day or week or observe a cooking demonstration for a few hours (**Le Cordon Bleu, Ritz-Escoffier**)? Food in Paris has much greater meaning than just satisfying one's need for sustenance.

Many of Paris' great restaurants and cafés have remained great for decades, with some dating from the 19th century. But where should you go and what can you expect to spend for breakfast, lunch, and dinner? A whole publishing industry has emerged to assist you in making the proper Parisian dining choices. Indeed, we recommend consulting the following dining guides for the latest information on the best of the best for different categories of dining:

❑ *Michelin, Guide France Hôtels et Restaurants*: Published annually, this red "bible" rates France's top restaurants. When a restaurant is anointed the much-coveted Michelin one, two, or three stars, it joins the ranks of the world's very best. This is the restaurant guide all others try to emulate. They do so with little success. Published in French.

❑ *The Best of Paris* (Los Angeles, CA: Gault Millau, Inc.). Published annually, this Gault Millau guide gives grades (10-20) and anoints toques (chef's hats) to the best of Paris' restaurants. This is one of the most respected and reliable restaurant rating guides, the major competitor to *Michelin*.

❑ *Restaurants of Paris* (New York: Alfred A. Knopf). One of the newest entries into the restaurant recommendation business. Essentially a coffee table book which some people try to travel with, this beautifully illustrated book provides enormous details on French barnyards and Parisian food and restaurants, most of which you can live without and is truly esoteric (Have you ever wanted to know what part of a French cow your veal comes from, or how the kitchen is laid out at the Les Ambassadeurs restaurant in the Hôtel de Crillon?). After digging through all the glossy photos and busy illustrations, you'll find some useful dining information, especially in the appendix appropriately entitled "Guide to the Restaurants of Paris."

❑ *Cheap Eats in Paris* (San Francisco, CA: Chronicle Books). Written by the always reliable Sandra Gustafson (also see her *Cheap Sleeps in Paris* for reliable hotel recommendations) who has a passion for eating and sleeping cheaply throughout Europe, this book provides detailed information on some of the best value restaurants in Paris. She really does her homework. While her restaurants are not always cheap (US$30 is considered cheap in Paris these days!), they will not bust your budget. Using this guide, you'll find lots of good restaurants where you can dine for under 130F (US$30) per person, with many eateries in the 50-100F (US$11-22) range, which is relatively cheap these days in Paris. Insightful annotations and user-friendly.

❑ *The Food Lover's Guide to Paris* (New York: Workman Press). Written by Patricia Wells, this is one of the best restaurant guides to Paris. Organized by arrondissements, it includes lengthy annotations as well as an occasional recipe from some of Paris' best restaurants.

❑ *Paris Bistros and Wine Bars* (Hopewell, NJ: Ecco Press). Authored by Robert and Barbara Hamburger, this guide tells you everything you ever wanted to know about bistros and wine bars in Paris. Includes detailed summaries of the best such establishments.

SHOCKING PRICES

A question always arises, are Parisian restaurants really worth the high prices they charge? Absolutely not compared to many fine restaurants elsewhere in the world. If coffee costs US$5 a cup and a Coke Cola is US$8, if US$30 per person is considered cheap dining, if you must pay US$60 for lunch, and if your restaurant bill comes to US$200 per person for dinner, what is it you're getting that's so special? Nothing, really. Just the privilege of being in one of the world's most exciting and expensive cities. You're in France. And the French have a very high cost and standard of living which has little to do with getting good value for your franc or dollar. You may pay three to five times more in Paris for comparable cuisine you might find back home. Differences in quality do not explain nor rationalize such high prices. High taxes, high rents, high costs of labor, and the economies of scale, or the lack thereof (small restaurants with few customers each day), go a long way to explaining the high costs of Parisian restaurants.

Let's face the high costs and get on with the realities of spending money. The truth of the matter is that everything is outrageously expensive in Paris. You'll simply have to pay the price if you want to experience the "best of the best" in Parisian restaurants.

MAJOR CHOICES

Paris' eating establishments fall into several distinct yet sometimes confusing categories, from restaurants to wine bars. Just what is a restaurant versus a bistro, brasserie, or café? It's not always clear, nor need it be clear for most people. These are all more or less different types of restaurants. In fact, some cafés also call themselves café brasseries, and some bistros also call themselves brasseries and cafés. Regardless of attempts to make clear distinctions, it's difficult to do so once you see these eating and drinking establishments. These distinctions may be more academic than practical. Here are some basic distinctions which hopeful will help clarify what are essentially fuzzy distinctions:

❏ **Restaurants:** Restaurants are a particular type of eating establishment exhibiting five major characteristics. First, they only serve lunch and/or dinner. Second, all meals are served in three complete courses. Third, restaurants usually offer a lengthy list of wines and an extensive wine cellar. Fourth, dining takes time—up to two hours for lunch and two to three hours for dinner; the table belongs to you, no one will rush you unless you linger beyond closing time, and you'll have difficulty getting the bill! Fifth, patrons tend to be well-dressed and well-mannered in restaurants. In contrast to what you may call "restaurants" back home, restaurants in Paris are not places you go for a quick bite to eat nor stop in to eat a salad or dessert. In fact, one of the major reasons prices tend to be high in French restaurants is the economies of scale—they tend to be very small and only serve a few customers each day (remember, the dining culture does not turn over tables) while their rent, labor, and product costs remain high.

❏ **Cafés:** Functioning as a combination coffee house, snack bar, tavern, and club, these are wonderful Parisian institutions where you can grab a cup of coffee and croissant for breakfast, nurse a drink while reading the newspaper, converse with friends or a business associate, people-watch, or just watch the world go by. Cafés encourage idleness, introspection, conversation, and spontaneity. They do not do much for the palate since they offer limited food selections. Some observers believe cafés are the main reason the French have little use for psychologists—they do self-therapy by talking through their problems in cafés! These are places where business gets conducted; where problems get resolved; where dreams and ideas evolve; and where you can use a toilet. One could not imagine Paris nor the French without their cafés. Every Parisian seems to have his or her favorite café for breakfast, lunch, or a break. In addition to serving coffee, cafés offer limited menus of other drinks, snacks, and sandwiches. Most have an outdoor portion with tables and chairs lining the sidewalk. Some have large outdoor terraces which also are glassed in and heated during the winter. When inside a café, it's always cheaper to order and consume drinks standing at the bar than to be served at a table. Despite public anti-smoking campaigns, you can expect cafés to be smoke-filled rooms. The most popular cafés also tend to be very noisy and crowded. These establishments could well become one of your cheapest forms of entertainment for people-watching and absorbing the local culture. While you can expect to pay US$4-6.00 for the privilege of sipping a small cup of coffee at a café—there are no free refills—you can at least keep your table for as long as you like. Expect a cultural experience in many of these places. The three most famous cafés are **Les Deux Magots** (170, Boulevard Saint-Germain, 6th arr.), **Café de Flore** (172, Boulevard Saint-Germain, 6th arr.), and **Fou-quet's** (99, Avenue des Champs-Élysées, 8th arr.).

❑ Some cafés also call themselves café brasseries, and some bistro call themselves brasseries and cafés. All are more or less different types of restaurants.

❑ Restaurants in Paris are not places you go for a quick bite to eat nor stop in to eat a salad or grab a dessert.

❑ Cafés encourage idleness, introspection, conversation, and spontaneity. Some observers believe they are the main reason the French have little use for psychologists—they do self-therapy by talking through their problems in cafés!

❑ Brasseries tend to be big and noisy, and they serve lots of food all day long, from early morning to late at night.

❑ **Bistros:** These eateries tend to be small, relatively unpretentious, and friendly neighborhood restaurants serving popular home-cooked French dishes. The atmosphere is much less formal than large restaurants, and their hours are more restricted than brasseries. However, many of them can be large, elegant, and noisy, which means they are graduating to the status of a brasserie.

❑ **Brasseries:** These are larger versions of bistros and cafés. In fact, it's very confusing whether a café is a brasserie or simply a café. Many large cafés also refer to themselves as brasseries. You can expect these eateries to be big and noisy, and they serve lots of food all day long, from early morning to late at night. Many of them display iced seafood on display racks in front of the restaurant. Several of Paris' famous cafés are actually brasseries.

❏ **Wine bars:** These places (*bars à vin*) primarily serve a large variety of wines and light meals consisting of salads, cold meats, cheeses, and main dishes. They are usually open from noon until late evening. One of the best and most innovative is **Willi's Wine Bar** (13 Rue des Petits-Champs, 1st arr., Tel. 42-61-05-09) with its 250 wines, fixed-price menu, and weekly specials.

❏ **Tea rooms:** *Salons de thé* serve a light lunch, brunch, or a late afternoon snack with tea. Many of them are very elegant and offer a relaxing setting for lunch or a nice afternoon tea break with pastries and deserts. One of the most attractive tea rooms is **A Priori-Thé** (35-37, Galerie Vivienne, 2nd arr., Tel. 42-97-48-75).

Other dining choices include fast-food restaurants, such as McDonald's, Burger King, Pizza Hut, and Quick Hamburger, Hippopotamus, pizzerias, corner stands, and, of course, the local grocery store or supermarket. Fast-food restaurants appear popular. However, don't expect to find your US$1.99 Big Mac at the McDonald's in Paris. Big Mac is closer to US$4, and a complete fast-food meal can set you back nearly US$10. Given such prices, you might want to try other Parisian dining alternatives which may not cost much more and may be a more interesting cultural experience. Also look for *charcuteries* (self-service food bars), *boulangeries* (bakeries), *pâtisseries* (pastry shops), and *fromageries* (cheese shops). Amongst these alternatives, we tend to have an addiction for the many wonderful *pâtisseries* found throughout Paris. We've ruined more lunches and dinners snacking from different *pâtisseries*, our own form of moveable feast!

BREAKFAST, LUNCH, AND DINNER

You may have to modify your eating habits somewhat. Dining hours and menus are probably not the same as you are used to back home. Here are some basic tips for making such adjustments.

Breakfast (*petit déjeuner*) is usually served between 7:00am and 10:00am at most cafés and hotel restaurants. American breakfasts are not particularly popular in France. And when you find one, especially at a top hotel restaurant, it can be very expensive. If you want to do it in style, head for the **Restaurant des Ambassadeurs** in the elite Hôtel de Crillon (10 Place de la Concord, 8th arr., Tel. 44-71-15-00) for an elegant breakfast.

You may want to skip the American breakfast altogether and do what many Parisians do in the morning—stop at a café for coffee or hot chocolate (*café au lait, grande crème,* or *chocolat chaud*) and a croissant. You can have the same breakfast at your hotel, but it is likely to cost you two or three times what you will pay at a café. In fact, if breakfast is included in the price of your hotel room, you can save money, maybe as much as US$15-20 a day, by asking for a room without breakfast. Alternatively, since breakfast is not a particularly exciting French experience, you may want to visit a grocery store or pastry shop where you can compile a relatively inexpensive and quite acceptable breakfast to be eaten in your hotel room or on the street.

Lunch (*déjeuner*) is normally served between noon and 2:00-2:30pm. For many Parisians, lunch is a major meal which takes time at their favorite restaurant and is usually presented in three-courses. Lunch normally is not an eat-and-run experience. In fact, many restaurants offer a fixed-price (*prix-fixe menu*) luncheon special (45-100F). You'll see signs posted outside many restaurants advertising such specials. This is really one of the best dining buys in Paris. If you only want a salad for lunch, don't go to a restaurant. When you're taking a table, the restaurant expects you to order a full meal. Salad lovers should try an excellent, yet relatively inexpensive, chain of restaurants that serves wonderful salads as meals—**Oh!..Poivrier!** Branches of this popular restaurant are found in various districts of both the Left and Right Banks. It's one of our favorites for both lunch and dinner. Do check to see if a recommended restaurant is open for lunch. Many restaurants are only open for lunch or dinner—but not for both meals. If you're looking for something fast and inexpensive for lunch, you might try eating at a café, brasserie, wine bar, tea room, or fast-food outlet. On a nice day, lunch time also is a good time to put together a picnic in a park, along the banks of the Seine River, or on one of the bridges overlooking the river. Grocery stores, food markets, street vendors, and pastry shops are good sources for creating your own picnic. In fact, eating on the streets can be one of the great joys of dining in Paris!

- ❑ You may want to skip the American breakfast altogether and do what many Parisians do in the morning—stop at a café for coffee or hot chocolate and a croissant.

- ❑ Lunch is really one of the best dining buys in Paris, especially the fix-priced menus.

- ❑ Dinner usually starts late in Paris—after 8:00pm—and lasts 1½-3 hours. In Parisian restaurants, good food and conversation are to be savored rather than quickly consumed.

- ❑ Many restaurants close on Saturdays and Sundays as well as during the month of August.

- ❑ To arrive in Paris without reservations for dining at one of the city's top restaurants is to invite disappointment.

Dinner (*dîner*) is normally served in most restaurants from 7:30-8:00pm to 10:00-10:30pm, although a few restaurants open as early as 7:00pm and close at 11:00pm. Early-birds often find themselves dining with the staff who are finishing their meal in the dining area before retiring to the kitchen or waiting on tables. If this is the meal you've been waiting for all day, it may seem to come very late and very expensive. Most Parisians don't start dining until after 8:30pm. It's usually the half-starved tourists who arrive early because they are not used to eating at such late hours. Keep in mind that an 8:30pm reservation means the food doesn't start moving in front of you until 9:00 or 9:30pm. Many restaurants offer two menus—à la carte and set. The set menu may represent some of the chef's best creations for the evening rather than good value. Most restaurants are not in the business of turning over each table two or three times an evening. The table you get is probably your table for the evening. Expect a meal to take one and a half to three hours to complete. When dining in Paris, good food and conversation are to be savored rather than quickly consumed. If you are looking for faster service and more convenient serving hours, try a bistro or brasserie rather than a formal restaurant. Many brasseries serve food all day long, from 8:00am to 2:00am.

ARE YOU OPEN TODAY?

While many restaurants are open seven days a week, especially those in hotels, others may close on Saturday and/or Sunday and on major public or school holidays. Some may be closed for lunch on Saturday, Sunday, and/or Monday. In many parts of the city, you may have difficulty finding a restaurant open on Sunday.

Many restaurants also close during the months of July and August, France's ritual annual vacation period. Others many close for a week around Christmas time. It's best to check ahead to make sure your favorite restaurant will be open during your visit. Again, be sure to make reservations well ahead of time so you won't be disappointed.

DINING ETIQUETTE

The French have their own set of spoken and unspoken rules about dining in Paris. If you want your culinary experience to go well and avoid disappointments, it's best to observe several of these rules.

RESERVATIONS

If you plan to experience Paris' best of the best in dining pleasures, we advise you to identify your favorite restaurants before arriving in Paris. Since many of these restaurants are small and have long waiting lists of patrons, you may need to make reservations well in advance—perhaps three to six months in advance in some cases. If, for example, you wish to spend a romantic evening dining at the famous **Jules-Verne** restaurant in the Eiffel Tower or the **Tour d'Argent** overlooking Notre Dame Cathedral, you should make reservations at least six weeks in advance. Forget experiencing the culinary pleasures of **Joël Robuchon** unless you've reserved a table six weeks in advance or **Ambroisie, Taillevent, Guy Savoy**, and **Lasserre** three weeks in advance. To arrive in Paris without reservations at such places is to invite disappointment. Don't even try to use your hotel concierge or influential "pull" to get a coveted last minute reservation; there aren't any. Even a Prime Minister may not get in without such reservations! Maybe you'll get lucky with a last minute cancellation, but don't count on it. Our rule of thumb is this: Any restaurant that has received a Michelin star or a Gault Millau toque requires a reservation at least five days in advance; some will need two to eight week advance reservations, especially the really top restaurants known for their haute cuisine. Make reservations at other recommended restaurants at least a day or two before. Same day reservations may be possible, but your choice of dining hours may be very limited—very early (you may find yourself dining with the staff) or very late. If you decide to go to a restaurant without reservations, your best times will be early (7:30pm) or late (9:30pm).

If you are making reservations from abroad, do so by fax (ask for a confirming fax), telephone, or letter. Offer to put 300F (US$70) down on your credit card to hold your reservation. By prepaying part of your check in this manner, the restaurant assumes you are a serious patron.

If you must cancel a reservation, be sure to do so immediately. Since many restaurants are very small, they need to fill all of their tables every night in order to remain profitable in Paris' highly competitive restaurant game. "No shows" are simply rude and inconsiderate.

If you feel uncomfortable making or canceling a reservation by phone, ask your hotel concierge or front desk personnel to do so for you. Most hotels are wired into a computerized information system that makes such restaurant calls very easy and convenient for you.

BRING YOUR PUPPY

Don't be surprised, or look aghast, if you find patrons bringing their dogs into restaurants. The French obsession with pet dogs is carried over with many eateries permitting owners to dine with their dogs. The puppies are usually clean, well behaved, and often become topics of table conversation. However, the best restaurants only permit dead animals (not pets) on their premises, which are found in the kitchen being prepared for consumption!

ARRIVAL

Try to arrive five or ten minutes before your reservation time. If you arrive without a reservation, you may be turned away, or you may have to wait for an hour or more. Arriving very early or very late may ensure a table. Peak reservation hours tend to be 8:30pm and 9:00pm.

DRESS

Restaurants in Paris these days are more accepting of casual or smart casual dress. Nonetheless, individuals dining at fine restaurants are expected to dress appropriately—men in suits or sport coats and ties and women in dresses or smartly tailored pant suits. Elegant restaurants require elegant dress. Patrons in small neighborhood restaurants often dress up for the occasion, although smart casual dress is acceptable. Avoid dressing down for restaurants.

❑ If you make reservations from abroad, do so by fax, telephone, or letter. Offer to put 300F down on your credit card to hold your reservation.

❑ Don't be surprised to see patrons bringing their dogs into restaurants.

❑ You should address waiters as *monsieur* and all waitresses as *mademoiselle*.

❑ The wine expert in restaurants is called the *sommelier*.

❑ Wine can be very expensive when served in restaurants—$50 to $100 or more per bottle. Ask the price before ordering so you won't be surprised later!

❑ Water does not automatically come with the meal nor is the bottled variety free.

❑ The bill doesn't come automatically in French restaurants. You'll have to ask for it.

❑ Most major restaurants accept credit cards, but some restaurants only accept cash.

❑ By law all restaurants must display their menus outside their front doors. However, it may only be printed in French.

❑ Your best restaurant buy will be on the fixed-price menu.

❑ French restaurant portions may seem small compared to portions back home.

PERSONNEL

Many of Paris' restaurants are small Mom and Pop operations where you may be greeted, seated, and served by members of the family. Larger operations may be fully staffed with the following personnel: car parking attendant, doorman, maître d'hôtel, cloakroom attendant, sommelier, waiter, and chef. Restaurant personnel consider themselves professionals rather than part-time workers or moonlighters who do their jobs to make ends meet. They expect to be treated like professionals— politely and as food experts (they will advise you on the best selections). As a polite foreigner, you should address waiters as *monsieur* and all waitresses as *mademoiselle* rather than use the local term, *garçon*. You may have difficulty finding room for your coat in a small restaurant. If so, the waiter or owner will usually take care of it for you, which may mean it ends up in the kitchen!

TABLES

Tables in many restaurants are very small and crammed together, and personal space tends to be limited. If you have a choice, try to get a corner table where you don't have to worry about bumping into other patrons and where it may be less noisy and smokey. Avoid tables next to the front entrance or kitchen since you'll be in a major traffic thoroughfare. In some cases, where two tables are placed next to each other, you may find yourself dining with other patrons. In other words, you may feel a little uncomfortable since your personal space is very limited. On the other hand, this is a good way to meet the locals or fellow travelers! In crowded cafés you may have to share your table with others.

SMOKING

Nonsmokers often have unpleasant experiences in French restaurants. It's especially irritating when smokers manage to ruin a US$200 per person meal with thick clouds of noxious smoke! While some restaurants set aside obligatory nonsmoking tables, these are a joke since most French restaurant patrons smoke. They quickly fill up with smoke what are often poorly ventilated restaurants. Many restaurants even encourage the practice by offering male diners the traditional cigar at the end of the meal. If you arrive early, you may be able to get through the first two courses of your meal before the later-arriving guests blow smoke your way.

ORDERING FOOD AND BEVERAGES

Dinner menus include three **courses**: appetizers, main course, and dessert. You may want to order **wine** with your meal, although don't feel obligated to do so because you're in France. The wine expert in restaurants is called the *sommelier*. While wine is very cheap on the street, it can be very expensive when served in restaurants; ask the price before ordering so you don't have any surprises (many restaurants don't carry wines under US$50 a bottle!). The custom for **coffee** is to serve it at the very end of the meal rather than with the meal. **Water** does not automatically come with the meal nor is the bottled variety free. You'll have to order it. If you order a bottle of water, your choices are mineral water "with gas" (carbonated—*gazeuse*) or "without gas" (*plat* or *non-gazeuse*). This water is not free—US$6-12 per bottle. Tap water (*une carafe d'eau*), which seems just as good as the noncarbonated bottled water, is free. Although somewhat plebeian to order tap water, we have yet to taste any difference that would warrant drinking the pricy bottled stuff. And we're not into consuming fizz water.

THE BILL, THE BILL PLEASE!

This is where service seems to unexpectedly disappear! Hopefully you're not in a hurry to get elsewhere. Contrary to what you may be used to, the bill doesn't come automatically in French restaurants. You'll have to ask for it, which can take some time since waiters are usually preoccupied with serving other patrons and, after all, they really don't want to bother you since you are supposed to be enjoying a leisurely evening of dining. You'll just have to keep an eye on your waiter and try to get his attention at an opportune moment—eye contact with a discrete hand motion will suffice. When asking for the bill, ask for *la note* rather than the more provincial *l'addition*. Don't be shocked when you do get your bill. It probably won't be cheap (under US$30 per person is considered cheap). Indeed, in some restaurants the tab may be so high that you may think you've just bought the table and chairs!

PAYMENT METHODS

Most major restaurants accept one or more major credit cards—Visa, American Express, MasterCard, and Diners Card. However, some restaurants only accept cash. When making a reservation, always ask whether or not the restaurant accepts your particular credit card or cards. If not, you may be embarrassed to learn you are unable to pay a "cash only" bill.

TIPPING, TIPPING, TIPPING

All restaurants include a 12-15 percent service charge in their bills. This is usually clearly stated on the menu as *service compris* or *prix nets*. Since this service charge does not appear as a separate line item, because it's included in the price of each item, you may think you need to leave a tip. This situation is especially confusing if you use your credit card to pay your bill. Many restaurants put the total amount on the first line of the credit card slip, thus leaving "tip/gratuity" blank. You may mistakenly think you need to include something in this blank. You don't. Just draw a line from the total to the bottom of the slip and reenter the total again. If you decide to tip, you're probably a very nice person, or naive, since you've already tipped 12-15 percent! Tipping is not necessary under these circumstances. Nonetheless, restaurant personnel appreciate receiving tips on top of the service charge. It's really up to you if you want to do such tipping. We really don't feel obligated to do so nor do we feel guilty for not over-tipping, especially given the already high cost of food and service. Other writers recommend leaving extra tips. We can be moved to do so under very exceptional circumstances, which we have yet to experience in Paris. The story is a little different in the case of cafés. Patrons often leave small change behind in cafés.

MENU MADNESS

The good news is that by law all restaurants must display their menus outside their front doors. The bad news is that you may not understand what's on them if you don't read French! However, many restaurants simultaneously post English-language menus for tourists, or they have such menus available inside the restaurant. You might also find this to be a good occasion to strike up a conversation with someone who is also reading the posted menu. They may be happy to translate for you, if their English is better than your French. After all, Paris is used to handling 20 million visitors a year, many of whom only speak English and who must eat! Most restaurants understand the economies of this situation and accordingly are quite adept at dealing with the language barrier to dining.

If you are able to understand the menu, the practice of displaying menus outdoors gives you an opportunity to survey dining options before committing to a specific restaurant. If you are in a restaurant that gives you a French-language menu and you do not understand French, ask your waiter if the restaurant has an English-language menu. Many do. If they don't, someone in the restaurant should be able to translate the menu for you. If this becomes too awkward, just ask what they would recommend or what are their most popular dishes. Your language problem should quickly go away as someone assists you with the menu.

Many restaurants have a special menu for the day or a special main course (*plat du jour*) in addition to their standard offerings on their printed menu. The special may be printed or written on an overhead chalk board. Be sure to look for these specials since many of them represent the kitchen's best productions for the day. Also, waiters often volunteer frank advice on the different selections rather than just say *"everything is good here."* After all, many of them have sampled the kitchen's offerings earlier in the evening. Don't be afraid to ask them *"What are you especially well noted for here—the dishes that people come back for again and again?"* You may be pleasantly surprised with their recommendations!

Your best restaurant buys in most restaurants will be selections on the fixed-price menu (*menu prix fixe* or *menu conseille*). Most of these menus divide a meal into three-courses: *entrée* (first course), *plat* (main course), and dessert and/or cheese.

Keep in mind that French restaurant portions may be small compared to what you get back home. Thus, a four-course meal may not be as awesome as it initially sounds.

Watch what you order at restaurants on Sundays and Mondays. Fish, for example, may not be very fresh on Sunday because the fish market at Rungis is closed that day. The same is true for the outdoor markets that are closed on Monday.

BEST OF THE BEST

If you are looking for truly great restaurants, focus most of your attention on the Right Bank where over 80 percent of them will be found. The Left Bank has some exceptional restaurants, such as the famous **La Tour d'Argent** (5th arr.), **Jacques Cagna** (6th arr.), **Arpège** (7th arr.), **Le Bourdonnais** (7th arr.), and **Jules-Verne** (7th arr.), but most of Paris' really fine restaurants are found in various arrondissements of the Right Bank. Reflecting the nature of its less affluent and more artistic clientele, the Left Bank is especially noted for its cafés, bars, ethnic restaurants, and inexpensive eateries.

The following restaurants represent the best of the best in dining pleasures. Most of them are expensive (**$$$$**—350-600F) or very expensive (**$$$$$**—600F+), although a few are on the moderate (**$$$**—200-350F) side. Since many of them are very popular, be sure to make reservations well in advance.

We've organized our recommendations by arrondissements for ease of location. However, we do not include all arrondissements (10th-14th, 18th) because several of them do not yield exceptional restaurants that would warrant making special trips beyond the more popular districts in search of what are not truly great restaurants. There are plenty of very good restaurants found throughout Paris, but truly exceptional ones are disproportionately found in only a few areas. Here we focus on the best of the best.

1ST ARRONDISSEMENT (RIGHT BANK)

❑ **Gérard Besson:** 5 Rue Coq-Héron, Tel. 42-33-14-74, Fax 42-33-85-71. Closed Sunday. Open until 10:30pm. This elegant dining room run by noted Chef Gérard Besson produces the perfect meal. Try the pan-roasted sweetbreads, poached sea bass, or sardine fillets. Wonderful selection of desserts. Expensive (**$$$$**).

❑ **Carré des Feuillants:** 14 Rue de Castiglione, Tel. 42-86-82-82, Fax 42-86-07-71. Closed Saturday for lunch and during August. Open until 10:30pm. Experience some of Paris's finest dining with Alain Dutournier's inventive dishes, such as pheasant consommé with chestnuts, Pauillac lamb, and veal shank. Expensive to very expensive (**$$$$**½).

❑ **Espadon:**Hôtel Ritz, 15 Place Vendôme, Tel. 42-60-38-30, Fax 42-61-63-08. Closed the month of August. Open until 11:00pm. Guy Legay's classic dishes are a real winner in this elegant restaurant with its superb terrace. Try the turbot with fava beans, veal, or foie gras. Outstanding desserts and service. Expensive to very expensive (**$$$$**½).

❑ **Les Cartes Postales:** 7 Rue Gomboust, Tel. 42-61-02-93. Closed Saturday for lunch. Open until 10:30pm. Operated by Yoshimasa Watanabe, this small and quaint restaurant produces fine cuisine with a touch of the exotic. Try the scallops in papaya sauce and oxtail braised in Médoc wine. Offers a good value set lunch for 135F. Moderate to expensive (**$$$½**).

❑ **Goumard-Prunier:** 9 Rue Duphot, Tel. 42-60-36-07, Fax 42-60-04-54. Closed Sundays (summer) and Mondays. Open until 10:30pm. Chef Georges Lardiot offers the freshest seafood dishes—shellfish fricassée, braised sole, Brittany prawns, and crab with Sherry aspic. Expensive to very expensive (**$$$$½**).

❑ **Grand Véfour:** 17 Rue de Beaujolais, Tel. 42-96-56-27, Fax 42-86-80-71. Closed Saturdays, Sundays, and August. Open until 10:15pm. Served in one of Paris' most beautiful restaurants, Chef Guy Martin's dishes win the praise of most gourmet diners—prawns in olive oil, baked turbot with anchovy purée, roast Bresse chicken Miéral, and braised eel in Port sauce. One of Paris' most expensive culinary experiences (**$$$$$**).

❑ **Le Meurice:** Hôtel Meurice, 228 Rue de Rivoli, Tel. 44-58-10-50, Fax 44-58-10-15. Open until 11:00pm. A grand and sumptuous restaurant. The kitchen of Marc Marchand continues to produce superb dishes, from crab cake with stuffed squid to stewed veal. Expensive (**$$$$**).

2ND ARRONDISSEMENT (RIGHT BANK)

❑ **Le Céladon:** Hôtel Westminster, 15 Rue Daunou, Tel. 47-03-40-42, Fax 42-60-30-66. This elegant and romantic dining room served by Chef Emanuel Hodencq presents such wonderful dishes as lamb chops with lamb sausage and timbale of crèpes, macaroni, and snails. Terrific desserts (try the sautéed pears with licorice ice cream). Moderate to expensive (**$$$½**).

❑ **Drouant:** 18 Rue Gaillon, Tel. 42-65-15-16, Fax 49-24-02-15. Open until 10:30pm. Offers Louis Grondard's fine bourgeois cooking. Try the fillet of Pauillac lamb in an herbal crust, molded prawns with eggplant, and roast beef with bone marrow. Popular with business crowd for lunch and theater-goers for dinner. Expensive (**$$$$**).

3RD ARRONDISSEMENT (RIGHT BANK)

❑ **Ambassade d'Auvergine:** 22 Rue du Grenier-St-Lazare, Tel. 42-72-31-22, Fax 42-78-85-47. Closed August 1-16. Open until 10:30pm. With hams hanging from the rafters, you get a hint of what's on the menu—country ham, sausages, duck daube with fresh pasta and smoky bacon, and cabbage and Roquefort soup. Good desserts. Moderate (**$$$**).

❑ **Au Bascou:** 38 Rue Réaumu, Tel. 42-72-69-25. Closed Saturdays, Sundays and three weeks in August. Open until midnight. Operated by Jean-Guy Loustau, the kitchen here turns out excellent lamb kidney with eggplant caviar, shirred eggs with foie gras, and caramel mousse with walnut brittle. Good value lunch at 85F. Moderate (**$$$**).

4TH ARRONDISSEMENT (RIGHT BANK)

❑ **L'Ambroisie:** 9 Place des Vosges, Tel. 42-78-51-45. Closed Sunday, Monday, February school holidays, and the first 3 weeks of August. One of Paris' very best restaurants set under the arcades of the lovely Place des Vosges and run by Bernard and Danièle Pacaud. Try the lobster soup with scallops, turbot braised with celery and celery root, or saddle of Pauillac lamb in a truffled persillade. Great desserts. Very Expensive (**$$$$$**).

❑ **Miravile:** 72 Quai de l'Hôtel-de-Ville, Tel. 42-74-72-22, Fax 42-74-67-55. Closed Saturday lunch and Sundays. Open until 10:30pm. Operated by Gilles Épié, this is a good value restaurant offering a fixed price menu for 220F. Expect to find several inventive dishes on the menu—pimientoes with codfish and crushed potatoes, sea urchins and spinach, and rabbit with olives. Moderate (**$$$**).

5TH ARRONDISSEMENT (LEFT BANK)

❑ **La Tour d'Argent:** 15-17 Quai de la Tournelle, Tel. 43-54-23-31, Fax 44-07-12-04. Closed Monday. Open until 10:30pm. Offering a gorgeous view of Notre Dame

Cathedral (the restaurant pays part of the electric bill to illuminate the cathedral at night for its patrons!), this remains one of Paris's finest restaurants for gourmet diners. Chef Manuel Martinez turns out truly fine dishes, such as crab-stuffed turbot, double veal chop, ravioli de foie gras et homard, and truffled brouillade. Incredible wine cellar. And you'll never forget the incredible prices which don't seem to deter diners who may wait for more than a month to get in! You'll need reservations well in advance to spend this much money. Very, very, very expensive (**$$$$$$**).

❑ **La Timonerie:** 35 Quai de la Tournelle, Tel. 43-25-44-42. Closed Sundays and for Monday lunch. Open until 10:30pm. Noted Chef Philippe de Givenchy turns out inventive contemporary dishes. Try the sea bream roasted with tarragon and chilis in a red-wine sauce and his mackerel fillet. Moderate to expensive (**$$$½**).

6TH ARRONDISSEMENT (LEFT BANK)

❑ **Jacques Cagna:** 14 Rue des Grands-Augustins, Tel. 43-26-49-39, Fax 43-54-54-48. Closed Saturday lunch, Sundays, 3 weeks in August and 1 week at Christmas. Open until 10:30pm. Operated by Jacques Cagna and his sister, this elegant establishment serves excellent lobster, suckling pig, and sturgeon as well as a wonderful selection of desserts. Expensive (**$$$$**).

❑ **Le Paris:** Hôtel Lutétia, 45 Boulevard Raspail, Tel. 49-54-46-90, Fax 49-54-46-64. Closed Saturdays, Sundays, and the month of August. Open until 10:00pm. Operated by the inventive Philippe Renard, the kitchen produces wonderful asparagus, crayfish, red mullet, lobster, and veal dishes. Expensive (**$$$$**).

❑ **Yugaraj:** 14 Rue Dauphine, Tel. 43-26-44-91, Fax 46-33-50-77. Closed Monday lunch. Open until 11:00pm. If you enjoy Indian cuisine, look no further. This is the best Paris has to offer. Try the herbed chicken sausages, crab balls, and lamb and cod dishes. Moderate (**$$$½**).

7TH ARRONDISSEMENT (LEFT BANK)

❑ **Arpège:** 84 Rue de Varenne, Tel. 45-51-47-33, Fax 44-18-98-39. Closed Saturdays and Sunday lunch. Open until 10:30pm. Here's where you will find the creative kitchen of one of Paris' top three chefs, Alain Passard. Everything is good here, from lobster and lamb to pheasant and baby boar. But it doesn't come cheap. Very, very expensive (**$$$$$**½).

❑ **Jules-Verne:** Tower Eiffel, 2nd floor, Tel. 45-55-61-44, Fax 47-05-29-41. Open until 10:30pm. Be sure to make reservations 4-8 weeks in advance (ask for a window table) since this is one of the hardest places to get into any time of the year. In addition to commanding the most fabulous view of Paris for lunch or dinner, this is also one of the city's best restaurants for fine cuisine. Operated by talented Chef Alain Reix, the restaurant serves excellent grilled scallops, veal chops with figs, and baby eels along with many other fine selections. Expensive to very expensive (**$$$$**½).

❑ **Le Bourdonnais:** 113 Avenue de la Bourdonnais, Tel. 47-05-47-96, Fax 45-51-09-29. Open until 11:00pm. This gem of a restaurant consistently turns out some of Paris' finest dishes in an intimate and romantic setting. Under the innovative Philippe Bardau, the kitchen produces wonderful lobster soup, grilled salmon, stuffed tuna, scallops, and roast lamb. Moderate to expensive (**$$$**½).

❑ **Le Divellec:** 107 Rue de l'Université, Tel. 45-51-91-96, Fax 45-51-31-75. Closed Sundays. Open until 10:00m. Jacques Le Divellec's turns out some of Paris' most fabulous fish dishes. Try his steamed scallops, smoked sea bass, and raw oysters and sea urchins. Very expensive (**$$$$$**).

❑ **Paul Minchelli:** 54 Boulevard Latour-Maubourg, Tel. 47-05-89-86, Fax 45-56-03-84. Closed during the month of August. Open until 10:30pm. Chef Paul Minchelli, famous for seafood delights, continues to wow diners with his inventive seafood dishes. You can't go wrong trying the sea bass, salmon, tuna, and lobster. Moderate to expensive (**$$$**½).

8TH ARRONDISSEMENT (RIGHT BANK)

❏ **Au Petit Montmorency:** 5 Rue Rabelais, Tel. 42-25-11-
19. Open until 10:30pm. Closed Saturdays, Sundays,
and the month of August. Chef-owner Daniel Bouché
offers wonderful selections soupe aux crèpes, pâté in
caramelized sauce, and truffled potato tourte. Top this
off with hazelnut soufflé. Very expensive (**$$$$$**).

❏ **Chiberta:** 3 Rue Arsène-Houssaye, Tel. 45-63-77-90,
Fax 45-62-85-08. Closed Saturdays, Sundays, and the
month of August. Open until 11:00pm. Still popular
with the powerful and celebrities, chef Philippe Da Silva
manages to create truly exciting dishes with wonderful
herbs and seasoning, such as turbot braised with bay
leaves in a Riesling-based sauce and red mullet salad with
a coriander jus. Very expensive (**$$$$$**).

❏ **La Marée:** 1 Rue Daru, Tel. 43-80-20-00, Fax 48-88-04-
04. Closed Saturdays, Sundays, and the month of
August. Open until 10:30pm. Offers imaginative fare of
vegetables and seafood. Very expensive (**$$$$$**).

❏ **Lasserre:** 17 Avenue Franklin-Roosevelt, Tel. 43-59-53-
43, Fax 45-63-72-23. Closed Sundays, Monday lunch,
and July 30 - August 28. Fabulous service awaits you in
this culinary palace with a retractable roof. Try the duck
à l'orange, tournedoes béarnaise, and crêpes flambées.
Very, very expensive (**$$$$$**½).

❏ **Laurent:** 41 Avenue Gabriel, Tel. 42-25-00-39, Fax 45-
62-45-21. Closed Saturday lunch, Sundays, and holidays. Open until 11:00pm. Chief Philippe Braun produces superb fare using the freshest of ingredients. Try
the veal chop and duck liver. The best deal here is the
fixed-price menu for 380F. Otherwise, Lauret is very,
very expensive (**$$$$$**½).

❏ **Le Jardin du Royal Monceau:** Hôtel Royal Monceau,
35 Avenue Hoche, Tel. 42-99-98-70, Fax 42-99-89-94.
Open until 10:30pm. Chef Bruno Cirino's wonderfully
authentic Provençal cuisine make this a stand-out
restaurant. Vegetable and fish dishes are excellent as are
the tempting desserts. Very expensive (**$$$$$**).

❑ **Ledoyen:** Carré des Champs-Élysées, Tel. 47-42-23-23, Fax 47-42-55-01. Closed Saturdays, Sundays, and the month of August. Open until 10:30pm. One of Paris' top chefs, Ghislaine Arabian offers Flemish cuisine with all the trimmings—smoked mussels, gingerbread, cheeses, crayfish, waffles, lobster, duck, and smoked chicken. Very expensive (**$$$$$**).

❑ **Les Ambassadeurs:** Hôtel de Crillon, 10 Place de la Concorde, Tel. 44-71-16-16, Fax 44-71-15-02. This gilted dining room offers the outstanding cuisine of chef Christian Constant. Try his peppered whiting on polenta with crushed black olives and sautéed pollack with puréed white beans. Very expensive (**$$$$$**).

❑ **Lucas-Carton:** 9 Place de la Madeleine, Tel. 42-65-22-90, Fax 42-65-06-23. Upon until 10:30pm. Closed Saturday lunch, Sundays, December 22 - January 4, and July 29 - August 25. Operated by one of Paris' truly great chefs, Alain Senderens, this restaurant represents his talent well. Try the foie gras de canard steam in a cabbage leaf, lobster, and saddle of rabbit. Take tons of money—you'll need it in what is one of Paris' most expensive restaurants (**$$$$$$**).

❑ **Taillevent:** 15 Rue Lamennais, Tel. 44-95-15-01, Fax 42-25-95-18. Closed Saturdays, Sundays, and July 23 - August 22. Open until 10:30pm. One of Paris' great restaurants, chief Philippe Legendre continues to produce outstanding fare. Try the red mullet stuffed with black olives, sea bass with carrots, or rabbit and spinach pie. Great desserts. Very very expensive (**$$$$$½**).

9TH ARRONDISSEMENT (RIGHT BANK)

❑ **La Table d'Anvers:** 2 Place d'Anvers, Tel. 48-78-35-21, Fax 45-26-66-67. Closed Saturday lunch, Sundays. Open until 10:30pm. From the inventive kitchen of Christian Conticini comes a vast array of dining pleasures. Try the oyster gnocchi with baby peas, ravigote, grilled red mullet, sea bass with fava beans, and desserts galore. Includes different menus. Expensive (**$$$$**).

❑ **Venantius:** Hôtel Ambassador, 16 Boulevard Haussmann, Tel. 48-00-06-84, Fax 42-46-19-84. Closed Saturdays, Sundays, February 17-27, and July 28 - August 28. Open until 10:30pm. Chef Gérard Fouché offers fine duck foie gras in a peppery pineapple marmalade, crab gazpacho, sole stuffed with celery root rémoulade, and breast of Bresse chicken. Expensive (**$$$$**).

I 5TH ARRONDISSEMENT (LEFT BANK)

❑ **Morot-Gaudry:** 8 Rue de la Cavalerie, Tel. 45-67-06-85, Fax 45-67-55-72. Closed Saturdays and Sundays. Open until 10:00pm. Excellent quality cuisine on this rooftop restaurant overlooking the city. Offers a good value (220F) lunch of calf's foot croustillant, rabbit stewed in white wine with wild thyme, cheeses, and a tartelette de poires Bourdaloue. À la carte menu can be expensive (**$$$$**).

I 6TH ARRONDISSEMENT (RIGHT BANK)

❑ **Faugeron:** 52 Rue de Longchamp, Tel. 47-04-24-53, Fax 47-55-62-90. Closed Saturdays (except dinner October - April), Sundays, December 23 - January 2, and the month of August. Open until 10:00pm. Sample the classic and creative cooking of chef Henri Faugeron. Try the scallops, lobster tournedoes, and dilled rabbit in a potato blanket. Very expensive (**$$$$$**).

❑ **Jean-Claude Ferrero:** 38 Rue Vital, Tel. 45-04-42-42, Fax 45-04-67-71. Closed Saturdays (except for dinner in winter), Sundays, May 1-15, and August 8 - September 5. Open until 10:30pm. The innovative chef Jean-Claude Ferrero presents a variety of intriguing menus. Try his red mullet, mussel gratin, or calf's head rémoulade. Expensive to very expensive (**$$$$½**).

❑ **Joël Robuchon:** 55 Avenue Raymond-Poincaré, Tel. 47-27-12-27, Fax 47-27-31-22. Closed Saturdays, Sundays, and July 8 - August 6. Open until 10:15pm. Many seasoned observers of the Paris restaurant scene consider this to be the number one restaurant in France, if not in the world! It's owned and operated by Paris' number one chef, Joël Robuchon and Madame Robuchon. Be sure to make reservations several weeks in advance. Housed in a wonderful 19th century townhouse, the restaurant only seats 45 for which there is a long waiting list. It offers an incredible menu, from rock lobster roasted with cumin and rosemary to roasted guinea fowl, in which everything is outstanding. After you've been lucky to get a reservation, you'll be the unlucky one to get the astronomical bill! This could kill your travel budget for France at US$300+ per person. On the other hand, you'll always remember this special culinary experience. Very, very, very expensive (**$$$$$$**).

❑ **Le Pré Catelan:** Bois de Boulogne Route de Suresnes, Tel. 45-24-55-58, Fax 45-24-55-58. Closed for Sunday dinner, Mondays, and February 27 - March 13. Open until 10:00pm. This beautifully decorated and cosy restaurant is home to Chef Roland Durand's delightful creations. Try his mackerel rillettes with green bean salad, lightly cooked salmon, and langoustines in black risotto. Very expensive (**$$$$$**).

❑ **Vivarois:** 192 Avenue Victor-Hugo, Tel. 45-04-04-31, Fax 45-03-09-84. Closed Saturdays, Sundays, and the month of August. Open until 10:00pm. Claude Peyrot, one of Paris' finest chefs, keeps turning out wonderful selections, from turbot with wild mushrooms and hare à la royale to oxtail braised with mustard. And it's all very expensive (**$$$$$**).

I 7TH ARRONDISSEMENT (RIGHT BANK)

❑ **Amphyclès:** 78 Avenue des Ternes, Tel. 40-68-01-01, Fax 40-68-91-88. Closed Saturday lunch and Sundays. Open until 10:30pm. Chef Philippe Groult creates outstanding dishes including crab soup with cavair, lamb à l'ancienne, and rack of veal ménagère. Includes several theme menus that attract the crowds. Very expensive (**$$$$$**).

❑ **Apicius:** 122 Avenue de Villiers, Tel. 43-80-19-66, Fax 44-40-09-57. Closed Saturdays, Sundays, and the month of August. Open until 10:00pm. Jean-Pierre Vigato continues to offer outstanding cuisine in this charming restaurant. Try his escalope de foie gras, truffle risotto, fried prawns, and cod. Offers great desserts. Very expensive (**$$$$$**).

❑ **Clos Longchamp:** Hôtel Méridien, 81 Boulevard Gouvion-St-Cyr, Tel. 40-68-30-40, Fax 40-68-30-81. Closed Saturdays, Sundays, last week of December, and July 29 - August 30. Open until 10:30pm. Talented chef Jean-Marie Meulien combines Southeast Asian spices with Mediterreanean flavors to create a wonderful selection of dishes. Try his spiced scallops, terrine of duck liver, squash blossoms stuffed with cardamom-spiced salmon, and sea bass with toasted buckwheat. Very expensive (**$$$$$**).

❑ **Guy Savoy:** 18 Rue Troyon, Tel. 43-80-40-61, Fax 46-22-43-09. Closed Saturday lunch and Sundays. Open until 10:30pm. Newly rebuilt from a devastating fire in 1993, the ever-popular Guy Savoy is back with his creative dishes. Food here is a work of art. New items appear on the menu daily. Try the croustillant of calf's foot, pheasant and bean soup, and roast John Dory. Watch your wallet! This is all very expensive (**$$$$$**).

❑ **Michel Rostang:** 20 Rue Rennequin, Tel. 47-63-40-77, Fax 47-63-82-75. Closed Saturday lunch, Sundays, and August 1-15. Open until 10:15pm. This popular chef serves a wonderful array of provincial dishes. Look for pumpkin soup, pan-roasted lobster en anchoïade, and lamb's tongue. Very expensive (**$$$$$**).

❑ **Sormani:** 4 Rue du Général-Lanrezac, Tel. 43-80-13-91. Closed Saturdays, Sundays, holidays, end of December, Easter, and first three weeks of August. Open until 10:30pm. Pascal Fayet creates Paris' finest and most innovative Italian cuisine in this popular restaurant. Try the diaphanous ravioli stuffed with sea urchins or truffled goat cheese; pizza topped with onion purée, lobster, and arugula; and white-truffle risotto. Expensive (**$$$$**).

THE 50 BRIGHTEST STARS

Most restaurant experts agree that the following establishments deserve to be ranked as the "best of the best" in Paris. The difference in quality between our five star (★★★★★) and three star (★★★) restaurants is probably very little in many cases, although most of our five-star restaurants are indeed exceptional haute cuisine establishments. The numbers and abbreviations in the third column refer to the arrondissement (1st, 8th, 17th) and whether it's located on the Right Bank (RB) or Left Bank (LB). Paris' truly outstanding restaurants are disproportionally found in the 1st, 7th, 8th, and 16th arrondissements, the centers for Paris' wealth, power, and opulence. Here's where the action is—where you can easily spend US$75 per person on lunch and US$200 per person for dinner, and that may not include wine! If you're on a tight budget, you might want to save your money for splurging on at least one of these fine restaurants. Lunch at these restaurants, which often includes a fixed-price menu, usually offers the best dining value.

★★★★★	Arpège	7th/LB	$$$$$½
	Carré des Feuillants	1st/RB	$$$$½
	Guy Savoy	17th/RB	$$$$$
	L'Ambroisie	4th/RB	$$$$$
	L'Espadon	1st/RB	$$$$
	La Tour d'Argent	5th/LB	$$$$$$
	Lucas-Carton	8th/RB	$$$$$$
	Robuchon	16th/RB	$$$$$$
	Taillevent	8th/LB	$$$$$½
	Vivarois	16th/RB	$$$$$
★★★★	Amphyclès	17th/RB	$$$$$
	Apicius	17th/RB	$$$$$
	Chiberta	8th/RB	$$$$$
	Drouant	2nd/RB	$$$$
	Espadon	1st/RB	$$$$½
	Faugeron	16th/RB	$$$$$
	Gérard Besson	1st/RB	$$$$$
	Goumard-Prunier	1st/RB	$$$$½
	Grand Véfour	1st/RB	$$$$$
	Jacques Cagna	6th/LB	$$$$$
	Lasserre	8th/RB	$$$$$½
	Laurent	8th/LB	$$$$$½
	Le Bourdonnais	7th/LB	$$$½
	Le Divellec	7th/LB	$$$$$
	Le Pré Catelan	16th/RB	$$$$$
	Les Ambassadeurs	8th/RB	$$$$$
	Ledoyen	8th/RB	$$$$$
	Michel Rostang	17th/RB	$$$$$
	Paul Minchelli	7th/RB	$$$½
★★★	Ambassade d'Auvergine	3rd/RB	$$$
	Au Bascou	3rd/RB	$$$
	Au Petit Montmorency	8th/LB	$$$$$

Chiberta	8th/LB	$$$$$
Clos Longchamp	17th/RB	$$$$$
Jean-Claude Ferrero	16th/RB	$$$$½
Jules-Verne	7th/LB	$$$$½
La Marée	8th/LB	$$$$$
La Table d'Anvers	9th/RB	$$$$
La Timonerie	5th/LB	$$$½
Le Céladon	2nd/RB	$$$½
Le Meurice	1st/RB	$$$$
Le Paris	6th/LB	$$$$
Le Jardin du Royal Monceau	8th/LB	$$$$$
Les Cartes Postales	1st/RB	$$$½
Miravile	4th/RB	$$$
Morot-Gaudry	15th/RB	$$$$
Paul Minchelli	7th/LB	$$$½
Sormani	17th/RB	$$$$
Venantius	9th/RB	$$$$
Yugaraj	6th/LB	$$$½

BEST CHEFS

So much of a Parisian restaurant's reputation in tied up with its specific chef. Without the renowned chef, Paris' renowned restaurants could not retail their stellar reputations. Many of Paris' chefs are world famous for their inventive dishes and for training many of today's young talented chefs. These chefs receive the attention and respect normally reserved for celebrity artists and actors. After all, they are a very special type of artist.

If you want to experience the creative genius of some of the world's greatest chefs, make reservations well in advance to experience the works of these outstanding chefs. Most of the best chefs also are chef-owners:

❑ **Joël Robuchon:** Robuchon, 55 Avenue Raymond-Poincaré, 17th arr., Tel. 42-27-12-27, Fax 47-27-31-22. Open until 10:15pm. Closed Saturdays, Sunday, and July 8 - August 6.

❑ **Alain Passard:** Arpège, 84 Rue de Varenne, 7th arr., Tel. 45-51-47-33, Fax 44-18-98-39. Open until 10:30pm. Closed Saturdays and Sunday lunch.

❑ **Alain Senderens:** Lucas-Carton, 9 Place de la Madeleine, 8th arr., Tel. 42-65-22-90, Fax 42-65-06-23.

Upen until 10:30pm. Closed Saturday lunch, Sundays, December 22 - January 4, and July 29 - August 25.

❑ **Henri Faugeron:** Faugeron, 52 Rue de Longchamp, 16th arr., Tel. 47-04-24-53, Fax 47-55-62-90. Open until 10:00pm. Closed Saturdays (except for dinner, October - April), Sundays, December 23 - January 2, and August.

❑ **Jean-Pierre Vigato:** Apicius, 122 Avenue de Villiers, 17th arr., Tel. 43-80-19-66, Fax 44-40-09-57. Open until 10:00pm. Closed Saturdays, Sundays, and the month of August.

❑ **Alain Dutournier:** Le Carré des Feuillants, 14 Rue de Castiglione, 1st arr., Tel. 42-86-82-82, Fax 42-86-07-71. Open until 10:30pm. Closed Saturday lunch, Sundays, and the month of August.

❑ **Philippe Bardau:** Le Bourdonnais, 113 Avenue de la Bourdonnais, 7th arr., Tel. 47-05-47-96, Fax 45-51-09-29. Open until 11:00pm.

❑ **Daniel Bouché:** Au Petit Montmorency, 5 Rue Rabelais, 8th arr., Tel. 42-25-11-19. Open until 10:30pm. Closed Saturdays, Sundays, and the month of August.

❑ **Bernard Pacaud:** L'Ambroisie, 9 Places des Vosges, 4th arr., Tel. 42-78-51-45. Open until 10:30pm. Closed Sundays, Mondays, school holidays, and first three weeks of August.

❑ **Ghislaine Arabian:** Ledoyen, Carré des Champs-Elysées, 8th arr., Tel. 47-42-23-23, Fax 47-42-55-01. Open until 10:30pm. Closed Saturdays, Sundays, and the month of August.

❑ **Guy Savoy:** Guy Savoy, 18 Rue Troyon, 17th arr., Tel. 43-80-40-61, Fax 46-22-43-09. Open until 10:30pm. Closed Saturday lunch and Sundays.

❑ **Michel Rostang:** Michel Rostang, 20 Rue Rennequin, 17th arr., Tel. 47-63-40-77, Fax 47-63-82-75. Open until 10:15pm. Closed Saturday lunch, Sundays, and August 1-15.

❏ **Philippe Legendre:** Taillevent, 15 Rue Lamennais, 8arr.,
Tel. 44-95-15-01, Fax 42-25-95-18. Open until 10:30pm.
Closed Saturday, Sunday, July 23 - August 22.

❏ **Manuel Martinez:** La Tour d'Argent, 15-17Quai de la
Tournelle, 5th arr., Tel. 43-54-23-31, Fax 44-07-12-04.
Open until 10:30pm. Closed Mondays.

❏ **Pascal Fayet:** Sormani, 4 Rue du Général-Lanrezac,
17th arr., Tel. 43-80-13-91. Open until 10:30pm. Closed
Saturdays, Sundays, holidays, end of December, Easter,
and first three weeks of August.

❏ **Claude Peyrot:** Vivarois, 192 Avenue Victor-Hugo, 16th
arr., Tel. 45-04-04-31, Fax 45-03-09-84. Open until
10:00pm. Closed Saturdays, Sundays, and the month of
August.

❏ **Jean-Claude Ferrero:** Jean-Claude Ferrero, 38 Rue
Vital, 16th arr., Tel. 45-04-42-42, Fax 45-04-67-71.
Open until 10:30pm. Closed Saturdays (except for
dinner during winter), Sundays, May 1-15, and August
8 - September 5. Famous for his truffles and mushrooms.

BEST FOR A VIEW

What better way to enjoy the City of Lights than to have a
table at a fine restaurant overlooking romantic Paris at night.
These much-in-demand restaurants may require reservations
two months in advance! So be forewarned to plan a reservation
well in advance rather than be disappointed upon arriving in
Paris and discovering there is no room for you. And even during
the day, you can dine at some wonderful restaurants that have
terrific views of the city. Here are some nice options:

❏ **Jules-Verne:** Tour Eiffel (Eiffel Tower), 2nd Floor, 7th
arr., Tel. 45-55-61-44, Fax 47-05-29-41. Open until
10:30pm. Terrific food along with the best view in Paris.
Yes, make your reservation two months in advance!

❏ **La Tour d'Argent:** 15-17Quai de la Tournelle, 5th arr.,
Tel. 43-54-23-31, Fax 44-07-12-04. Open until 10:30pm.
Closed Mondays. One of Paris' finest restaurants with
the best view of Notre Dame Cathedral. You are well
advised to make reservations two months in advance.

❑ **15 Montaigne:** 15 Avenue Montaigne, 8th arr., Tel. 47-23-55-99. Wonderful view of Paris, the Eiffel Tower, and the Seine River.

❑ **Restaurant du Musée d'Orsay:** 1 Rue de Bellechasse, Tel. 45-49-42-33. Open for lunch and dinner on Thursday evenings. Great view of the Seine River in this beautifully appointed restaurant.

MOST BEAUTIFUL EATERIES

Tasteful French architecture, art, and design are well represented in some of its most beautiful restaurants. If you love dining in places that are simply beautiful, try a few of these stand-out restaurants:

❑ **Maxim's:** 3 Rue Royale, 8th arr., Tel. 42-65-27-94, Fax 40-17-02-91. Considered by many observers to be the most beautiful restaurant in the world. Includes erotic mural frescoes and a gorgeous glass roof. Owned by Pierre Cardin.

❑ **Grand Véfour:** 17 Rue de Beaujolais, 1st arr., Tel. 42-96-56-27, Fax 42-86-80-71. Open until 10:15pm. Closed Saturdays, Sundays, and the month of August. An elegant restaurant of Directoire chairs, carved boiserie ceilings, bronze chandeliers, and painted panels set in the gardens of the Palais-Royal.

❑ **Lapérouse:** 51 Quai des Grands-Augustins, 6th arr., Tel. 43-26-68-04, Fax 43-26-99-39. Open until 11:00pm. Closed Sundays and for Monday lunch. Gilded windows, decorated ceilings, gorgeous carpets, and paintings make this an exceptionally beautiful restaurant.

❑ **Le Train Blue:** Gare de Lyon, 20 Boulevard Diderot, 12th arr., Tel. 43-43-09-06, Fax 43-43-97-96. Incredible interior design—murals, bronze chandeliers, sculptures, and huge bay windows. Some claim this is Paris' most beautiful restaurant. However, it gets few marks for quality cuisine.

❑ **Lasserre:** 17 Avenue Franklin Roosevelt, 8th arr., Tel. 43-59-53-43, Fax 45-63-72-23. Open until 10:30pm. Closed Sundays, Monday lunch, and July 30 - August

28. This well appointed and festive restaurant includes a retractable ceiling that opens to the stars.

 BEST WINE BARS AND BISTROS

Wine bars offer an opportunity to sample France's great variety of wines as well as relax. Larger wine bars tend to be bistros. And large bistros tend to become brasseries. Who knows what today's wine bar might grow up to be! Some of the best choices in wine bars and bistros include:

❑ **Willi's Wine Bar:** 13 Rue des Petits-Champs, 1st arr., Tel. 42-61-05-09. Open noon to 11:00pm. Closed Sundays. Extremely popular wine bar serving a wide range of excellent wines from around the world. Serves good food.

❑ **Au Sauvignon:** 80 Rue des Saints-Pères, 7th arr., Tel. 45-48-49-02. Open 8:30am to 10:00pm. A popular Left Bank bistro serving Beaujolais wines on a glass-covered terrace.

❑ **Le Relais Chablisien:** 4 Rue Bertin-Poirée, 1st arr., Tel. 45-08-53-73. Open 8:00am to 10:00pm. Closed Saturdays and Sundays. Wines of Northern Burgundy.

❑ **Ma Bourgogne:** 133 Boulevard Haussman, 8th arr., Tel. 45-63-50-61. Open 7:00am to 10:00pm. Closed Saturdays and Sundays. Noted for serving Beaujolais. Draws a loyal lunchtime crowd for coq au Juliénas, bœuf bourguignon, and parsleyed ham terrine.

❑ **Le Bistrot de l'Etoile:** 75 Avenue Niel, 17th arr., Tel. 42-27-88-44, Fax 42-27-32-12. Closed Sunday lunch. Open until midnight. Owned by the noted chef Guy Savoy who operates his famous restaurant a few blocks away at 18 Rue Troyon. Serves excellent raviolis, rabbit, escargot, fresh sardines, and desserts.

❑ **Le Bistrot d'à Côté:** 16 Boulevard St-Germain, 5th arr., Tel. 43-54-59-10. Closed Saturday lunch and Sundays. Open until 11:00pm. Operated by the noted chef Michel Rostang, this popular bistro offers such specialties as veal kidney in red-wine sauce, codfish fricassée à la lyonnaise, and lentil soup with garlic sausage.

BEST CAFÉS AND BRASSERIES

Paris's café culture is well displayed along its many streets and boulevards. Many of the most popular cafés are virtual Parisian institutions, famous for their illustrious patrons (artists, writers, intellectuals, politicians, actors) and location rather than for their drinks and foods. Some have long histories dating from the 19th century or pre-World War II days. Some of the older establishments are worth a visit just to see their interesting architecture, art, and interior decorations. Each has its own particular character, including lots of nostalgia. The coffee is usually good and the food acceptable, although not remarkable. Many of these places are crowded and noisy all day long. Several of them function as brasseries. The paying custom is to ask for your bill when you're ready to leave rather than when you are served. Some people say you haven't really experienced Paris until you try one of these cafés:

❑ **Le Bourbon:** 1, Place du Palais-Bourbon, 7th arr., Tel. 45-51-58-27, Monday-Saturday, 7:30am to 10:30pm; Sunday 7:30am to 7:00pm. Located near the Assemblée Nationale and offering a nice view of the square, this is a favorite stop for politicians, models, and fashion writers.

❑ **Brasserie Lipp:** 151, Boulevard St-Germain, 6th arr., Tel. 45-48-53-91, 8:00am to 2:00am. (restaurant serves from noon to 12:30am). Originally established in 1870, this famous café/brasserie/restaurant has a fascinating history centered around its famous patrons. Go here for the atmosphere rather than the food and drinks.

❑ **Café de Flore:** 172, Boulevard Saint-Germain, 6th arr., Tel. 45-48-55-26, 7:00am to 1:30am. A Parisian institution where most famous 20th century writers, artists, intellectuals, actors, and hangers-on have passed. Still draws a similar crowd these days along with numerous tourists in search of the "real Paris." Its crowded competitor, Les Deux Magots, is located next door.

❑ **Café de la Paix:** 12, Boulevard des Capucines (Place de l'Opéra), 9th arr., Tel. 40-07-30-20, 10:00am to 1:30am. Originally opened in 1863, this famous café has seen better days when it was a favorite stop for Émile Zola, Ernest Hemingway, and F. Scott Fitzgerald. Located near the famous Opera de Paris Garnier, this huge, crowded, and noisy café still draws the crowds, especially tourists. Its impressive architecture is still worth a visit. The restrooms (Second Empire) alone warrant a visit.

❑ **La Coupole:** 102, Boulevard du Montparnesse, 14th arr., Tel. 43-20-14-20, 7:30am to 2:00am. A once popular hang-out for Bohemian artists and writers in the Montparnasse area in pre-World War II Paris. It still remains popular. Worth a visit for its interesting Art Deco architecture, painted pillars, and lighted ceiling. Renovated in 1988 to recapture some of its former glory, this huge café is filled with history and nostalgia. A great place for people-watching.

❑ **Les Deaux Magots:** 170, Boulevard Saint-Germain, 6th arr., Tel. 45-48-55-25, 7:30am to 1:30am. Adjacent to and similar in atmosphere and clientele as Café de Flore. Actually, this café is more popular than its neighbor. It has a better location facing the intersection and a terrific view of the famous church, St. Germaine des Pres. Many a famous writer, artist, intellectual, and actor have frequented this establishment. Today, it's crowded with tourists and wannabes.

❑ **Fouquet's:** 9 Avenue des Champs-Elysées, 8th arr., Tel. 47-23-70-60, 8:00am to 2:00am. This is the most famous café on the Champs-Elysées with its bright red awning and expansive terrace. More celebrities have probably passed through this café than any other in Paris—Chaplin, Chevalier, Dietrich, Churchill, Roosevelt, and Jacqueline Onassis. You'll still see an occasional celebrity come here along with throngs of tourists. The coffee and wine are some of the most expensive in Paris —25F for coffee and 40F for a glass of wine. Fouquet's also has a restaurant on the second floor, although most people come here for coffee, wine, and sandwiches served on the street-level terrace.

BEST TEA ROOMS

Tea rooms can be one of the best dining experiences in Paris. After a long day of visiting museums, walking the streets, and shopping, tea time may become one of your favorite dining times. Remember, it's a long time between lunch (noon to 2:00

pm) and dinner (9:00pm). Tea rooms provide a wonderful bridge between lunch and dinner. In many cases, tea room selections may become your lunch.

Paris has numerous small tea rooms. Some of the best include these delightful places:

❑ **A Priori-Thé**: 35-37 Galerie Vivieene, 2nd arr., Tel. 42-97-48-75. Open noon-7:00pm. This charming setting is popular for lunch and afternoon tea with journalists and iintellectuals.

❑ **Angelina**: 226 Rue de Rivoli, 1st arr., Tel. 42-60-82-00 (and other locations in city). Offers excellent tea, coffee, hot chocolate, and light meals.

❑ **Grande Mosquée de Paris**: 39 Rue Geoffroy Saint-Hilaire, 5th arr., Tel. 43-31-18-14. Open from 10:00am to 9:30pm. Serves North African and Middle Eastern pastries, sweet mint tea, and Turkish coffee.

❑ **La Maison du Chocolat**: 52 Rue François-ler, 8th arr., Tel. 47-23-38-25. Open 10:00am to 6:00pm. Closed Sundays. Here's the tea room that doesn't serve tea— only hot chocolate which comes in five varieties. Nice selection of pastries.

❑ **Ladurée**: 16 Rue Royale, 8th arr., Tel. 42-60-21-79. Open 8:30am to 7:00pm (Sunday 10:00am to 7:00pm). This popular tea room serves an expensive lunch as well as wonderful tea with macaroons.

BEST PLACES FOR DESSERTS

Paris abounds with great places to indulge your sweet tooth. Tempting pastry shops (*pâtisseries*) are found throughout Paris. Indeed, every other block seems to have a wonderful pastry shop displaying delectables in their window. It's difficult to end up with a bad pastry. But if you want something special, try these pastry shops:

❑ **Fauchon**: 26 Place de la Madeleine, 8th arr., Tel. 47-42-60-11. Open 8:30am to 8:00pm. Closed Sundays. This is pastry heaven! You'll find everything here in addition to a fine pastry shop.

❑ **Michel Couderc:** 6 Boulevard Voltaire, 11th arr., Tel. 47-00-58-20. Open 8:30am to 1:30pm and 3:00pm to 8:00pm. Closed Monday. Terrific selection of pastries, chocolates, ice creams, and candies nicely displayed. Try the apricot tarts.

❑ **Peltier:** 66 Rue de Sèvres, 7th arr., Tel. 47-34-06-62. One of the city's best pâtisseries. Try their tarte au chocolate. Also has a nice selection of cheeses, quiches, salads, and sandwiches.

For excellent ice cream, try **Bertillion** (31 Rue St-Louis-en-I'lle, 4th arr., Tel. 43-54-31-61). Offering nearly 70 flavors of ice cream and sorbets, this shop occasionally draws long lines of eager ice cream fans who pay 28F ($6.00) for two scoops of this devine creamy substance. While not on par with Italian *gelato*, at least in Paris this unique concoction stands out from the local competition.

Most tearooms have a wonderful pastry cart from which you can choose your favorite dessert.

BEST GROCERY AND GOURMET SHOPS

If you want to see a full range of quality food products available in Paris, you need not go much further than these three delightful food emporiums offering everything from meats, cheeses, breads, and pastries to wine, beer and fruit juices. You can quickly put together a wonderful, although not always cheap, picnic in each of these places:

❑ **La Grande Épicerie de Paris:** Bon Marché Department Store, 38 Rue de Sèvres (Magasin 2, main floor), 7th arr., Tel. 44-39-81-00. Open Monday-Friday, 8:30am to 9:00pm; Saturday, 8:30am to 10:00pm. Closed Sunday and major holidays. This upscale Left Bank supermarket packs in the crowds with its wonderful selections of cheeses, meats, wines, pastries, and packaged foods. If you're wandering the Left Bank and don't know where to go for breakfast, lunch, or dinner, come here for some ideas. Trust us. You'll find several solutions along their tempting aisles! This is the Left Bank's answer to the Right Bank's Lafayette Gourmet and Fauchon.

❑ **Lafayette Gourmet:** Galeries Lafayette Department Store, 1st Floor, 48 Boulevard Haussmann, 9th arr., Tel. 48-74-46-06. Open 9:30am to 6:30pm. Closed Sunday and holidays. Wow! This floor is a real surprise—especially if you're visiting Galeries Lafayette to do some serious shopping for clothes and accessories—as your escalator gives you a preview of this food mecca. Forget what you ostensibly came for, get off the escalator, and feast your eyes on all the delectable goodies crammed on the shelves and in the display cases. You'll have no problem putting together the perfect picnic in this incredible food department. You also can eat here at the different food stations that offer salads, fruits, cheeses, pastries, pasta, sushi, and wines.

❑ **Fauchon:** 26 Place de la Madeleine, 8th arr., Tel. 47-42-60-11. Open 9:40am to 7:00pm. Closed Sundays and holidays. Tired of visiting museums and shopping for clothes? Here's the real thing for food lovers, and a cultural experience, too. This is the ultimate upscale food emporium you'll have to see to believe! Just bring lots of money, a healthy appetite, and a big shopping bag. Indeed, a visit here could well be one of the highlights of your visit to Paris. It simply doesn't get any better in France, or even in the world, than the famous Fauchon with its more than 30,000 food products from around the world; its wonderful crowd-pleasing window displays; its staff of 300; and its associated restaurants. Founded in 1886, few food shops in the world can claim such a vast collection of gastronomic delights. You will literally find everything here and in abundance: fruits, vegetables, salads, meats, cheeses, smoked salmon, coffees, teas, spices (4,500!), candies, pastries, and wines. The huge shop is divided into different departments, including a gifts department, a cocktail department, and a section offering Fauchon-signature china, crystal, and tableware. Fauchon includes a reasonably priced self-service cafeteria and rotisserie in the basement that is literally packed for lunch (11:30am to 2:00pm); it becomes a brasserie in the evening (7:00pm to 2:00am). Fauchon also operates four restaurants located around Place de la Madeleine: **Le Trente** (#30), **Le Bistro du Caviar** (#30), **La Trattoria** (#26), and **Bistro de la Mer** (#6). Le Trente takes honors for being the best of the four.

BEST FOOD MARKETS

Paris has numerous colorful outdoor food markets offering wonderful varieties of fruits, vegetables, meats, and fish. If you want a unique cultural experience of observing Parisians and learning about daily food rituals, spend some time visiting these markets. They also offer great photo opportunities and you'll probably pick up some items for yourself.

France's largest wholesale food market is the **Rungis Market** on the southern outskirts of the city, near Orly Airport. You may be able to get in to observe this huge 625 acre complex that is the major food source for Paris' other food markets and restaurants. It's only supposed to be open to bonafide wholesalers. However, it's probably best to go with an organized tour such as those conducted by **Mme. Gillot** (Société Semmaris, 1 Rue de la Tour, 94152 Rungis Cedex, Tel. 46-87-35-35, Fax 46-87-56-77) or **Robert Noah** (Paris en Cuisine, 49 Rue de Richelieu, 75001 Paris, Tel. 42-61-35-23). Gillot's tour is conducted in French and English and primarily focuses on the fish market. Noah's tour is in English and covers all of the major markets. Call both tour leaders for details on current prices and itineraries.

Each neighborhood has is own food shopping street (*rue commerçante*) or roving market (*marché volant*). The major shopping streets with permanent food markets include the following:

2nd arrondissement:	Rue Montorgueil
5th arrondissement:	Rue Mouffetard
6th arrondissement:	Rue de Buci
7th arrondissement:	Rue Cler
9th arrondissement:	Rues des Martyres
16th arrondissement:	Rue de L'Annonciation
17th arrondissement:	Rue de Levis and Rue Poncelet
18th arrondissement:	Rue Lepic

These markets are normally open from 8:30am to 1:00pm and from 4:00pm to 7:00pm, Tuesday through Saturday, and in the morning on Sunday; many of the merchants take off for holidays and during July and August.

Roving markets are constantly on the move, but make their moves on specific days in specific neighborhoods.

5th arrondissement:	**Carnes**, Place Maubert (Tuesday, Thursday, & Saturday)

5th arrondissement:	**Monge**, Place Monge (Wednesday, Friday, & Saturday)
6th arrondissement:	**Raspail**, Boulevard Raspail, between Rue du Cherche-Midi and Rue de Rennes (Tuesday, Friday, & Sunday; Sunday becomes the organic market, *marché biologique*)
7th arrondissement:	**Breteuil**, Avenue de Saxe, between Avenue de Ségur to Place Breteuil (Thursday & Saturday)
11th arrondissement:	**Richard-Lenoir**, adjacent to the Bastille, beginning at Rue Amelot (Thursday & Saturday)
15th arrondissement:	**Dupleix**, between Rue Lourmel and Rue du Commerce (Wednesday & Sunday)
17th arrondissement:	**Cours de la Reine**, between Rue Debrousse and Place d'Iéna (Wednesday & Saturday)

Wherever and whenever they function, these markets are open from 7:00am to 1:00pm.

FAVORITE BUDGET RESTAURANTS

As you'll quickly discover, frequenting Paris' many all-star restaurants create havoc on any semblance of a travel budget. Most travelers cannot sustain more than one or two visits to such expensive establishments.

Paris abounds with many wonderful budget restaurants that offer good meals for under 130F (US$30) per person; many offer three-course fixed-price meals for under 65F (US$15). Some of the best of the best are outlined in Sandra Gustafson's *Cheap Eats in Paris*. A few of our favorites include these:

❏ **Bistrot Le P'tit Troquet:** 28 Rue de l'Exposition, 7th arr., Tel. 47-05-80-39. This small and romantic neighborhood restaurant operated by Patrick and Dominique Vessière serves excellent dishes, from smoked duck and salmon to filet of pork, tuna, and lamb.

❑ **Oh!..Poivrier!** 25 Quai des Grands Augustins, 6th arr. This chain of restaurants (also in 8 other locations) serves an excellent selection of salads, sandwiches, and drinks at reasonable prices.

❑ **Perraudin:** 157 Rue St-Jacques, 5th, Tel. 46-33-15-75. Open for lunch (noon to 2:30pm) and dinner (7:30pm to 10:00pm) Does not take reservations. This charming eatery serves excellent French home-style dishes. Good wine selection and desserts.

JOIN A COOKING SCHOOL

If you're really into French cuisine, you may want to join a cooking school. A few companies offer cooking tours of France. You should contact them for details before you arrive in Paris:

❑ **Le Cordon Bleu:** 8 Rue Léon Delhomme, 75015 Paris, Tel. 48-56-06-06 (from the U.S., call toll free 800/457-2433 or write to: 404 Irvington St., Pleasantville, NY 10570). Established in 1895, this world-famous French cooking school operates 10-week courses as well as four-day workshops and three-hour demonstration classes for both beginners and professionals. Prices vary from 200F (US43) for a three-hour demonstration class to 4,590F (US$1000) for a four-day workshop. Also offers other alternative programs. Call for information and brochures.

❑ **Ritz-Escoffier Ecole de Gastronomie Française:** 75001 Paris, Tel. 43-16-30-50 (from the U.S., call toll free 800/966-5758). Operated at the Ritz Hotel, this popular program includes daily demonstration classes (US$49, Mondays through Thursdays) as well as weekly cooking courses. Learn the art of French cooking, bread, and pastry making from the experts. Call for rates and information.

7

Shopping Seductive Paris

Paris is seductive in many different ways. But shopping is really where it gets you. You can float through its museums, circle and climb its monuments, stroll through its gardens and along the river Seine, sit and people-watch from its charming sidewalk cafés, stay at its opulent hotels, or dine at its exquisite restaurants. But it's shopping that pulls it all together.

In many respects, Paris is all about shopping. Whether you like it or not, you'll probably be seduced by Parisian shopping.

CONTEMPORARY MUSEUMS

Paris' shops are the city's contemporary museums, displaying the best of the best France has to offer the world today. But unlike museums, hotels, and restaurants, you can buy what's in the shops, take it with you, and enjoy it for many years to come. That's why we like to spend most of our money on things we can take with us and continue to admire rather than on consumables we must leave behind and only remember as pleasurable experiences (hotels, restaurants, and museums).

For us, one of the high points of visiting Paris is to acquire its many treasures by shopping its many shops, department stores, and markets. In so doing, we meet a lot of interesting people and learn a great deal about France and the French. Shopping becomes an important window to really understanding and enjoying this fascinating city and its people.

THE ULTIMATE SHOPPING HIGH

Paris is the world's most fashionable shopping center for clothes and accessories as well as a major center for quality jewelry, antiques, arts, and crafts. Few places in the world, except perhaps Milan, can claim to offer such a wide range of top quality clothing and accessories. On every other shopping front, Paris seems to have an advantage over most other cities.

If you've come to Paris to shop, you won't be disappointed. Shopping is everywhere, but it's especially concentrated in the same districts where you will find many of Paris' best hotels, restaurants, and popular attractions—1st, 4th, 6th, 7th, 8th, and 16th arrondissements. Shop after shop beckon you to come-on-in and sample their treasures. Just watch your wallet, for you are about to engage in a truly budget-bleeding activity!

And shopping in Paris is fun, entertaining, and educational. It also can be dirt cheap. Indeed, you can have a great time without spending a single franc by just window-shopping for clothes, jewelry, art, and antiques; taking in free fashion shows that announce the latest in Parisian fashions; discovering discount haute couture shops; browsing through flea markets for unique antiques and exotic treasures; surveying the sumptuous surroundings and offerings of major department stores; or exploring the many art, antique, and ethnographic shops that line the streets of Paris.

For us, shopping is one of the major highlights of visiting Paris. It's our street entertainment. But it's also serious business aimed at rounding out our closets, decorating our home, and adding to our art collection. Having visited the Parisian museums, monuments, buildings, and churches, we now focus on our real Paris passion—shopping for unique quality products.

QUALITY AND STYLE HAVE A PRICE

Let's get one fact straight from the very beginning—you don't go to Paris to do bargain shopping nor to save money. That's not what this city is all about. Yes, Paris has its flea markets and discount shopping, but you won't find many bargains you'll want to take home with you at these ostensibly bargain shopping centers. You're more likely to encounter a lot of mediocre discounted items you neither need nor want to take home. For example, you might find a US$300 sweater discounted to US$100 but, on second thought, you wouldn't even think of paying US$50 for it back home.

On the other hand, you may find a gorgeous Christian Lacroix jacket originally priced at US$2000 discounted to US$800. While you might never pay that much for a jacket back home, the discounted price does make it a real steal. And it's really gorgeous, you look great and feel terrific in it, and all of a sudden you can't live without it! That's shopping seductive Paris. Something tells you to go ahead and buy it, even though it is still very expensive and you feel a little guilty about splurging on this great deal.

That "something" is called Parisian quality and style. You see it, you feel it, you try it on, and you fall in love with it. You can't find it back home because shops back home aren't into stocking such quality and stylish items. Indeed, many of your hometown shops may start looking mediocre once you return home from Paris. Quality and style are what make you pull out your credit card and buy things you never thought you were capable of buying!

Once you get home, you'll love such Parisian purchases. Not only are they excellent quality. They are very fashionable, and you still look great and feel good in them.

Paris does offer bargains, but they are only bargains if you fall in love with them. What you are most likely to fall in love with are top quality products, such as haute couture and designer label clothes and accessories at 20 to 60 percent discount. Chances are these are things you are not used to purchasing even at what appear to be nicely discounted prices.

For dedicated shoppers, Paris is all about quality and how to acquire it. This is not an easy concept to explain to someone who has never visited Paris. You have to go to Paris and visit its many shops to know exactly what we mean about quality shopping.

You have to face the fact that this city offers wonderful

- ❑ Paris' shops are the city's contemporary museums, displaying the best of the best France has to offer the world today—and it's all for sale!

- ❑ Shopping is an important window to really understanding and enjoying this fascinating city and its people. It's our street entertainment.

- ❑ Basic fact of shopping life—you don't go to Paris to do bargain shopping nor to save money. This city offers wonderful shopping that may bust your budget within an hour or two!

- ❑ Paris is unique for its shopping quality and style—you see it, you feel it, you try it on, and you fall in love with it.

- ❑ The basic rules of shopping in Pais are to bring lots of money, a good pair of walking shoes, and a sense of adventure as you seek out the city's many treasures.

shopping that may bust your budget within an hour or two. If, for example, you're used to buying blouses for US$150 back home, how does US$800 sound in Paris? If you pay US$50 for nice leather belts back home, what will you do when you find a gorgeous and stylish French designer belt for US$200? And what about that US$1500 jacket you've just fallen in love with but you've never paid more than US$300 for this type of garment?

Spend a few days window shopping and browsing through Paris' many quality shops and you may quickly become addicted to quality shopping that has made Paris so famous. This "quality" thing tends to slowly creep up on you and, before long, you are buying things at prices you never thought you would ever pay. You may feel guilty spending so much, but you love what you bought. It's pure quality that you will admire for years to come.

❑ Many shops close during the month of August, the traditional French vacation period.

❑ Most shops put prices tags or signs in their display windows.

❑ Don't forget to calculate the value-added tax that is refundable on purchases of US$400 or more in a single store.

❑ The two major department stores run huge sales during March and September.

❑ Pack a comfortable pair of walking shoes since Paris is a walking city for shopping.

❑ The best buys in Paris are those things Paris is especially well noted for and which can not be easily found elsewhere at cheaper prices.

If you thought your hotel room and restaurants were expensive, you haven't seen anything! Welcome to the wonderful world of expensive Parisian shopping. For some visitors, it's unbelievable. For others, they've fallen into shopper's heaven. Many French products scream quality and style unlike you may have ever seen. After awhile, you begin understanding want real quality is all about. And you discover you don't get much of this quality back home, even in some of the best shops.

SOME BASIC RULES

The basic rules for shopping in Paris are to bring lots of money, a good pair of walking shoes, and a sense of adventure as you seek out this city's many treasures. You'll walk its many streets exploring interesting small shops, expensive boutiques, unique shopping centers, grand department stores, and exotic markets. In between your shopping sojourns, you'll probably want to do some people-watching from a quaint café, take afternoon tea at a charming tea room, or picnic along the river or on a park bench.

HOURS AND DAYS

There are no hard and fast rules on shopping hours and days, only general guidelines and lots of exceptions to the general rules.

Most shops are open from 9:00am to 7:00pm, Tuesday through Saturday. However, many shops do not open until 9:30 or 10:00am. Bookstores and drugstores may stay open late. Most shops are closed on Sunday and Monday, although some do remain open. Sunday and Monday are slow shopping days since many shops close on these days or are only open for half a day. Some close early on Saturday, others stay open on Sunday but take a half day off on Monday, and still others stay open seven days a week.

Expect department stores to open at 9:30am or 9:35am and close at 6:45 or 7:00pm, Monday through Saturday. Some of these stores, such as Galeries Lafayette and Au Printemps, stay open until 9:00pm and 10:00pm respectively on Thursday. They close on Sunday but remain open on Monday.

Small shops may close each day for a two-hour lunch break. You'll see a sign informing you of their reopening hours.

The huge flea market, Marché Des Puces de Paris Saint-Ouen, is open every Saturday, Sunday, and Monday from 9:00am to 6:00pm, although some markets within this market keep later hours. Many street markets also are open on these days. Since most city shops are closed on Monday, one of the best days to visit the flea market is on Monday. Prices may also be better because this is the last day before they close for another four days. In fact, we normally plan to spend all day Monday visiting the flea market. If we have extra time, we may visit one of the major department stores that also are open on Monday. Other than that, you're taking a chance you'll be disappointed trying to shop elsewhere on Monday.

Remember that August is traditionally the French vacation month. Many shops close during this month, although many others stay open. Just don't plan to visit Paris in August with the expectation of finding all shops open.

MONEY MATTERS

Thank God for plastic money! Most shops in Paris, including those in the flea market, take major credit cards. Your purchases will be charged in French francs, but you will receive the bank's exchange rate when the charge is processed, which is usually the best daily rate. Most shops also accept traveler's checks, but they will probably need to call the bank to get the current exchange rate before translating US dollar traveler's checks into French francs. And some shops may even accept a personal check.

PRICING

One of the nice things about shopping in Paris is that most shops put prices in their display windows. The prices are either attached to the item, as in the case of jewelry and shoes, or written on a board next to each labeled display item. You'll know ahead of time what type of prices you can expect to encounter inside the shop. This also makes for appealing window-shopping.

RINGING IT UP

Some department stores have their own unique payment systems that eat up precious shopping time. They work like this. When you select an item, the store clerk gives you a receipt. You then take the receipt to a cashier who accepts your payment and stamps your receipt paid. You then retrieve your purchase with the paid receipt. This system is somewhat confusing and leads to standing in more than one line to make purchases.

DISCOUNTS AND TAXES

Most prices in shops are fixed prices as stated on the price tags. However, there are occasions when you can and should bargain for better prices. Art, antique, and jewelry shops, for example, may discount five or ten percent on big ticket items. They also may give you a three to five percent discount if you pay cash rather than use your credit card. But don't expect much more. Shops will often tell you that you're getting a discount when you apply for the value-added tax (VAT) refund. Many shops in flea markets will give discounts (15-30 percent) if you ask, especially on Mondays, the last day before closing for four days. When you ask for a discount, do so with class. Rather than ask *"Can you give me a 20 percent discount,"* ask *"Is it possible to do any better on the price?"* Life is fully of possibilities if you ask nicely!

Don't forget to consider the value-added tax that is refundable on purchases costing 2000F (US$400) or more in a single store. The average refund is about 13 percent, although refunds range from 12 to 18 percent, depending on the items purchased. Therefore, if you purchase a US$1000 piece of jewelry, you may be entitled to a US$160 tax refund. But you'll have to work for this refund if you take the item with you. First, make sure you ask the shop if the item qualifies for a tax refund and what percentage if you purchase the item and take it with you. Second, be sure to complete the necessary paper work—you show your passport and the merchant completes an export sales form in triplicate and signs it. Third, when you leave France or the final EU country, take the form and a self-addressed envelope with you, which you will present to a certifying Customs official. Be sure you have packed your purchase in your carry-on luggage or go to the desk to process the paper-work for your VAT refund before you check your luggage through to your next destination. You must have the item available to show along with your tax form, when you leave Europe. (If item is too large to carry home, many shops can ship the item for you and will take care of formalities to have the VAT deducted as well). Mail the form that has been stamped by Customs to the shop or the tax refund company for a refund (the company takes a commission and leaves you with maybe 15 percent). You normally receive your tax refund within four months. The French refer to this refund system as *détaxe*. Remember, you must complete the paper work at the time of your purchase. If you don't remember the *détaxe* system, you can easily miss out on hundreds of dollars in refunds. You won't be able to go back later to get the refund. Shipped purchases also qualify for *détaxe*, but you don't have to process the paper work with Customs—the shop does this for you.

A few department stores periodically offer discounts to tourists who present a special coupon to the store's welcome desk in exchange for a discount card. Au Printemps and Galeries Lafayette currently offer tourists a 10 percent discount on several store items (books, food, services, red dot merchandises exempted) upon presentation of the discount card. You'll find such coupons in much of the tourist literature or just go to the welcome desk and inquire about the special discount card. Be sure to take your passport with you to show that you are a bonafide tourist qualifying for this discount.

PACKAGING

One of the real joys of shopping in Paris is the lovely packaging that accompanies your purchases. The art of fine packaging is very much alive and well in Paris. Indeed, shops seem to literally gift wrap your purchases in beautiful papers, boxes, bows, and bags. If you're buying gift items in Paris, you probably won't need to gift wrap them when you get home!

SALES AND SPECIAL SHOPPING EVENTS

Shops and department stores periodically run sales. When you see a sign that says "SOLDES," it means a sale is in progress. Such sales normally discount items by 20-30 percent and maybe as much as 50 percent. The major sale periods in Paris take place during the first three weeks of January and July. The two major and highly competitive department stores catering to tourists, **Au Printemps** and **Galeries Lafayette**, run huge sales during March and October.

Some stores have annual sales. **Hermès**, for example, holds its popular annual sale in October when many items are sold at nearly half price. Several shops donate quality merchandise to the semi-annual (June and December) **Braderie de Paris** (bazaar) which takes place at the Porte de Versailles.

You also may want to look for special shopping events, such as fairs and trade shows, that are often held at the Grand Palais; most are open to the public. For example, every other year in September the world's largest antiques fair, the **Biennale Internationale des Antiquaires**, is held at the Grand Palais. Several other annual sales are held here in late November and early December. Check with the French Government Tourist Office (444 Madison Avenue, New York, NY 10022) for information on these special events prior to your departure for Paris. Once in Paris, check with the tourist office and your hotel concierge or survey the tourist publications and *Allo Paris* for information on current or upcoming special shopping events.

NO TOUCHY-FEELY PLEASE

While you may be used to picking up merchandise and examining it in a shop, this is not an accepted custom in Paris and other parts of France. Customers are expected to ask for assistance rather than take initiative by touching and feeling items, especially highly breakable items. If you walk into a shop and pick up something, chances are you will get a disapproving look or store personnel will ask you not to handle the merchandise. Some shops will put up signs in English saying "Do not touch." Since we're touchy-feely American shoppers, we frequently generate disapproving looks. We can't help it—it's our custom! You may want to be more culturally adaptive than us by keeping your hands to your side and ask for assistance to see things close up. Ask for permission to touch and feel it. On the other hand, touch-feely shoppers can have a great time in department stores where the clerks leave you alone to play with the merchandise!

SHIPPING

Most shops can arrange for shipping merchandise abroad or your hotel concierge can find a reliable shipper to help you. Keep in mind that you still qualify for *détaxe* if you ship your purchases from Paris. The shipper will take care of the *détaxe* form required for Customs certification.

TREAT YOUR FEET RIGHT

We surely hope you pack a comfortable pair of walking shoes. Paris is a walking city. You'll be on your feet much of the time, and you will probably cover long distances in a single day. The good news is that Paris is filled with numerous park benches and cafés where you can rest your feet. But comfortable walking shoes are essential to enjoying your Paris shopping experience.

VENTURE INTO THE UNKNOWN

Don't be afraid to go into shops, even though many may seem intimidating. The joy of shopping in Paris is the adventure of discovering new shops and products and meeting interesting shopkeepers and salespeople. Many shops, especially some of the top jewelers, boutiques, and haute coutures, may appear to be too exclusive for your shopping tastes. But don't hesitate to go into these places. Entry is free and you'll get a real education about quality French products and French shopping culture. You also may discover some things you really can't live without or ones you plan to return to Paris for someday!

If you don't think a flea market is to your shopping tastes, think again. The huge Marché des Puces de Paris Saint-Ouen is a wonderful shopping, if not cultural, experience. You may even surprise yourself by making some unique purchases here. And you may discover this market is one of your all-time memorable shopping experiences, one you may try to repeat on subsequent visits to Paris. It's the type of shopping experience that makes Paris such a special place.

Whatever you do, approach shopping as an adventure from which you will learn a great deal about Paris, France, and the French. The shops of Paris represent a kind of living museum that may be more interesting than the many official museums that dot Paris' urban landscape. In so many ways these shops express the very best of what Paris and the French have to offer the world today. In the process of shopping, you may even acquire some wonderful items that will constantly remind you of some very magical moments you had in Paris. That's what this adventure is all about. Enjoy!

BEST BUYS

A truly best buy in Paris is one you can't live without at any price. Hopefully, you won't find too many of those buys because, if you do, you're in big financial trouble!

The best buys in Paris are those things Paris is especially well noted for and which can not be easily found elsewhere at cheaper prices. For the most part, best buys are not cheap nor do they represent bargain basement prices. As noted earlier, Paris is simply a very expensive city in every way except public transportation. The emphasis here is on **quality shopping**. And you'll see what we mean by quality shopping once you begin venturing into our many recommended shopping streets and shops.

FASHION AND ACCESSORIES

This is more than just clothes, shoes, and purses. In Paris we say "fashion" because that is what the designers produce and the shops and department stores offer. You see it everywhere, from fashionably dressed Parisian women and men walking the streets or sitting at cafés and restaurants to shops and department stores filled with enticing fashions and accessories. This city abounds with all types of clothing and accessory shops. Street after street is lined with the latest fashions. Here you will find the world's best haute coutures along with numerous exclusive boutiques, designer label shops, and your run-of-the-mill department store clothes. You'll find discount outlets offering last season's designer garments at half price as well as numerous other garments and accessories at discounted prices. Window shopping for fashion and accessories is one of the great pastimes in Paris. We'll see what hundreds of Paris' fashion designers are introducing each season. Store windows display the latest chic fashions that make Paris such a famous center for clothes.

You may even want to attend a free weekly fashion show at Au Printemps and Galeries Lafayette department stores (see *Where Paris* and other tourist literature for information on dates and times) where you can see the latest fashion creations modeled.

You'll also find beautiful leather goods, such as shoes, purses, gloves, and belts, in Paris' many shops. The selection of fashion belts is especially outstanding. French designers are especially talented in creating fashionable belts that can really dress-up basic outfits.

The good news is that shops offering the latest in chic Parisian fashions and accessories are concentrated along a few key streets. The latest fashions also are abundantly on display in the major department stores, especially at Au Printemps and Galeries Lafayette which are located adjacent to each other on Boulevard Haussmann (9th arr.). For a quick introduction to Parisian fashions and accessories, head for the following streets:

Right Bank

Rue du Faubourg-St-Honoré	8th arr.
Avenue Montaigne	8th arr.
Boulevard Haussmann	9th arr.
▪ Au Printemps Department Store	
▪ Galeries Lafayette Department Store	
Avenue Victor Hugo	16th arr.

Left Bank

Rue du Grenelle/Saint Pères	7th arr.
Rue du Dragon	6th arr.

Just walk along these streets and look at the wonderful window displays and occasionally go inside for a closer look. If you really want to see the best of the best, be sure to visit **Hermès** at 24 Rue du Farbourg-St-Honoré. Their beautiful and creative window displays may seem intimidating, but go on in and see what's happening in the various rooms of this incredible two-storey shop. This is one of Paris' chicest and most popular fashion and accessory shops. It will give you a good introduction into the fabulous world of quality Parisian fashion, especially for leather goods and signature scarves. It also will help you develop a mind-set as to what such fashions and accessories are likely to cost at many of the other top Parisian shops that offer the very best in French fashions and accessories.

Look for lots of very fashionable clothes under such famous French, European, and Japanese designer labels as Giorgio Armani, Pierre Cardin, Céline, Cerruti 1881, Chanel, Christian Dior, Louis Féraud, Ferragamo, Givenchy, Gucci, Kenzo, Emmanuelle Khanh, Christian Lacroix, Karl Lagerfeld, Lanvin, Guy Laroche, Matsuda, Issey Miyake, Claude Montana, Missoni, Moschino, Révillon, Nina Ricci, Sonia Rykiel, Yves

Saint Laurent, Joan-Louis Scherrer, Trussardi, Emanuel Ungaro, Valentino, Gianni Versace, Louis Vuitton, Yohji Yamamoto, and Ermenegildo Zegna. The list goes on and on. Any designer worth anything has one or more shops in Paris.

FABRICS AND LINENS

The French are well known for producing fine fabrics and bed, bath, and table linens. Gorgeous designer fabrics for wall coverings, draperies, and upholstery are found in several shops along Rue Bonaparte (**Besson** and **Nobilis Fontan**), Rue des Saints-Pères (**Casal**), Rue Jacob (**Pierre Frey**), and Rue de la Paix (**Henri Maupiou**). **Marché Saint-Pierre** at Place due Marché Saint-Pierre in the 18th arrondissement is the largest discount fabric market in Paris. It includes a huge selection of cotton, silk, velvet, satin, and felt fabrics for clothes, upholstery, and curtains. For excellent quality bed, bath, and table linens, be sure to visit **Porthault** (18 Avenue Montaigne, 8th arr.), **Agnès Comar** (7 Avenue George-V, 8th arr.), and **La Châtelaine** (170 Avenue Victor-Hugo, 16th arr.).

JEWELRY

It doesn't get much better than Paris when it comes to jewelry, both real and fake. Only six jewelers carry the title *Haute Joaillerie de France*: **Gianmaria Buccellati** (4 Place Vendôme), **Mauboussin** (20 Place Vendôme), **Mellerio** (9 Rue de la Paix), **Poiray** (46 Avenue Georges-V), **Rene Boivin** (49 Avenue Montaigne), and **Van Cleef & Arpels** (22 Place Vendôme). These jewelers design and mount their own jewelry as well as guarantee the quality of their gems.

If you want to see the best of the best in jewelry, head straight for the Place Vendôme and adjacent Rue de la Paix. Place Vendôme is lined with Paris' finest jewelers. Here you will find the incredible designs and craftsmanship of the Italian jeweler **Gianmaria Buccellati**. In the same square you'll find **Alexandra Reza**, **Boucheron**, **Van Cleef & Arpels**, **Mauboissin**, **Piaget**, **Chaumet**, **Mikimoto**, **Repossi**, **Chanel**, and **Cartier** offering exquisite jewelry. Rue de la Paix, which crosses Place Vendôme, is home to such fine jewelers as **H. Stern**, **Poiray**, and **Corum**.

Paris also abounds with shops offering estate jewelry. Some of the best such shops are located just around the corner from Place Vendôme, west along Rue St.-Honore. Here you'll find two excellent shops offering estate jewelry—**G. Linde** (#374) and **Albuquerque** (#376).

We've also discovered several shops offering excellent quality jewelry made with semi-precious stones. One of our favorites is **Cipanyo** (14 Rue de L'Echaude, 6th arr.), a small shop located behind St-Germain des Prés, which produces unique pieces using antique Venetian glass beads, coral, pre-Columbian crystals, seed pearls, and silver. **Elena Cantacusine** (47 Rue du Cherchi Midi, 6th arr.) produces creative and colorful (red and gold) necklaces, bracelets, and earrings using natural materials, African beads, molten glass, ceramics, wood, and semi-precious stones.

One of the favorite jewelry purchases for many visitors is the excellent quality faux jewelry offered by several shops. Considered by most experts to be costume jewelry, the products are so good they deserve a different classification. They also can be expensive. **Burma** (72 Rue du Faubourg-St-Honoré), which also includes branches throughout Paris and elsewhere in France, offers some of the best designs along with high prices. For more affordable costume jewelry, look for **Agatha** which has numerous branches in Paris, France, Europe, United States, Canada, and Japan. You also can see their selections at Paris' three major department stores, Au Printemps, Galeries Lafayette, and Le Bon Marché.

- ❑ You may want to attend the free fashion shows at Au Printemps and Galeries Lafayette department store.

- ❑ It doesn't get much better than Paris when it comes to jewelry, both real and fake. Place Vendôme is home to most of Paris' top jewelers.

- ❑ Art galleries tend to be disproportionately concentrated along Avenue Matignon and Rue de Seine.

- ❑ Paris is the ultimate city for antique shops.

- ❑ The best English-language bookstore is Brentano's at 37 Avenue de l'Opéra.

- ❑ The underground shopping mall at Les Halles is somewhat confusing and depressing. There are better things to do with your time than to go underground here.

- ❑ The 8th arrondissement is Paris' most decadent shopping area. You'll lose your shopping innocence here!

Also look for **Anemone** (7 Rue de Castiglione, 1st arr.), **Biche de Bere** (348 Rue St- Honoré, 1st arr.), and **Octopussy** (255 Rue St-Honoré, 1st arr.).

PERFUMES

French perfumes are readily available in several shops on the Right and Left Banks. Some of the best shops for perfumes include **Annick Goutal** (14 Rue de Castiglione, 1st arr., and 12 Place St. Sulpice, 6th arr.), **Artisan Parfumeur** (24 Boulevard Raspail, 7th arr., 22 Rue Vignon, 9th arr., and 32 Rue du Bourg Tibourg, 4th arr.), **Guerlain** (68 Avenue des Champs-Elysées, 8th arr.), and **L'Occitane** (55 Rue St. Louis en L'Ile, 4th arr.). For discounted perfumes (20-40%), try **Freddy of Paris** (3 Rue

Scribe, 9th arr.), **Michael Swiss** (16 Rue de la Paix, 2nd arr.), and **Catherine** (6 Rue de Castiglione, 1st arr.).

ARTS AND CRAFTS

The streets of Paris also abound with arts and crafts, from the inexpensive to the astronomical. Try to pick up a free copy of the latest fold-out map/guide to Paris' art galleries, "Programme des Galeries." It's available in most participating art galleries and covers the major districts of Paris.

Art galleries tend to be disproportionately concentrated along Avenue Matignon (8th arr.) and Rue de Seine (6th arr.). Here you will find everything from original oil paintings and prints to sculptures produced by French, European, and American artists. Many museums, but especially the Louvre, have art shops selling original art, posters, and art books.

Street artists also abound in Paris. The largest concentration of such artists is found along the bridges that pass over the river Seine in the 4th, 5th, 6th, and 7th arrondissements. They set up their easels and paint or draw their favorite scenes, which always seem to include Notre Dame Cathedral or the Eiffel Tower. Most of these budding artists also sell their paintings to anyone who approaches them. Other street artists paint or draw portraits or they will inscribe your name on a grain of rice (just what you need!). Be careful with the portrait artists who may overcharge you. These artists are disproportionately found near the Eiffel Tower, Sacré Cœur Basilica, and the George Pompidou Centre.

Paris' one and only Vietnamese fine art and home decorative shop is **Ambiance—Thé Galerie** (3 Rue Chomel, 7th arr.). Here you will find the works of Vietnam's top artists. The selections here are outstanding.

Numerous craft shops also are found throughout Paris. While many of the shops import ethnographic arts and crafts from Africa and Asia (see below), other shops offer the best of contemporary French and European crafts. We especially like the selections at **Artcurial** (9 Avenue Matignon, 8th arr.), an international gallery representing the works of twelve artists and craftsmen who produce outstanding arts and crafts ranging from jewelry and ceramics to furniture and carpets. If you enjoy woodcrafts, you'll enjoy the unique selections found at **Design 95** at 23 Rue de Bac. The shop represents the works of 24 artists and craftsmen who work in wood, producing inlaid boxes, bowls, pins, clocks, and a large assortment of fun pieces. **Heller Artisanat** (259 Rue St-Honoré) represents the unique works of French artists and craftsmen producing paintings, glass works, fountains, and scarves. Another good source is the craft shop at the **Musée des Arts Décoratifs** (107 Rue de Rivoli, 1st arr.). Be sure to explore the area immediately southeast of the Opéra de Paris Bastille along Avenue Daumesnil. Several new arts and crafts shops have recently opened in this newly developing area. The **Viaduc des Arts** (9-129 Avenue Daumesnil) houses numerous shops and craftsmen.

ANTIQUES

Paris is the ultimate city for antique shops. You can literally spend weeks just shopping for antiques in Paris. Indeed, given the sheer volume of antique shops, one gets the distinct impression that Parisians must be obsessed with collecting antiques. After visiting a few of these shops, one also gets the impression that this is a very serious business in which prices on antiques can be very very expensive.

Paris boasts several large antique centers where you can get a quick initiation into the world of French antiques. You might want to start at **Le Louvre des Antiquaires** (2 Place due Palais-Royal, 1st arr.), an upscale antique emporium located across the street from the Louvre Museum and housing nearly 250 antique dealers on three floors. The **Village Suissee** (78 Avenue de Suffren and 54 Avenue de La Motte-Picquet, 15th arr.), located not far from the Eiffel Tower, is one of our favorite antique centers with its cluster of nearly 150 shops offering everything from antique guns and artillery to furniture and china. The **Village Saint-Paul** (23-27 Rue St-Paul, 4th arr.) and **La Cour aux Antiquaires** (54 Rue du Faubourg-St Honoré) also have several small antique shops. But for the ultimate antique experience, head for the huge weekend (Saturday, Sunday, Monday) antique market at Saint-Ouen (**Marché des Puces de Paris Saint-Ouen**) in the 18th arrondissement. You'll find antiques everywhere, from trash to treasures, from small collectibles, such as postcards and books, to large pieces of furniture and chandeliers. There's so much here that you may experience antique sensory overload!

The streets of Paris are literally lined with antique shops on both sides of the river. On the Left Bank, Rue de l'Université, Rue Bonaparte, Rue de Bac, Rue de Seine, Quai Voltaire, all in the 6th arrondissement, are filled with antique shops offering furniture, crystal, paintings, sculptures, chandeliers, clocks, porcelain, and architectural pieces. In fact, **Le Carre Rive Gauche**, which extends from Quai Voltaire to Rue du Bac, includes 130 exclusive antique dealers. On the Right Bank, Rue de Faubourg-St-Honoré, Rue de Monceau, Avenue Matignon,

Rue de Miromesnil, Boulevard Haussmann and Place des Vosges are home to numerous antique shops.

Remember, Paris also hosts the world's largest antiques fair (the Biennale Internationale des Antiquaires) every other year in September. It's held at the Grand Palais. If you're lucky to be in Paris at that time and you're a real antique lover, you will be in for a real treat.

ETHNOGRAPHIC ARTS, CRAFTS, AND ANTIQUES

You really begin understanding what an incredibly international and cosmopolitan city Paris is when you discover its many ethnographic art, crafts, and antique shops. France's long colonial history is well and alive in its many shops that offer a large range of collectibles and home decorative items from Africa and Asia. You'll find them at the flea market in Saint-Ouen as well as in many shops of the Right and Left Banks. Many of the shops and stalls at the flea market essentially offer airport African art. Other shops offer good quality Asian arts, crafts, and antiques.

Some of our most treasured purchases from Paris have come from several of Paris' ethnographic shops. One of the largest concentrations of such shops is found in and around Rue de Seine and Rue Boneparte in the 6th arrondissement. Here you will find an excellent pre-Columbian art shop, **Arts des Amériques** (42 Rue de Seine) along with two excellent quality African art shops (**Galerie Pierre Robin** and **Primitif**) just off of Rue de Seine at Rue Jacques Callot. Further down Rue de Seine is another excellent street on the left for ethnographic arts and antiques, Rue des Beaux Arts. Here you will discover some truly first-rate shops for Southeast Asian and Oceanic primitive art— **Alain de Monbrison, Galerie Antipodes**, and **Galerie Meyer-Oceanic Art**. If you are a collector of Oceanic art, the Galerie Meyer-Oceanic Art should be a "must visit" stop. Bring lots of money since this is a collector's collector shop. During our last visit, their most expensive piece was a small Papua New Guinea mask for US$200,000! A few other shops are located just around the corner on Rue Bonaparte.

You'll find additional ethnographic shops elsewhere in the city. Within the Village Suisse (78 Avenue de Suffren, 15th arr.), for example, **Maud and René Garia** offer good quality African art. **Le Singe Blanc** (15 Rue Saint-Jacques, 5th arr.) offers nice quality Asian artifacts. **Galerie Bamyan** (1 Rue des Blancs-Manteaux, 4th arr.) has a terrific collection of furniture, carpets, and jewelry from Central Asia. **Galerie du Scorpion** (9 Rue de la Huchette, 5th arr.) offers a wonderful selection of artifacts from Africa and Asia. You'll make your own interesting ethnographic discoveries as you walk the streets of Paris.

TABLEWARES

The French know how to decorate a table with exquisite crystal, china, porcelain, silver, candles, glasses, tablecloths, napkins, and center pieces. You'll find several shops offer excellent quality tablewares with the French flare for class and style. Two of our favorite shops for candles, table clothes, napkins, plates, and glasses are **Dîners en Ville** (27 Rue de Varenne, 7th arr.) and **Point à la Ligne** (25 Rue de Varenne, 7th arr., and 67 Avenue Victor-Hugo, 16th arr.). For fine quality tableware, try **Baccarat** (11 Place de la Madeleine, 8th arr.), **Lalique** (Galerie du Carousel du Louvre, 99 Rue de Rivoli, 1st arr.), **Pavillon Christofle** (24 Rue de la Paix, 2nd arr., plus three other Parisian locations), and **Bernardaud** (11 Rue Royale, 8th arr.).

DRIED FLOWERS AND FRUITS

We've fallen in love with the beautifully displayed arrangements of dried flowers, especially roses, and fruits that are supposed to last for at least five years. Several shops offer these unique arrangements. One of the best is **Herve Gambs** (24 Boulevard Raspail, 7th arr.).

HOME FURNISHINGS AND DECORATIVE ITEMS

The French emphasis on design and style is well represented in the many home decor shops found throughout Paris. These shops stock a wide range of home furnishings and decorative items: furniture, vases, lamps, objets d'art, upholstery fabrics, wallpaper, linens, rugs, Many of them are found on the Left Bank along Rue de Bac and Boulevard Raspal. One of the largest such shops is **The Conran Shops** (117 Rue du Bac, 7th arr). Also look for **Elle** (30 Rue Saint-Suylpice, 6th arr.), **Étamine** (63 Rue du Bac, 7th arr.), and **David Hicks** (12 Rue de Tournon, 6th arr.).

BOOKS

Paris is a book city. You'll find numerous used bookstores, book stalls lining the river Seine, and specialty bookshops. The best English-language bookstore is **Brentano's** (37 Avenue de l'Opéra, 2nd arr.). It has a terrific selection of maps, travel books, periodicals, music, and books about Paris and France. However, English-language books tend to be very expensive, twice what you might pay back home. Other good English-language bookstores include **Galignani** (224 Rue de Rivoli, 1st arr.), **La Librairie Internationale** (78 Boulevard Saint-Michel, 6th arr.), **Shakespeare & Company** (37 Rue de la Bûcherie, 5th arr.), **W.H. Smith** (248 Rue de Rivoli, 1st arr.), **Tea and Tattered Pages** (24 Rue Mayet, 6th arr.), and **Village Voice** (6 Rue Princesse, 6th arr.).

MUSIC

The largest music store in Paris is the **Virgin Megastore** (52-60 Avenue des Champs-Elysées, 8th arr.). You'll find a large selection of CDS and tapes here. This store with its massive crowds and tight security has it all. If you can't satisfy your music needs here, chances are you won't be about to satisfy them elsewhere in Paris.

FOOD AND WINE

One of the great shopping adventures in Paris is to shop for gourmet food and wine. As we noted in Chapter 7, be sure to visit **Fauchon** (26 Place de la Madaleine, 8th arr.), the huge and extremely popular food emporium. Also, try **Debauve & Galais** (30 Rue des Saints-Pères, 6th arr.) for chocolates; **Hediard** (21 Place de la Madeleine, 8th arr.) for wines, teas, coffees, jams, exotic fruit and caviar; and **Verger de la Madeleine** (4 Boulevard Malesherbes, 8th arr.) for an excellent selection of wines. **Galeries Lafayette** (40 Boulevard Haussmann, 9th arr.) and **Le Bon Marché** (5 Rue de Babylone, 7th arr.) department stores both have extensive gourmet food sections.

THE SHOPPING STREETS OF PARIS

Most shopping in Paris takes place along a few major streets of both the Right and Left Banks. For ease of locating the major shopping areas and shops, let's examine the shopping streets of Paris by arrondissements. We'll only focus on the major areas of Paris.

1 ST ARRONDISSEMENT (Right Bank)

Some of Paris' best quality shopping is found in this district of the Louvre, Les Halles, Palais Royal, and Place Vendôme. A heavily touristed area, it is a mixture of top quality jewelry, antique, and clothing stores as well as some disappointing centers and souvenir shops. You can literally spend hours shopping the main streets in the district.

The major shopping streets here are Rue St-Honoré, Rue de Rivoli, and the shops at Place Vendôme, Palais Royal, and Les Halles. One of the best places to start is the Ritz Hotel at **Place Vendôme**. This somewhat stark but elegant square is home to most of Paris' top jewelers. If you start just north of the square, at the intersection of Rue de la Paix and Rue Danielle Casanova, which extends a few feet into the 3rd arrondissement, you'll see three fine jewelry shops on Rue de la Paix—**Poiray**, **Corum**, and **H. Stern**. Across the street and on the corner is a very nice fabric and accessory shop, **Henri Maupiou** (2 Rue de la Paix). Moving south into the square, you become overwhelmed with top quality jewelry shops, unlike any you may have ever seen before. These are some of the world's very best jewelers. The stand-out jeweler here is Italian **Gianmaria Buccellati** who has set a new standard for jewelry making. Simply incredible jewelry, the classiest of the bunch. We're always impressed by the extreme quality that goes into Buccellati jewelry. Someday we'll be back here or to one of the Buccellati family shops in Milan or Rome to actually buy one of their gems. Other outstanding jewelers include **Mauboissin**, **Van Cleef & Arpels**, **Boucheron**, **Alexandre Reza**, **Miki-moto**, **Chaumet**, **Chanel**, and **Cartier**. You also find a few exclusive shops offering clothes (**Emporia Armani, Charvet, Giorgio Armani**), accessories (**Morabito, Comptoir sud Pacific**), watches (**Piaget**), and perfumes (**Guerlain**). Shopping for jewelry in Paris will not get better—though perhaps less expensive—after you leave Place Vendôme!

As you leave Place Vendôme walking south along Rue de Castigione, turn right onto **Rue St.-Honoré**. This is one of Paris' most chic streets for clothes and accessories, although this section of the street is more mixed than the more upscale western end of this street—the Rue du Faubourg-St.Honoré section that extends into the 8th arrondissement. This section of the street has several clothing, accessory, jewelry, art, and home decor shops. The **Godiva** chocolate shop stands at the corner of Rue de Castiguone and Rue St-Honoré. Moving west along Rue St.-Honoré, you'll see **Georg Jensen** (#241) for quality silver tableware; **Ilins Lalaounis** (#364) for unique gold jewelry; **Burma** (#247) for gorgeous faux jewelry; **Yves Saint Laurent** (#372) and **Valentino** (#378) for designer-label clothes; **G. Linde** (#374) and **Albuquerque** (#376) for excellent quality estate jewelry, including pieces from such top jewelers as Poiray, Cartier, Boucheron, and Bvlgari); and **Heller Artisanat** (#259) for quality French arts and crafts (laces, paintings, bronzes, enamels, miniatures, silks, crystals, porcelain, bronze and stone carvings and tableware, and leather cases). When you reach Rue Royale, which forms the western border of the 1st arrondissement, turn right and walk north to the Place de la Madeleine which also lies in the far eastern section of the 8th arrondissement. On the corner of Rue Royale and Boulevard de la Madeleine is **Les Trois Quartiers** shopping center which encompasses more than 50 boutiques and related shops and restaurants. Here you will find Diffusion Yves St. Laurent, Gentleman Givenchy, Heyraud, Kenzo Hommes, Mondi, and Stéphane Kélian for clothes and accessories and Agatha and Burma for faux jewelry. A heavily promoted shopping arcade, it is relatively new and hopefully will see better days ahead. For now, it's very quiet and lacks a distinctive character. It can be skipped altogether with little consequences for your Parisian shopping experience. You will find a handy currency exchange booth in front of the shopping center (along Boulevard de la Madeleine) which is open on Saturdays and Sundays.

Another major shopping area in the 1st arrondissement is the **Louvre** where the Palais Royal meets both Rue St-Honoré and Rue de Rivoli. If you visit the Louvre, be sure to stop at the bookstore and gift shop which are housed under the glass pyramid. The bookstore has a terrific selection of art books, postcards, and films on the Louvre. The gift shop offers reproduction pieces, engravings, jewelry, and sculptures for sale. This is one of the better museum gift shops and shopping centers we've encountered. Across the street from the Louvre, at 2 Place du Palais-Royal, is **Le Louvre des Antiquaires**, an antique emporium of nearly 250 small antique shops. After visiting the Louvre, this may be one of those anti-climatic experiences. At least you can buy the antiques whereas you could only view the Louvre's holdings! Most shops in this emporium offer 18th and 19th century European antiques, although a few shops offer Asian antiques. These are top quality antique shops for serious collectors and decorators. Look for special monthly exhibits on the second floor.

Another major shopping area in this arrondissement is the

Forum Les Halles, the former city market that has been converted into a major underground shopping and cultural center. This is a very mixed area which you may or may not want to visit or spend much time. It tends to appeal to a young crowd that cruises the walkways and frequents the many cafés, snack bars, and fast food restaurants in the adjacent areas. We find the area somewhat confusing and depressing, more of a cultural experience to be escaped from than a worthwhile shopping destination. You'll find numerous souvenir shops and inexpensive eateries in this area. An underground shopping mall extends four-levels and includes more than 200 boutiques as well as numerous restaurants, snack bars, cafés, a branch of the FNAC, and cinemas. Further underground is the Châtelet-Les Halles, a huge métro station linked to the REF, métro stations, and parking lots. While you will find a few upscale boutiques and shops here (Bally, Benetton, NAF NAF), most of the area has little appeal to visitors who seem to get caught up with hundreds of roving teenagers. In addition, you may have difficulty finding the entrance to the underground mall. Just look for the tallest glass structure at the center of the Forum. If you miss the entrance, no great loss. There are better things to do with your time than to go underground here.

Just north of Forum Les Halles are several kitchen supply shops along Rue Montmartre which also extends into the 2nd arrondissement. These shops are well stocked with a large assortment of cooking and eating utensils, including pots, pans, electrical appliances (220V only), and flatware, as well as tablewares. Look for **Mora** (#13), **Duthilleul & Minart** (#14) and **La Corpo** (#19).

❑ Place Vendôme is home to most of Paris' top jewelers. The stand-out jeweler here is Italian Gianmaria Buccellati.

❑ The city's major garment district is found at Sentier which has numerous wholesalers selling to the trade.

❑ The major street for art in the 6th arrondissement is Rue de Seine.

❑ Most writers overrate the discount outlets in the 6th arron-dissement. We find them disappointing.

❑ If you visit only one discount haute couture shop in Paris, make sure it's Anna Lowe at 35 Avenue Matignon (8th arr.).

❑ Hermès is the ultimate shop for chic accessories. The quality and craftsmanship here are second to none.

❑ A good time to the department stores in the 9th arrondissement is on Monday when most other shops in Paris are closed.

❑ The discount outlets along Rue d'Alésia in the 14th arrondissement also disappoint us—lots of mediocre clothes and accessories at high prices.

❑ Since opening in 1989, the Opéra de Paris Bastille in the 12th arrondissement has encouraged the development of air galleries along Avenue Daumesnil.

2ND ARRONDISSEMENT (RIGHT BANK)

Located immediately north of the 1st arrondissement and known as the Bourse for its stock market, this area includes the districts of Gaillon, Vivienne, Mail, and Bonne-Nouvelle. There's not much here to recommend for shopping. A few of the jewelry shops associated with the Place Vendôme extend into this area. The city's major garment district is found at **Sentier** which has numerous wholesalers selling to the trade. A few kitchen supply shops are found along Rue Montmartre (look for A. Simon at 38 Rue Montmartre), an area which extends north from the Forum Les Halles in the 1st arrondissement. One of Paris' interesting shops which manufactures unique and fashionably chic studded belts, vests, and handbags at excellent prices is located nearby—**José Cotel** (10 Rue Mundar, Tel. 40-41-95-66). This shop is one of the best kept secrets in the 2nd arrondissement. A less well kept secret is **C. Mendès** (65 Rue Montmartre, Tel. 42-36-83-32), one of Paris' best discount shops for chic womenswear. Its two shops, located on two different floors, offers quality Yves Saint Laurent (ground floor) and Christian Lacroix (1st floor) garments at half price.

3RD ARRONDISSEMENT (RIGHT BANK)

Immediately east of the 2nd arrondissement and north of the 4th arrondissement, this area includes part of the Marais and is adjacent to the Place Des Vosges of the 4th arrondissement. It's best known for its Picasso Museum. We've not found a great deal of quality shopping here to recommend. Rue du Temple constitutes another garment district with numerous wholesale clothing shops lining this central street. If you decide to walk this street, don't expect to find many good quality garments at discounted prices. The discounted shops here tend to be overrated. **Biderman** (114 Rue du Temple), for example, is a large outlet for men's clothes that also includes a small women's section. Here you will find suits, coats, belts, ties, and sweaters under such popular labels as Yves St. Lauren, Kenzo, and Andre Balzac. When we visited the selections were disappointing (lots of dated styles and unattractive colors) and even the discounted prices seemed high—not our idea of a good shopping time. A lot depends on the timing of your visit and your degree of patience in sorting through a lot of merchandise to find a gem. The area is a bit rundown and somewhat depressing. Nonetheless, you will find several wholesale clothing shops here. One of the best places for having fashionable women's suits made is **Farnel** at 71 Rue Charlot (Tel. 42-72-80-01). It's a manufacturer for Chanel and Dior. You will find several art galleries near the Picasso Museum along Rue Vielle du Temple, Rue Debelleyme, Rue du Perche, and Rue Charlot.

Most of the quality shopping in this area is found along Rue Rambuteau and Rues des Frances Bourguois which border on the 4th arrondissement.

4TH ARRONDISSEMENT (RIGHT BANK)

This heavily touristed area offers some interesting shopping opportunities around the Place Des Vosges, Ile St. Louis, Rue de Rivoli, Rue Rembuteau and Rue des Frances Bourguois and the George Pompidou Centre. The **Village Saint-Paul** (23-27 Rue St-Paul) includes several small art and antique shops offering furniture, jewelry, pictures, glass and crystal, ceramics, and numerous decorative items. A few interesting ethnographic shops (Mexico, India, Tibet, Nepal) are located immediately to the south of the Place des Vosges, along **Rue de Birague**. Immediately around the perimeter of Place des Vosges you will find a few art and antique shops. If you walk down **Rue des Francs-Bourgeois**, you will encounter several boutiques and gift shops. Look for **Imex** at 8 Rue Des Francs-Bourgeois for women's coats and sewing supplies. It's located in a courtyard (La Cour des Pancs-Bourgeois). **Rue de Sevigne** also includes several nice clothing shops, especially **Romeo Gigli** (46 Rue de Sévigné) for beautiful men's and women's overcoats and sweaters. Several interesting clothing and accessory shops also are located along Rue Vielle du Temple and ethnographic shops along Rue des Blancs Manteaux (**Galerie Bamyan** for Central Asian rugs and furniture).

The **George Pompidou Centre** has a large book shop that stocks a good selection of 20th century art books, most of which are in French. It also has an extensive post card collection of the major modern art pieces displayed in the museum. Several art galleries are found near the Centre, along **Rue Quincompoix**.

5TH ARRONDISSEMENT (LEFT BANK)

This is the famous Latin Quarter of students and the Sorbonne, and the Panthéon. This is a very mixed shopping area you may want to skip altogether. Much of the shopping here deals with books, souvenirs, and ethnographic arts and crafts. The major shopping streets are Rue Saint Jacques and Boulevard Saint Germain. A small street off of Rue Saint Jacques, Rue de la Huchette, includes a few shops and numerous ethnic restaurants. One of our favorite ethnographic shops is located here (**Galerie du Scorpion**, 9 Rue de la Huchette, Tel. 43-26-06-16). This shop has some wonderful ethnographic art pieces from Ethiopia, the Sudan, India, and Nepal. **Le Singe Blanc** (15 Rue Saint-Jacques, Tel. 43-26-14-70) offers nice quality artifacts from Indonesia, Thailand, China, and Tibet.

6TH ARRONDISSEMENT (LEFT BANK)

Here's where much of the Left Bank shopping is centered. You can literally spend two or three days shopping this interesting area of mixed shops offering everything from the latest in fashions and accessories to arts, antiques, and home decorative items. While the major shopping streets are Boulevard Saint Germain, Rue de Sévres, Rue de Seine, Rue Bonaparte, Rue du Cherche Midi, and Rue St. Placide, you'll find lots of interesting shops along small streets leading into these major thoroughfares.

It might be best to start your shopping adventure in this area at **St.-Germain-des-Pres**. Other than famous and not so famous cafés along Boulevard Saint Germain, there's not much shopping along this street. One of Paris's major concentrations of art, antique, ethnographic, and home decorative shops is found east and north of this landmark church. If you walk along the narrow street north of the church, Rue de L'Abbaye, you'll see several art and home decorative shops along the way. One of our favorites is **Salon** (4 Rue de Bourbon le Château, Tel. 43-25-40-47), a very small home decorative shop that constantly changes its eclectic displays. You're likely to find interesting pieces of furniture, art, or accessories here. Just around the corner is **Cipanyo** (14 Rue de L'Echaude) which produces lovely neckpieces using Venetian glass beads, coral, crystals, seed pearls, Indian silver, and semi-previous stones. Most of these artistic pieces sell in the US$800-1000 range. The owner-designer-artist is usually in the shop.

The major street in this area for art is **Rue de Seine**. Both sides of this street are mostly lined with art galleries offering oil paintings, prints, and sculptures. Look for **Protée** (38 Rue de Seine) for large abstract paintings and **Galerie Jeanne Bucher** (53 Rue de Seine). A few shops offer excellent ethnographic art.

For a fabulous collection of pre-Columbian art (pottery and figures), stop at **Arts des Amériques** (42 Rue de Seine, Tel. 46-33-18-31). A few small side streets also have large concentrations of art galleries. Rue Jacques Callot, for example, has one of Paris' best African art galleries, **Galerie Pierre Robin** (10 Rue Jacques Callot, Tel. 43-26-31-38). Rue des Beaux Arts is lined with excellent quality galleries. Some of our favorites include **Alain de Monbrison, Galerie Antipodes**, and **Galerie Meyer-Oceanic Art** for ethnographic art. Rue Bonaparte also has a few art shops.

If you return to St. Germain des Pres, you may want to walk south along Rue de Sèvres and Rue de Four. These two streets are somewhat confusing because they are actually the same street but the name changes at the intersection of Rue de Rennes. This shopping area is filled with small but chic boutiques offering the latest in Paris fashions and accessories. Several excellent quality shops are found at the intersection of Rue de Four and Rue de Rennes: **Kenzo, Celine, Lancel**, and **Kashiyama**. You'll also find another branch of the faux jeweler **Burma** at 50 Rue de Four.

The intersection of Rue de Sèvres, Rue de Grenelle, Rue de Dragon, and Rue du Cherche Midi, also known as the Carrefour de la Croix-Rouge square, poses a dilemma—which way should you go? First of all, circle this square and survey its shops. It has some very fine boutiques beckoning you to window-shop and come-on-in. Look for **Lisa Frey** (10 Rue de Grenelle), a small but top quality couture; **Revillon** (44 Rue du Dragon) a famous furier offering gorgeous but very expensive coats (terrific styling); **Sonia Rykiel, Inscription Rykiel**, and **Sonya Rykiel Enfant** at 4/6 Rue de Grenelle for a large range of elegant (Sonia Rykiel) and trendy (Inscription Rykiel) clothes. **Yves St. Laurent, Prada, Longchamp, Givenchy**, and **Salvatore Ferragamo** also have nice shops at this intersection. If you would like to circle back to St. Germain des Pres, turn right and go north along **Rue du Dragon** which is well noted for its high concentration of excellent shoe stores along with small boutiques, galleries, and restaurants. If you go northwest, you enter **Rue de Grenelle** and the 7th arrondissement, one of the Left Bank's most fashionable streets.

If you turn left, you'll head down **Rue de Cherche Midi**. Let's go this direction as we head past several boutiques and antique, home decorative, and ethnographic shops. After you cross Boulevard Raspail look for **Elena Catacusene** at 47 Rue du Cherche Midi. This delightful shop offers creative and colorful affordable jewelry (earrings, necklaces, bracelets) made from natural materials. If you're looking for some small gift items, this shop might just meet your needs.

When you come to the intersection of Rue Saint Placide, turn right (northwest)and head toward the end of the block which connects with Rue de Sèvres and meets one of Paris' finest department stores, **Bon Marché** (22 Rue de Sèvres). This section of Rue Saint Placide is famous for its discount outlet shops. The best shop here is the **Mouton à Cinq Pattes** (16 Rue Saint Placide) and its children's shop five doors away (#8). However, try as we may several times, we found both the women's and men's selections disappointing and the prices still seemed high in these outlets. Quite frankly, we think most writers overrate these shops, or they must be finding some treasures we haven't found yet. You, too, may have better things to do with your time than to paw through the racks and bins to find a "diamond in the rough." Nothing matches and the colors and styling may not be for you. Many of the items (clothes, jackets, sweaters, blouses, shirts, vests, slacks, belts) of the clothes looks cheap and truly discontinued. You'll have more fun at the Bon Marché department store which technically puts you into the 7th arrondissement.

7TH ARRONDISSEMENT (LEFT BANK)

This is the area of the Eiffel Tower, Invalides, and the Musée d'Orsay. Essentially an upscale extension of the western end of the 6th arrondissement, this area is one of our favorites. Most shopping is concentrated in and around Rue de Grennelle, Rue des Saints Pères, Rue de Bac, Rue de l'Universite, Rue de Verenne, and Rue de Babylone.

If you're visiting the **Musée d'Orsay** and you're interested in the 19th century art on display in the museum, be sure to stop at the museum shop. You can also enter the shop from the street, without having to pay admission to the museum. The shop has a good selection of art books. However, it's not as well organized as the shop at the Louvre.

Rue de Grenelle is the chicest shopping street in the 7th arrondissement. A relatively narrow street with an occassional pastry and grocery store and antique shop, the area between Rue du Bac and Rue des Saints Pères it is lined with some of the biggest names in Parisian fashion and accessories—**Kenzo, Barbara Bui, Roberto Verino, Montana, Robert Merlox, Patrick Cox, Mani, Dona Anna** (Versace, Gianfranco Ferre, Fendi), **Sergio Rossi, Stéphane Kélian**, and **Charles Krammer**. As noted in our examination of the 6th arrondissement, the climax to this street is the intersection of Rue de Grenelle and Rue des Saints Pères which flows into the Carrefour de la Croix-Rouge square with its high concentration of chic boutiques.

Rue du Bac is another popular shopping street lined with home decorative, linen, tableware, jewelry, antique, and art and craft shops interspersed with excellent pastry shops—the ultimate high caloric shopping adventure! Look for **Magnolia** (78 Rue du Bac) for its porcelains, jewelry, inkwells, and vases, **Play Bac** (62 Rue du Bac) for affordable sportswear and dresses, and **Missoni** (43 Rue du Bac) for trendy fashions. One of our favorite shops is located near the far end of this street: **Design 95** (23 Rue du Bac, Tel. 42-61-17-43). This shop offers wood creations produced by 15 different artists. The pieces are beautiful, ranging from wood inlaid boxes and bowls to large sculptured pieces. The shop also includes pins, letter openers, clocks, glass, and leather items produced by other artists. Since the shop does not advertise and is out of the mainstream for other shops in Rue du Bac, you'll have to make a special effort to go there. We think you'll be pleased with these treasures, many of which would make nice affordable gift items.

Rue de Varenne is home to two of our favorite tableware shops—**Point à la Ligne** (#25 Rue de Varenne, Tel. 42-84-14-45) with its wonderful collection of unique candles, and **Dîners en Ville** (#27 Rue de Varenne, Tel. 42-2278-33) with its extensive and colorful collection of tablewares, from napkins and tablecloths to goblets, flatware, and ceramics. You'll also find several art galleries and antique shops along this street.

Boulevard Raspail, which also extends into the 6th arrondissement, has several nice boutiques and home decorative shops. A few major Japanese designers are located in this area: **Issey Miyake** (17 Boulevard Raspail), **Matsuda** (26 Boulevard Raspail), and **Issey Miyake Homme** (33 Boulevard Raspail). **Herve Gambs** (24 Boulevard Raspail, Tel. 42-22-86-21) offers beautiful dried roses and other vegetation nicely framed for decorations. **Lumieres de Pais** (26 Boulevard Raspail, Tel. 45-48-36-77) has an extensive collection of uniquely designed metal lights, lamps, and chandeliers.

Rue Chomel, which links Boulevard Raspail to Rue de Babylone, has one of our favorite shops, **Ambience—Thé Galerie** (3 Rue Chomel, Tel. 45-44-60-88). This is the only shop in Paris offering top quality Vietnamese paintings, reproduction furniture, and ceramics. It represents nine artists, including Quách Dóng Phuong, Truong Dình Hao, and Huáng Sùng. The paintings by Hao are fabulous.

Don't forget to visit the Left Bank's most upscale department store, **Bon Marché** (5 Rue de Babylone) as well as the adjacent home decor shop, **The Conran Shop** (117 Rue du Bac). The department store also has a wonderful gourmet shop called **La Grande Épicerie de Paris** which is located across the street from the main building (38 Rue de Sèvres, Magasin 2, main floor).

8TH ARRONDISSEMENT (RIGHT BANK)

Welcome to Paris' most decadent shopping area, where block after block of money-is-no-object shops beckon you to come in and lose your shopping innocence. This is Paris' most upscale and expensive shopping district, the area where you also find its best hotels and restaurants. It's for people who have lots of money or for those who need to see things that will help motivate them to make more money. If you like fancy clothes and fine art, this arrondissement is for you.

The most famous street in this arrondissement is the broad Champs Élysées that links the Arc de Triomphe to the Place de la Concorde. While this street is interesting to stroll and to absorb the grandness of Paris, it is not a particularly interesting shopping street. Quality shops left this area long ago for several nearby streets. What's left are a lot of trendy shops catering to young people and tourists. You will find a few small shopping arcades, such as Galerie du Claridge, Galerie de Prestige, and Galeries Élysées Rond Point, with trendy boutiques and costume jewelry shops. You'll also find the huge **Virgin Records' Megastore** (52 Avenue des Champs Élysées) with its multi-media selections. With the advent of McDonald's, Planet Hollywood, and the Disney Store, this street does not offer the quality shopping one comes to expect in many other parts of the city. This is a heavily touristed area with visitors more interested in people-watching than in doing serious shopping. The most upscale part of this street is at **Rond-Point**, where Avenue Montaigne, Avenue Matignon, and Avenue Franklin D. Roosevelt intersect with the Champs Élysées. The north side of this intersection includes **Lancel, Boss,** and **Yves St. Laurent** boutiques.

Rond-Point is one of the best places to start your shopping adventure in the 8th arrondissement. The southwest corner of Rond-Point is the entrance into Paris' gold triangle for shopping, three streets with one of the highest concentrations of quality shops—Avenue Montaigne, Avenue Georges V, and Rue Francois 1er. The main shopping street here is **Avenue Montaigne**, Paris' most elegant and exclusive street for haute couture and designer labels. This street could easily be the envy of Rodeo Drive in Hollywood! Mega-boutiques set back from the tree-lined street, may appear intimidating at first. But go on in and look. Indeed, you're looking at the cream of the crop here. Start with **Nina Ricci** (39 Avenue Montaigne) with its beautifully designed lingerie, dresses, evening gowns, coats, shoes, hats, and purses. Just around the corner, at 19 Rue François-1er, is the Nina Ricci discount outlet that offers a limited selection of last season's clothes and accessories at bargain prices. Most items are slightly used—appeared on the catwalks eight or more months ago and worn by models with very slim figures (not everyone will find their size here!). Suits tend to be in size 38 and evening gowns in sizes 56-58. Be sure to examine its two floors of garments and accessories.

Nini Ricci is just a warm-up. Also along Avenue Montaigne look for **Valentino** (#17-19), **Christian Dior** (#30), **Chanel** (#42), **51 Montaigne** (#51), **Louis Vuitton** (#57), **Loewe** (#57), **Mugler** (#49), **Ungaro** (#2), **Porthault** (#18), **Céline** (#38), **Escada** (#51), **Krizia** (#48) and **Lacroix** (#26) for fabulous clothes and accessories. American jeweler **Harry Winston** (#29) and Italian jeweler **Bvlgari** (#27) have found homes here. In this area you'll also pass the Plaza Athénée Hotel, one of Paris' top three hotels, with its elegant red awnings.

At the end of Avenue Montaigne, turn right onto Cours Albert 1er and then right again onto **Avenue George V**. This street has some shopping, but not as concentrated as along Avenue Montaigne. It's most famous for the George V Hotel and one of Paris' top cabarets, Crazy Horse. A few big name designers have shops along this street: **Givenchy** (#3, 8, 29-31), **Gianfranco Ferre** (#8), **Balenciaga** (#10), **Kenzo** (#18), **Myrène de Prémonville** (#32), and **Gianfranco Ferré** (#44).

When you get to **Rue Francois 1er**, turn right onto this street and walk back to Avenue Montaigne. Along the way you'll pass several of Paris' very exclusive boutiques, many of which are for men: **Christian Dior Boutique Monsieur** (#11), **Nina Ricci** (#17-19), **Rochas** (#33), **Lapidus** (#35), **Courrèges** (#40), **La Maison Salon Versace** (#41), **Francesco Smalto** (#44), **Pierre Balmain** (#44), **Givenchy Gentleman** (#56), and **Harel** (#64).

From here you should return to Rond-Point and cross the Champes Élysées. Head for Avenue Matignon which stretches northeast from Rond-Point. This street is lined with several of the city's best art galleries. We especially like the contemporary offerings at **Artcurial** (9 Avenue Matignon) which represents 12 international artists creating unique jewelry, sculptures, ceramics, furniture, and rugs. This gallery also operates a large bookstore focusing on fine arts, crafts, and graphics. Also look for several other fine art galleries that line both sides of this street—**Galerie Piltzer** (#16), **Matigon** (#18), **Alain Daune** (#14), **Etinee Sassi** (#14), **Jean-Pierre Jobet** (#18), **Marcel Bernheim** (#18), **Taménaga** (#18), **Heraud** (#24), **Bernheim-Jeune** (#27), **Daniel Malingue** (#26), **Elysse Matignon** (#28), **Caplain-Matignon** (#29), and **Art France** (#36). Many of these galleries only represent top French and international artists as well as host special exhibits and shows.

As you walk further north on Avenue Matignon, the area seems to get a bit run down. However, you'll quickly discover one of Paris' best discount haute couture shops in this area, **Anna Lowe** (35 Avenue Matignon, Tel. 43-59-96-61). The two rooms of this spacious shop carry top quality designer fashions. The back room offers more trendy, "California-style" garments. Here you'll find last season's as well as this season's (from shows) fashions at 40-50 percent discount. The shop carries several major designer labels, such as Chanel, Montana, Mugler, Ungaro, Valentino, and Yve Saint Laurent. It also has some accessories as well as its own line of classic (Chanel-style) clothes produced under the new Anna Lowe label, a fashionable and affordable line offering a full range of sizes. Owned and operated by the delightful American expatriate Suzi Goei, who is usually in the shop, the selections and service here are excellent. If you only visit one discount haute couture shop in Paris, make sure it's Anna Lowe.

If you go a little further north on Avenue Matignon, you'll come to Rue de Penthiévre. Turn right and you immediately come to **Galerie Sordello** (25 Rue de Penthiévre, Tel. 42-25-41-62) with its gorgeous art glass pieces. Continue on to **Miss "Griffes"** (19 Rue de Penthiévre, Tel. 42-65-10-00), another popular discount couture shop. Don't be turned off by the smallness of this shop and its uninspiring window displays. You'll have to walk the narrow staircase from the ground floor to find the "good stuff" crammed on racks on the first floor. You'll find several name brand garments (jackets, suits, blouses, sweaters) produced by Chanel, Dior, Valentino, Ungaro, Givenchy, and Sonia Rykiel. You'll also find a limited selection of accessories (belts, purses, jewelry) on the ground floor. While not the same quality and selections as Anna Lowe, nonetheless, Miss "Griffes" has much to offer the discount shopper in search of quality Parisian clothes and accessories.

Continuing down Rue de Penthiévre, you'll come to another popular discount shop, **PWS** (1 Rue de Penthiévre, Tel. 47-42-64-30). This is a men's shop that nicely displays suits, coats, shirts, sweaters, and neckties as well as a few leather goods.

You'll find a good selection of men's suits here under the Pierre Cardin and Yves Saint Lauren labels. Neckties come under the Revillon label.

Between Miss "Griffes" and PWS is a narrow street called **Rue de Miromesnil**. Here you'll find a few excellent quality art galleries and antique shops. We especially like the selections at **A Colin-Maillard** (11 Rue de Miromesnil, Tel. 42-65-43-62) which include the works of the artist Carol Ivoy who produces beautiful painted screens with wildlife motifs.

Your next major shopping area is the incredible **Rue du Faubourg-St.-Honoré**, which you immediately come to at the southern end of Rue de Miromesnil. You've now moved from art and discount designer label clothes to chic boutiques offering the latest fashions and accessories. If you love to shop for the best of the best in women's Parisian clothes and accessories, you've just arrived at the ultimate shopper's heaven. You'll also find a few men's clothing stores and jewelers and an occasional antique shop here. Less intimidating than the haute couture emporiums lining Avenue Montaigne, nonetheless, the shops along this street are very exclusive and very expensive. The major concentration of shops is found between Rue de Miromesnil and Rue Royale, with the most exclusive ones concentrated on the eastern end of this street. It begins with the exclusive **Gucci** (clothes and accessories), at the corner of Rue de Faubourg-St.-Honoré and Rue Royale (21 Rue Royale), and proceeds to **Lanvin** (clothes) at 22 Rue de Faubourg-St.-Honoré.

But at the intersection of Rue Boissy D'Anglas you discover something very special. You've just come to the world's most famous and fabulous leather and accessory shop—Hermès (24 Rue de Faubourg-St.-Honoré). Sought-after for its colorful signature scarves, handbags, and gloves, Hermès is the ultimate shop for chic accessories. You may have to fight the crowds that at times overwhelm this shop in search of ultra-expensive scarves, gloves, handbags, neckties, perfume, or anything else with the Hermès name inscribed. The quality and craftsmanship here are second to none. If you want to get a quick introduction into Parisian design and quality, make this shop your first stop in Paris. Their window displays are some of the best you'll find anywhere in the world, true works of art. Look them over carefully.

After visiting Hermès, you'll be encountering numerous high quality boutiques representing some of Paris' and Europe's top designers. Next to Hermès is **Givenchy** (clothes) followed by **Guy Laroche** (clothes), **Jun Ashida** (clothes), **Brioni** (menswear), **Yves Saint Laurent** (clothes), and **Maxandre** (clothes).

In the same block but across the street is **Igin** (clothes), **Jaeger** (clothes), **Hanae Mori** (clothes), **Poiray** (jewelry), **Façonnable** (menswear), **Jean de Bonnot** (rare books), **La Baggagerie** (leather goods), **Istante** (clothes), and **Lanvin** (menswear). If you're not dizzy and broke by now, proceed on to the next block which begins with one of the world's most famous designers for women's clothing, **Karl Lagerfeld** (clothes), **Leonard** (clothes), **Cour aux Antiquaires** (a courtyard of small antique shops), **Chloé** (clothes), **Fratelli Rossetti** (shoes), **Au Vieux Venise** (antiques), **Ungaro** (clothes), **Revillon** (clothes and furs), **Trussardi** (men's and women's clothes), **Cartier** (jewelry), and **Lancôme** (cosmetics). The next block, beginning at Rue D'Aguesseau, has more of the same: **Zili** (menswear), **Gianni Versace** (clothes), **Pomellato** (jewelry), **Etro** (accessories), **Arfan** (jewelry), **Sonia Rykiel** (clothes), **La Tanneur** (leather goods), **Burma** (faux jewelry), and **Remy S.** (clothes). If you're not too exhausted by now, keep moving forward to the next block where you will come to **Maxim's** (clothes), **S. L. Dupont** (menswear and gifts), **Louis Féraud** (clothes), **Lilane Romi** (clothes), **Maud Frizan** (shoes), and **Jean Damien** (clothes). At this point you are facing both the Presidential Palace Palais de L'Élysée and the Interior Ministry. Just beyond these two landmarks are a few art galleries and antique shops as well as a **Pierre Cardin** (menswear) and **Christian Lacroix** (clothes).

Be sure to visit **Place de la Madeleine**, located just north of Place de la Concorde and at the eastern end of Rue de Faubourg-St.-Honoré within the 8th arrondissement. This square has numerous shops worth visiting. If food is on your mind, be sure to visit the world-famous **Fauchon**, the huge food emporium located at 30 Place de la Madeleine (see Chapter 7 description). Also look for **Polo Ralph Lauren** (men's and women's clothes), **Cerruti 1881** (menswear), **Odiot** (silverware), **Baccarat** (crystal), and **Cerruti** (clothes) as you walk clockwise around the square.

You've now completed the ultimate Parisian shopping adventure and, in the process, you've undoubtedly been wowed by the style and profusion of top quality goods. If you've already shopped Avenue Montaigne along with this street, shopping probably will never be the same for you again. You've been to the top of the mountain and you are about to come down as you leave the luxurious decadence of the 8th arrondissement.

9TH ARRONDISSEMENT (RIGHT BANK)

There's not much here to recommend for shopping other than a few major department stores and our favorite English-language bookstore. This arrondissement is famous for the grand Opéra Garnier which is near the center of most serious shopping in the 9th arrondissement. We recommend heading for Boulevard Haussmann where you will find two of Paris' best department stores which are located adjacent to each other— **Au Printemps** (64 Boulevard Haussmann) and **Galeries Lafayette** (40 Boulevard Haussmann). Both department stores are multi-level emporiums for the latest in fashions, accessories, perfumes, cosmetics, gift items, household goods, toys, and food items. They are shopper's meccas. If you felt somewhat intimidated by the boutiques along Avenue Montaigne and Rue de Faubourg-St.-Honoré, these two department stores might be the perfect places to visit. They both offer free weekly fashion shows and shopping services. Best of all, these are great places to view the latest fashions produced by major French, Italian, and Japanese designers. Both department stores have huge men's and women's departments, and both seem to carry similar lines of clothing and accessories. You'll see such familiar designer fashion names as Yves St. Laurent, Chanel, Mani, Louis Féraud, Karl Lagerfeld, Guy Laroche, Kenzo, Christian Dior, Valentino, Sonya Rykill, Laurel, Emanuelle Khanh, Ungano, and Hanae Mori. In the accessories departments, look for belts, handbags, gloves, umbrellas, and shoes by Gucci, Chanel, Longchamp, Squoia, Lorenzo, Escada, Moschino, Nina Ricci, Christian Lacroix, Yves Saint Laurel, Lancel, Christian Dior, Lagerfeld, Alfred Dunhill, Paloma Picasso, Celine, Coah, Mandarina Duck, and Claude Gérard. Each floor and/or counter display is arranged by designer with the name of the designer posted in big letters.

A third major department store is located across the street from Galeries Lafayette, the famous **Marks & Spencer** (50 Boulevard Haussmann). It has a decided British flavor to it, which reflects its home base.

A good time to shop this area is on Monday when most other shops in Paris are closed. These department stores stay opon on Monday until 6:45pm or 7:00pm. Be sure sure to look for special discounts, usually 10 percent, offered to tourists who present a discount card issued by the department store (contact their welcome desk for information on how to acquire the card and discount).

Paris' best English-language bookstore is found in the 9th

arrondissement. Located just south of the Opéra Garnier, **Brentano's** (37 Avenue de L'Opéra) offers a very large selection of books, magazines, and CDs. We especially like their extensive travel book and map sections as well as books on Paris and France. The personnel are very helpful, willing to go out of their way to find what you need. You should be able to find some excellent books about Paris and France here along with other types of reading material. In fact, you might want to make this bookstore one of your first stops in Paris if you feel you need more information on the city or you need to do additional trip planning on France or other countries in Europe. Don't be too shocked with the prices, which can be two to three times more than what you pay back home.

11TH & 12TH ARRONDISSEMENTS (RIGHT BANK)

There's not much to recommend for shopping or even other types of activities in the 11th and 12th arrondissements in this eastern section of Paris. A relatively poor area, it is generally avoided by most visitors to Paris, except for one or two sections.

We've grouped these two arrondissements together because what interesting shopping that exists is concentrated in an up-and-coming area that encompasses both arrondissements—Place de la Bastille and Opéra de Paris Bastille. Since opening in 1989, the **Opéra de Paris Bastille** has been responsible for encouraging the development of trendy restaurants, bars, night clubs, and art galleries along the nearby streets. The section of Avenue Daumesnil (12th arr.) near the opera house called the **Viaduc des Arts** (9-129 Avenue Daumesnil) now houses several arts and crafts shops that are built into a renovated viaduc. Rue Lucuée has a few shops such as **La Compagnie du Mexique** (3 Rue Lacuée) which offers furniture and tiles from Mexico. Overall, this area is expected to continue attracting more and more art shops and trendy shopping.

14TH ARRONDISSEMENT (LEFT BANK)

Located immediately to the south of the 6th arrondissement, this large district is best known for its discount outlets found along **Rue d'Alésia**. You'll find numerous clothing outlet shops lining both sides of this street, between Rue du Maine and Rue des Plantes. If you are a discount outlet junkie, this shopping area may be for you. However, we reached an instant verdict when we first arrived: *"You mean I came all this way for this? What* *a waste of time."* We're not impressed with the selections nor what we see as mediocre quality garments. Others may disagree. We've been very disappointed coming here after hearing a lot of hype about what great outlet shops can be found along Rue d'Alésia. Sorry, we can't recommend making the long trip to this area for this type of shopping. It may appeal to a younger bargain-seeking crowd. The real outlet shopping deals are found in the quality discount shops on the Right Bank (Anna Lowe, C. Mendès, and Miss "Griffes").

The open-air flea market, **Puces de Vanves** (Avenue Georges-Lafenestre at Place de Vanves) is popular with antique hunters. It's open Saturdays and Sundays from 2:00pm to 7:30pm.

15TH ARRONDISSEMENT (LEFT BANK)

There's not much shopping in this area except in the northern section along Avenue Suffren which borders the 9th arrondissement. One of our favorite antique centers is located here—**Village Suissee** (corner of Avenue de la Motte-Picquet and Avenue de Suffren). Here you'll find 150 antique shops offering a wide range of antiques from France, Europe, Africa, and Asia. Some of our favorites include **La Fille du Pirate** and **L'Echoppe Marine** for nautical pieces; **Arts Primities** for quality African Art; **C. Blondieau** for miniature soldiers; **Aux Armes d'Antun** for a huge collection of armaments (7 Avenue du Champaubert). Most shops in the Village Suissee are open Thursday through Sunday from 10:30 to 7:00pm.

16TH ARRONDISSEMENT (RIGHT BANK)

This is another one of Paris' upscale shopping areas. The main shopping street is **Avenue Victor Hugo** which stretches from the Arc de Triomphe that borders with the 8th arrondissement to just beyond Rue Paul Valery. Both sides of this street are lined with numerous exclusive boutiques—many of which have branches elsewhere in the city—offering gorgeous clothes, accessories, and jewelry. Look for **Céline** (#3, clothes), **Ophee** (#4, clothes), **Franceco Ferri** (clothes), **Guy Laroche** (#13, clothes), **Nina Ricci** (#14, clothes), **Emmanuel K.** (#15, clothes), **Cerruti 1881** (clothes), **Yves St. Laurent** (#19, clothes), **O.J. Perrin** (#33, jewelry), **Emmanuel Khanh** (#45, clothes), **Point à la Ligne** (#67, tablewares), and **François Pinet** (#83, shoes).

18TH ARRONDISSEMENT (RIGHT BANK)

This northern section of the city basically has two areas of interest to shoppers The huge flea market at **Saint-Ouen** draws thousands of shoppers every Saturday, Sunday, and Monday. You'll find numerous markets within this market that offer a wide selection of antiques and junk. It's a fun market where you can spend hours browsing, shopping, and eating.

The second major shopping area is near one of Paris' most popular tourist attractions, Sacré-Cœur Basilica. Known as Montmartre, the most popular shopping section is at **Place du Tertre**. Still a center for budding artists, here you will find street artists painting street scenes and portraits or cutting out silhouettes on black paper. You also will find a popular fabric market in this area, **Le Stand des Tissus** (11 Rue de Steinkerque).

SHOPPING CENTERS

Shopping centers in Paris tend to be small shopping arcades located on the Right Bank. Several are found along the Champs Élysées in the 8th arrondissement:

❏ **Galerie du Claridge:** Located next to Planet Hollywood (78 Avenue des Champs-Élysées), this relatively upscale shopping mall is filled with trendy boutiques and jewelry stores. Has a wonderful liquid clock spanning two levels that draws crowds of curious on-lookers. One of the best money exchange booths is located at the rear of this shopping mall—received our best exchange rate here.

❏ **Galerie de Prestige:** Includes 40 boutiques and jewelry shops with the popular Batifol restaurant set in the middle of this somewhat elegant looking shopping arcade lined with cheap lamps. **Infinitif**, a nice women's clothing and accessory shop, is the highlight of this area.

❏ **Galeries Élysées Rond Point:** Located at Rond-Point, this small shopping arcade includes two big-name boutiques that face the street—**Yves Saint Laurent** and **Boss**. Look for **Agatha** for trendy costume jewelry as well as shops selling perfumes, shoes, and optical goods. The downstairs area appears to be in transition with most shops deserted. Go there for the restaurant only.

You will find a few other very small shopping arcades, mostly nondistinct, in this general area.

If you're in the Place de la Madelaine area, you may want to stop at the following shopping mall:

❑ **Les Trois Quartiers:** 23 Boulevard de la Madeline (1st arr.). One of Paris' nicest shopping arcades. Includes 75 upscale boutiques with such famous names as **Diffusion Yves St. Laurent, Gentleman Givenchy, Heyraud, Inuit, Kenzo, Kookaï, Mondi,** and **Stéphane Kélian.** Two of Paris' major faux jewelry shops are also located here—**Burma** and **Agatha.**

The largest shopping mall is found at Les Halles in the 1st arrondissement:

❑ **Forum Les Halles:** This four-level underground shopping center is a labyrinth of over 200 shops. It is a popular center for young people who roam the walkways in search of trendy fashions and food. Includes a few upscale shops such as **Bally, Benetton,** and **NAF NAF.** Very mixed area. More of a cultural experience than a place to do serious shopping.

If you are near The Louvre (Rue Rivoli), be sure to stop at one of Paris' most interesting shopping malls:

❑ **Carrousel du Louvre:** Part of The Louve, this small but fine two-level underground shopping arcade is located at 100 Rue Rivoli in the 1st arrondissement. You can gain access to it from a small entrance on Rue Rivoli or through the glass pyramid entrance of the museum. The first level includes a food court; the second level includes shops found elsewhere in Paris—**Virgin Megastore, Esprit, Lalique,** and **Body Shop.** This level connects to the shops in The Louvre which include books, videos, jewelry, sculptures, art, and gift items.

If you're visiting the 16th arrondissement and want to see how the locals shop, head for Paris' newest shopping mall:

❑ **Passy Plaza:** Located in the center of Passy village, it includes two levels of shops as well as a nice supermarket. Most are boutiques. You'll find the American **Gap** and **Gap for Kids, Agatha** for costume jewelry and **Espace Chocalat.** Caters mainly to local residents. Don't recommend making a special trip here since you are likely to be disappointed with the offerings.

Overall, we've not been particularly impressed with Paris' shopping arcades, centers, or malls. Paris still is not into indoor shopping malls. Its best shopping is found in street shops and department stores.

DEPARTMENT STORES

We love Parisian department stores. Many of Paris' department stores are extremely impressive with beautiful glassed copulas. In many respects, they are the functional equivalent to huge American shopping centers. Their numerous departments are chock-full of specialty items, from clothes to housewares. If you've been wandering the streets shopping for fashions and accessories, you may want to head for the major department stores where you can see many of the same items nicely displaced next to each other. Many of the major department stores have branch stores elsewhere in the city. We're including only the major stores here.

The two major department stores, Au Printemps and Galeries Lafayette, run huge semi-annual sales in March and October. Both are extremely crowded during the sales months.

Our two favorite department stores, which also cater to tourists, are located adjacent to each other along Boulevard Haussmann in the 9th arrondissement:

❑ **Au Printemps:** 64 Boulevard Haussmann, Tel. 42-82-50-00, open 9:35am to 7:00pm, Monday-Saturday, and until 10:00pm on Thursday; closed Sunday. Wow, what a place! Claims it attracts over 100,000 shoppers a day. Includes three buildings jam-packed with the latest in fashions, accessories, and household goods. The fourth floor of the third building, Printemps de la Mode, is the designer fashion center. Here you'll find the latest fashions of Yves Saint Laurent, Chanel, Mani, Louis Féraud, Karl Lagerfeld, Guy Laroche, and Kenzo. You'll even find a Jean Louis David hair salon in the midst of this fashion center. The store also offers a "A Personal Image" service (Tel. 42-82-64-23) just in case you would like to have a Parisian make-over as well as try on clothes in your own personal salon. The ground floor includes one of the most extensive collections of leather accessories (handbags, belts, gloves) by major designers such as

Céline, Coach, Christian Lacroix, Nina Ricci, Mandarina Duck, Lorenzo, Yves Saint Laurent, Kenzo, Paloma Picasso, Longchamp, Claude Géraud, Lancel, Chanel, Sogo, Takashimaya, and Karl Lagerfeld. The men's department, Magasin Brummell, is located in a separate building. Printemps offers free 45-minute fashion shows twice a week under the beautiful Coupole Haussmann on the 7th floor of the Printemps de la Mode building. It's well worth attending if you would like a quick introduction into the Parisian fashion world. Be sure to check at the Welcome Desk to see if you qualify for a 10 percent discount card issued to tourists (a coupon is found on their free city maps and in the *"Where Paris"* magazine. It's good on everything in the store except food.

❑ **Galeries Lafayette:** 40 Boulevard Haussmann, Tel. 42-82-34-56, open 9:30am to 6:45pm, Monday-Saturday, until 9:00pm on Thursday; closed Sunday. Located just east of Printemps, this expansive department store consisting of four separate buildings is in heads-on competition with Printemps. They offer a similar 10 percent discount card to tourists, put on free fashion shows, provide free wordrobe consulting services to help you put together a smashing Parisian wardrobe, and display the latest in fashions. Their accessory department (ground floor of second building) is as extensive and impressive as Printemps'. Parts of the first floor of the first building (west) look seedy, a real bargain-basement look, especially if you've just come from Printemps. However, everything gets better as you move to the upper floors. Take the escalator to the first floor where you will discover one of Paris' best gourmet sections and grocery stores (Lafayette Gourmet). The next two floors are devoted to men's clothes and accessories offering such designer labels as Kenzy, Christian Dior, and Yves Saint Laurent. If you take the elevated walkway east, you'll enter a second building which is primarily devoted to women's clothes and accessories. You can't miss its beautiful Art Nouveau glass coupola and expansive atrium surrounded by several floors of boutiques. You'll probably recognize the famous designer labels here—Emanuelle Khanh, Louis Féraud, Yves Saint Laurent, Ungaro, Hanae Mori, Guy Laroche, Episode, Sonya Rykill, and Laurél. The ground floor is essentially a re-play of Printemps ground floor accessory department—same name brands and similar selections.

Other major department stores found in Paris include the following:

❑ **Bon Marché:** 22 Rue de Sèvres-Babylone, 7th arr., Tel. 44-39-80-00, open 9:30am to 7:00pm Monday-Saturday, closed Sundays and major holidays. This is Paris' oldest department store (founded in 1852) and the Left Bank's answer to Printemps, Galeries Lafayette, and Fauchon. While not as large as its Right Bank counterparts, this is definitely an upscale department store offering a large selection of designer-label clothing and accessories. It also has one of Paris' best gourmet food stores located across the street from the main building—**La Grande Épicerie de Paris** (38 Rue de Sèvre, Tel. 44-39-81-00; open Monday-Friday, 8:30am to 9:00pm and Saturday, 8:30am to 10:00pm; closed Sunday).

❑ **Marks & Spencer:** 33-45 Boulevard Haussmann, 9th arr., open 9:30am to 6:30pm, Monday-Saturday, with a 10:00am opening on Wednesday. Located across the street from Galeries Lafayette, this popular British-based department store carries things that are English, from British woolens to food. Includes a smaller and very popular branch store at 88 Rue du Rivoli in the 4th arrondissement.

❑ **Samaritaine:** 75 Rue de Rivoli, 1st arr., Tel. 40-41-20-20, open 9:30am to 7:00pm, Monday-Saturday, with extended hours on Tuesday and Friday (8:30pm) and Thursday (10:00pm); closed Sunday. Located at the Pont Neuf and consisting of four buildings, this is a full-service department store offering everything from clothes to sporting goods. Popular with locals, but not as upscale as other department stores catering to tourists. Great view of the area from the roof top garden.

❑ **BHV:** 52-64 Rue de Rivoli, 4th arr., open 9:30am to 6:30pm, Monday-Saturday, with extended hours to 10:00pm on Wednesday, Tel. 42-74-90-00. Officially known as Bazar de L'Hotel de Ville, this is a large hardware shop for Parisians. They find everything they need here to fix up their homes or acquire the latest in housewares and gadgets, and garden supplies. It also includes a perfume department and fashion section as well as a new "Beaux Arts" department on the first floor.

A few other departments stores, which offer cheap lines of goods, many of the dime store and K-Mart variety, are also found throughout the city: **Monoprix** (between Au Printemps and Galeries Lafayette on Boulevard Haussmann, 9th arr.); **Prisunic** (52 Avenue des Champs-Élysées, 8th arr.); and **Tati** (4-30 Boulevard Rouchechouart, 18th arr.). You'll find several branches of these department stores in other locations.

Since most of these department stores are open on Monday and have extended Thursday evening hours, when other shops in Paris are closed, you might want to plan to do your department store shopping on Mondays or Thursday evenings.

FLEA MARKETS

Flea markets can be one of the great shopping experiences in Paris. While we're generally not great flea market fans, in Paris we've learned these are much more than the stereotypical flea markets found in other countries. Many of them are top quality art and antique emporiums which are frequented by major dealers, designers, and decorators. Others look like tacky garage sales offering borderline trash and treasures. We're now dedicated flea market shoppers, especially when it comes to Paris' largest flea market. Most flea markets are open two or three days a week, usually Saturday, Sunday, and/or Monday. The best time to go is Monday when other shops in Paris are closed or on Sunday.

It's okay to attempt to bargain at flea markets, although discounts will vary (10-20 percent) and many vendors will refuse to give discounts. But it doesn't hurt to try!

Here's the rundown on what you can expect in the Parisian flea market shopping department:

❏ **Marché des Puces de Paris Saint-Ouen:** Simply known as the market at Saint-Ouen or Le Marché aux Puces, this is Paris' largest and most interesting flea market, a "must visit" for most visitors to Paris. It's located at the northern end of the 18th arrondissement (take the Metro to the Porte de Clignancourt stop). Open 10:00am to 6:00pm, Saturday-Monday, over 150,000 people flock to this market on a typical weekend. Occupying over 75 acres, it actually consists of several specialty markets, each with its own entrance and administration. Because of the expansive and rather confusing nature of this market, you may want to get a map or booklet explaining the various markets within the market. A few sidewalk vendors sell these maps and booklets. One of the best places to pick up a guide is the book stand in front of the Marché Malassis (Rue des Rosiers). They have the useful *Guide Emer des Puces* which sells for 20F and is in both French and English (limited). With this guide, the flea market begins to make a lot more sense.

Finding this market can be difficult as you emerge from the Metro station at Porte de Clignancourt. As you exit from the station, walk north along Avenue de la Port de Cligancount until you reach Rue René Binet. At this intersection you will begin seeing several make-shift covered stalls on your left selling a wide variety of cheap goods—shoes, leather coats, sweaters, jeans, African carvings, jewelry, T-shirts, and watches. If you decide walk through these stalls, be sure to walk north, keeping parallel with Avenue de la Porte de Clignancourt. You'll walk one long block until you get to an overpass. Walk under the overpass and immediately take a left into a street lined with numerous vendors selling more of same type of products you've just passed on the street. Walk one block and take a right. You've just entered the huge flea market via a small street that will take you to the first of several markets that define the flea market. You should be on Rue de Rosiers and **Marché Malassis** will be on your left. Look for the newstand in front of this market which sells the directory to the market. Marché Malassis is one of the best antique markets. Consisting of two floors with nearly 200 antique shops, you'll find the best quality antique shops on the ground floor. The range of art and antiques represented here is most interesting, including Japanese chests, Southeast Asian tribal artifacts, Indian architectual pieces, Syrian furniture, and French paintings, sculptures, porcelain, furniture, jewelry, and textiles. We especially like **Franck Antiquités** on the ground floor for Japanese furniture and lacquerware and **Sariling Atin** on the first floor for a nice collection of tribal artifacts from the Philippines and Borneo. Across the street from this market is **Marché Vernaison** with nearly 300 street stalls offering a wide assortment of interesting antiques and collectibles—furniture, silverware, clocks, pins, beads, drappery tie backs, jewelry, porcelain, bracelets, books, toys, uniforms, and hats. Be sure to go deep into this market and to your right since the first few shops primarily offer clothes and thus do not give you a good representation of what lies ahead. This is a fun place to poke around and find a very special treasure. Just wander the narrow lanes to discover some of the market's most interesting shopping. Bargaining is acceptable. Next door is a very small antique market, **Marché Antica**, with only seven shops offering collectibles. Quickly move through this area and head on to one of the best markets in the area, **Marché Dauphine**, which is located directly across the street. Housed in a two-storey glass enclosed building, it has 300 dealers offering a large range of antiques and collectibles from around the world. The shops here tend to be more expensive than elsewhere in the market with several nice art galleries (oil paintings) and major furniture dealers. The best quality shops are found on the ground floor. One of the best quality African art shops is found here, **Arts Africains Archéologie** (#135), a real stand-out shop after having passed by all the airport art vendors lining the streets leading into the market. If you need to exchange some money, the exchange booth at the end of this building offers one of the best exchange rates in Paris. Returning to Rue des Rosiers, cross the street and enter into Marché Biron. This is a dealer's market for top quality furniture, chandeliers, lamps, crystal, paintings, statuary, accessory pieces, and jewelry. Decorators and designers can have a field day here. If you're looking for top quality Japanese, Chinese, and African furniture, be sure to visit a shop at the very end this market, **Galerie Annie Minet** (#62). It also has a mini-warehouse nearby filled with gorgeous furniture. Returning to Rue des Rosiers, continue walking for another block until you come to **Marché Paul Bert** on your left. This is one of the most popular markets with 400 small street shops offering lots of antique furniture. After visiting the other markets, this one looks like one big garage sale. You may be able to find a few treasures amongst what looks like lots of trash. There are some good things here, so spend some time exploring the many shops. Next door is the enclosed **Marché Serpette** which has a few nice quality shops offering furniture, paintings, jewelry, and armaments. You'll find a few other markets in this area, such as **Marché de L'Usine, Marché Jules Valles, Marché Lecuyer, Marché Cambo,** and **Marché des Rosiers,** which you may want to explore.

❑ **Marché de Vanves:** Located on Avenue Georges-Lafenestre in the southern section of the 14th arrondissement and open Saturday and Sunday, 9:00am to 6:00pm.

Stretching for about one mile, this flea market includes about 200 vendors offering all types of collectibles generally associated with garage sales. Between March and October, on Sunday mornings the Square Georges-Lafenestra becomes an open-air art market where you can buy directly from artists.

❑ **Marché de Montreuil:** Located at Porte de Montreuil in the 20th arrondissement and open Saturday through Monday, 9:00am to 5:00pm. You'll have to walk through numerous trashy vendors before getting to the main market area. Lots of junk here, from used clothes to records and dishes.

STREET MARKETS AND VENDORS

Paris abounds with several colorful neighborhood food and flower markets that give Paris much of its street character. Some of the best such markets to visit include:

❑ **Rue de Buci:** Located behind the Saint-Germain-des-Prés church and spilling on to Rue de Seine, this colorful flower and food market is a delightful place to visit. You'll see fruits and vegetables pilled high (good photo opportunity), chickens roasting, and iced seafood on display. If you plan to visit the numerous art shops along Rue de Seine, you can't miss this market.

❑ **Rue Mouffetard:** Located in the heart of the Latin Quarter between Place de la Contrescarpe and the square St. Medard. Includes colorful stands and shops offering fruits, vegetables, meats, cheeses, pastries, pastas, and flowers as well as frequented by street artists, organ grinders, dancers, and theater troupes. A food and cultural experience.

❑ **Rue Cler:** Open on Sunday (8:30am to 1:00pm) and located in the 7th arrondissement near the Eiffel Tower and Invalides, this two-block long market is filled with foods. Includes supermarkets, cheese shops, and chocolatiers along with temporary street vendors.

You also will encounter numerous **street vendors** selling their wares and skills. One of the most colorful such shopping areas is along the river Seine in the 5th, 6th, and 7th arrondissements. Numerous used book dealers open their green display cases from which they offer an incredible range of old books, catalogs, posters, postcards, magazines, and prints. If you read French and love old books, you'll have a great time shopping this area. Even if you don't buy, it's just interesting "window-shopping" along the river Seine.

While you are strolling the river Seine, look for the sidewalk and bridge artists who set up their easels and paint various scenes along the river, especially Notre Dame Cathedral, the Eiffel Tower, and the boats plying the river. Most of these artists have a case full of paintings they offer for sale. If you see something you like, go ahead and approach the artist. Other sidewalk artists are found at **Place du Tertre** near Sacré-Cœur Basilica in Montmartre (18th arrondissement) and at the **Eiffel Tower** (7th and 16th arrondissements). They are either painting local scenes or doing portraits of tourists. Make sure you clearly agree to a price for doing your portrait before initiating the commission. Some portrait artists are noted for scamming tourists by charging two or three times more than expected.

Other street vendors are found in front of **Au Printemps** and **Galeries Lafayette** department stores in the 9th arrondissement (Boulevard Haussmann). They sell everything from belts to luggage. And still other vendors are usually found in areas leading into the flea markets. Many of them operate illegally.

THE PASSAGES

Paris also is famous for its passages or *galeries*, the original street arcades housed in skylighted passage ways. You can still find them near major commercial streets in the 2nd and 8th arrondissements. Most are small hole-in-the-wall shops offering collectibles, old books, model trains, toys, and handmade dolls. While you may not find much to buy in the passages, they are interesting to see as a cultural experience. The major passages are:

❑ **Galerie Vivienne:** 4 Rue des Petits-Champs, 2nd arr. The most beautiful of all the passages.

❑ **Galerie Colbert:** 6 Rue des Petits-Champs, 2nd arr.

❑ **Passage des Panoramas:** 11 Boulevard Montmartre, 9th arr.

❑ **Passage Jouffroy:** 12 Boulevard Montmartre. This is the oldest of all passages (began in 1800).

❑ **Passage Verdeau:** 31 Bis rue du Faubourg-Montmartre, 9th arr.

HAUTE COUTURE

You will find numerous fashionable boutiques in the major shopping districts of Paris. Many of them are referred to as "haute couture" but in reality they mainly offer off-the-rack designer labels that are not really haute couture. Many of them may represent the off-the-rack line of major haute coutures. Only a few designers qualify for the title of haute couture, the finest designers offering seasonal lines and personalized service at extremely high prices. These are considered to be the "best of best" in the fashion world. These are not your typical walk-in, buy-off-the-rack boutiques. In most cases you need an appointment for a private showing of their haute couture lines. Individuals expecting to spend several thousand dollars are good candidates for such haute couture appointments. These designers are registered with the Chambre Syndicate de la Couture Parisienne for their 1995/1996 collections. We've included the addresses where the of couture collections. Most are found in the 8th arrondissement in the Avenue Montigue area. The same designers have branch boutiques elsewhere in Paris where they offer off-the-rack clothes and accessories. Paris' current collection of haute coutures include the following:

❑ **Pierre Balmain:** 44 Rue François 1ᵉʳ, 8th arr, Tel. 47-20-35-34. Women.

❑ **Pierre Cardin:** 27 Avenue Marigny, 8th arr., Tel. 42-66-82-25. Men and women.

❑ **Carven:** 6 Rond-Point des Champs Elysées, 8th arr., Tel. 42-25-66-52. Women.

❑ **Chanel:** 31 Rue Cambon, 1st arr., Tel. 42-86-28-00. Women.

❑ **Christian Dior:** 30 Avenue Montaigne, 8th arr., Tel. 40-73-54-44. Women.

❏ **Louis Feraud:** 88 Rue du Faubourg-St. Honoré, 8th arr., Tel. 47-42-18-12. Women.

❏ **Givenchy:** 3 Avenue George V, 8th arr., Tel. 44-31-50-00. Women.

❏ **Lecoanet Hemant:** 24 Rue Vieille du Temple, 4th arr., Tel. 42-72-45-16. Women.

❏ **Christian Lacroix:** 73 Rue du Faubourg-St. Honoré, 8th arr., Tel. 42-65-79-08. Women.

❏ **Ted Lapidus:** 35 Rue François 1er, 8th arr., Tel. 44-43-46-70. Women.

❏ **Guy Laroche:** 29 Avenue Montaigne, 8th arr., Tel. 40-69-68-00. Women.

❏ **Hanae Mori:** 17-19 Avenue Montaigne, 8th arr., Tel. 47-23-52-03. Women.

❏ **Paco Rabanne:** 6 Boulevard du Parc, Neuilly, Tel. 40-88-45-45. Women.

❏ **Nina Ricci:** 39 Avenue Montaigne, 8th., Tel. 49-52-56-00. Men and women.

❏ **Jean-Louis Scherrer:** 51 Avenue Montaigne, 8th, Tel. 42-99-05-79. Women.

❏ **Torrente:** 1 Rond-Point des Champs Elysées, 8th arr., Tel. 42-56-14-14. Women.

❏ **Emanuel Ungaro:** 2 Avenue Montaigne, 8th arr., Tel. 46-23-61-94. Women.

❏ **Yves Saint Laurent:** 5 Avenue Marceau, 8th., Tel. 44-31-64-17. Women.

DISCOUNT HAUTE COUTURE

A few shops offer major designer label clothes at discount prices ranging from 30 to 50 percent. These shops can offer terrific bargains for those in search of such quality garments. Here you can find US$800 blouses for US$500, or US$2000 jackets for

US$1200, or US$200 belts for US$85. While the prices may still seem high, the prices reflect much better buys than many other discounted clothes you may find in Paris: you're getting top quality and unique garments at unusually good prices. However, selections may be very limited. The clothes are usually last season's fashions, with many chic items that were modeled on the runways of major fashion shows; they may be discontinued styles; or stock may have been returned to manufacturers because of bad debts. Don't expect to find a wide range of sizes since many are one-of-kind, and single-size, garments modeled in fashion shows. You may find something you fall in love with but then discover it's not in your size.

Some of the best discount shops for top quality clothes and accessories include the following:

❑ **Anna Lowe:** 35 Avenue Matignon, 8th arr., Tel. 45-63-16-95. Owned and operated by American expatriate Suzi Goei, this is one of the best shops for top name-brand French and Italian designer clothes. Look for labels by Chanel, Valentino, Christian Lacroix, Ungaro, and Thierry Mugler. You'll find gorgeous and stylish jackets, cocktail dresses, and elegant knits here. The spacious shop consists of two rooms, with the back room carrying garments with more flair ("California style"). The shop also produces its own Chanel-style clothing line (Anna Lowe) at affordable prices and offering a wide range of sizes. Also look for Anna Lowe's new trunk shows in the U.S. which offer the Anna Lowe line.

❑ **C. Mendès:** 65 Rue Montmartre, 2nd arr., Tel. 42-36-83-32. One of our very favorites. This nondescript shop (you can easily miss it and end up in the wrong shop) has two floors of fashions and accessories. The ground floor includes Yves Saint Laurent fashions. The first floor has Christian Lacroix fashions. Gorgeous stuff. This shop still does not have dressing rooms for privacy. As a result, customers change right in the aisles. Rather than construct dressing rooms, the shop has installed two couches outside the ground floor shop so men can sit there while the women undress in the aisles!

❑ **Miss "Griffes":** 19 Rue de Penthièvre, 8th arrondissement, Tel. 42-65-10-00. This small two-storey shop includes jackets, suits, blouses, purses, belts, sweaters, and accessories by Dior, Valentino, Ungaro, Armani, Lanvin, Givenchy, Chanel, and Sonia Rykiel. The real treasures are found on the first floor; the ground floor primarily stocks accessories. Take the narrow staircase upstairs where you will find clothes crammed on racks. If the shop looks closed, ring the door bell. Only one person operates this shop, who locks the door when upstairs.

❑ **PWS:** 1 Rue de Penthièvre, 8th arrondissement, Tel. 47-42-64-30. This is a discount menswear shop offering suits, slacks, shirts, coats, ties, and shoes under such noted labels as Yves Saint Laurent and Pierre Cardin.

❑ **Nina Ricci:** 19 Rue François 1er, 8th arr. This is the discount shop for the adjacent main shop at 39 Avenue Montaigne. Offers last season's fashions modeled on the runway at up to 50 percent discount. However, sizes are limited: 38 in suits and 56-58 in evening gowns. The basement level includes a large selection of evening gowns; the ground floor displays a limited selection of coats, blouses, shoes, handbags, and hats.

❑ **Solde Trois:** 3 Rue de Vienne, 8th arr., Tel. 42-94-93-34, open Monday-Friday, 10:30am-1:30pm and 4:30pm-6:00pm; Saturday, 10:30am-4:30pm; closed the first three weeks of August. Consisting of two boutiques, you'll find Lanvin fashions and accessories for both men and women at nearly 50 percent discounts. Does semi-annual sales in mid-January and mid-June when prices get discounted another 50 percent.

OTHER DISCOUNT SHOPPING

Several other streets and shops offer discount shopping for clothes and accessories that are basically last season's items that did not sell in other stores. However, we've not been particularly impressed with these places which tend to be popular with locals. Most of their selections still seem pricey, even after 30 to 50 percent discounts, and we're not into the trendy looks of many of the offerings. Nonetheless, you might have the time and interest in going to these places:

❑ **Rue Saint-Placide:** Located between Rue du Cherche Midi and Rue de Sèvres and just around the corner from Bon Marché department store in the 6th arrondissement of the Left Bank, this street has several discount shops offering women's clothes. The best discount shop here is

Moutin à Cinq Pattes (16 Rue Saint Placide). You'll have to dig a lot to find something appropriate. They also have a children's shop five doors away (#8).

❑ **Rue d'Alésia:** Located in the 14th arrondissement, this popular discount street is lined with boutiques selling last season's fashions at discounted prices. Most shops are clustered in a lengthy one-block section of this street, between Rue du Maine (Place Victor et Hélèna Basch) and Rue des Plantes. You may recognize some designer labels, but chances are you never heard of most labels. Many are **stock** shops offering factory overruns. Look for **SR** (Sonya Rykiel, #64), **Dorothée Bis** (#74, 76, 78), **Kookai** (#111), **Daniel Hechter** (#116-118), and **Alésia Discounts** (#139). Frequented by the young and trendy crowd. Check it out if you have lots of extra time. We have better things to do with our time.

You'll also find several used clothing, second hand, and consignment shops (thrift shops or *fripes*) that may look like discount shops. Many of these places offer hardly-ever-worn designer fashions (Chanel, Nina Ricci, Yves St. Laurent) and accessories. If you're in the Rue d'Alésia area, you'll see such a shop just around the corner at 230 Avenue du Maine—**Troc Mod**. While such shops are popular with locals, we can't get excited about buying used clothes in Paris, especially after coming so far and spending so much money on everything else. Just don't wander into one of these places by mistake and think you're buying new clothes and accessories at discounted prices.

However, you will find a few upscale consignment shops worth visiting, especially those in the 16th arrondissement: **Catherine Baril** (14-16 Rue de la Tour, Tel. 45-20-95-21), **Dépôt-Vente de Passy** (25 Rue de la Tour, Tel. 45-27-11-46), and **Réciproque** (89, 92, 93, 95, 97, 101, 123 Rue de la Pompe, Tel. 47-04-30-28). Most are open Tuesday-Saturday, 10:00am to 7:00pm, and on Monday, 2:00pm to 7:00pm; Réciproque is closed on Mondays). The first two primarily carry name-brand clothes and accessories whereas Réciproque also carries estate jewelry, gift items, antiques, and bags.

OTHER SHOPPING OPTIONS

Be sure to check newspapers and tourist literature and ask your hotel concierge about special shopping events, such as auctions, trade shows, and exhibits. Paris abounds with such events.

SHOPS AND MORE SHOPS

Paris is a city of villages and shops. While it has a few shopping centers and department stores, the ubiquitous street shop dominates the urban shopping landscape as much as the corner café, bistro, brasserie, and wine bar dominates its gastronomic landscape. To really enjoy Paris, you need to discover your own special shops. And the best way to do that is to walk its major streets and markets. Indeed, there's much more to shopping Paris than the shops we've identified here. Take our recommendations as starting points for positioning yourself in the major centers for discovering even more exciting shops and shopping. It's an adventure you'll soon come to relish as one of the highpoints of visiting seductive Paris!

8

Enjoying Your Stay

There's much more to Paris than hotels, restaurants, and shopping. Indeed, most visitors to Paris end up with a full schedule of sightseeing centered around the city's numerous museums, monuments, churches, and other attractions. After a full day of such activities, many visitors even find time and energy to enjoy Paris' varied nightlife. You may find yourself constantly on the go. You won't lack things to do in this city.

There's so much to see and do in this fabulous city of art, culture, and architecture that you may feel frustrated trying to select from amongst so many alternative choices. While you can't do everything, at least this is such a wonderful city that you will undoubtedly want to come back to continue enjoying its many pleasures. If you don't do everything, plan to come back and pick up where you left off.

As we noted earlier, some of the best things to do in Paris are free and they are on the streets. A city is a visual feast best enjoyed on foot. Indeed, one of the best things to do in Paris is nothing—just walk its streets, gardens, and parks and watch the world go buy. The streets of Paris are live theater involving interesting people and activities.

In this chapter we include checklists of major things to see and do in Paris. Rather than organize them alphabetically or by arrondissement, we've chosen to list them in descending order of popularity and importance. The first two or three listings in each section are the ones we feel are the "best of the best" for enjoying your stay.

If you love sightseeing and visiting museums, monuments, and churches, and welcome very detailed guidance on where everything is located and what you are likely to find at each location, we highly recommend getting a copy of the lavishly photographed and illustrated Eyewitness Travel Guide, *Paris* (New York or London: Dorling Kindersley Publishing). This book literally walks you through several popular sites, such as Notre Dame Cathedral and the Louvre, in sometimes excruciating detail, complete with floor plans and architectural cutouts. The book will help you decide which places to go as well as decide what to do at each place.

❑ Some of the best things to do in Paris are free and they are on the streets. The streets of Paris are live theater.

❑ If you are a museum junkie, you can easily spend a week or more visiting the major museums.

❑ The best museum deal is the Carte Musées et Monuments pass which provides entrance to 60 museums and monuments for one discounted price.

❑ The three most popular museums are the Louvre, Musée d'Orsay, and George Pompidou Centre. And these will just get you started for numerous other smaller but very interesting museums.

❑ Paris' three most enduring symbols are the Eiffel Tower, Arc de Triomphe, and Notre Dame Cathedral.

❑ For half-price theater tickets, contact the Kiosque Théâtre near 15 Place de la Madeleine and in the RER station at Châtelet-Les Halles.

MUSEUMS

Yes, museums are everywhere. Few cities in the world can claim such a high concentration of fine museums as does Paris. The French government, as well as many private groups, have assembled some of the world's finest museums in this city. If you are a museum junkie, you can easily spend a week or more visiting the major museums. If you're not into museums, you should at least visit a few to get a sense of French history and culture and the greatness of France. You don't need to spend a great deal of time in these places, but at least stop to see a few of Paris' best museums.

The best museum deal is the **Carte Musées et Monuments**, which can be purchased at the tourist office near the Arc de Triomphe (Champs-Elysées). Providing entrance to 60 museums and monuments, the pass costs 60F (1 day pass), 120F (2 day pass), and 170F (3 day pass).

Our first three museums are Paris' three top attractions, appealing to people with different centuries of art interest—BC to 18th (The Louvre), 19th (Musée d'Orsay), and 20th (George Pompidou Centre):

❑ **The Louvre:** 34-36 Quai du Louvre, 1st arr. Tel. 40-20-53-17. *Open Monday and Wednesday, 9:00am to 9:30pm; Thursday-Sunday, 9:00am to 6:00pm. Admission 40F before 3:00pm and 20F after 3:00pm; free on Sunday for under 18. English-language tours (90 minutes) given on Monday and Wednesday-Saturday at 10:00am, 11:30am, 2:00pm, and 3:30pm; costs 33F for adults and 22F for ages 13-18; free under 12.* Has two entrances—the newer crowded glass pyramid and the older and less crowded Porte Jaujard in the Pavilion de Flore. This is the world's largest museum and Paris' major tourist attraction exhibiting nearly 300,000 works of pre-19th century art. Famous for the controversial I.M. Pei glass pyramid covering the entrance to the world's largest palace, an underground shopping mall, the *Mona Lisa* and *Venus de Milo*, and acres and acres of displays, this is the ultimate museum. You'll either love it or want to escape it after an hour or two. The displays and crowds tend to overwhelm many visitors who may feel claustrophobic on a busy day. The museum is divided into seven departments each with its own extensive collections: Egyptian Antiquities; Oriental Antiquities and Islamic Art; Greek, Etruscan, and Roman Antiquities; Sculptures; Prints and Drawings; paintings; and Objets d'Art. The new Richelieu Wing has added 230,000 square feet of exhibition space which includes 165 rooms, three covered courtyards and 12,000 works of art. Includes a terrific museum shopping center which has a bookstore and gift shops offering guides, art books, reproductions, engravings, postcards, videos, gift items, jewelry, and casts.

❑ **Musée d'Orsay:** 1 Rue de Bellechasse or 62 Rue de Lille, 7th arr., Tel. 40-49-48-14. *Open Tuesday-Wednesday and Friday-Saturday, 10:00am-6:00pm; Sunday 9:00am-6:00pm; Thursday, 10:00am-9:45pm; Opens at 9:00am June 20-September 20. Admission 35F for adults and 24F for ages 18-24 and over 60; 17 or under free.* Many visitors prefer this museum over the Louvre and others. Housed in a beautifully restored old neoclassical railway station (Gare d'Orsay) across the river Seine from the Louvre and the Tuileries, the museum specializes primarily in 19th century art (1848-1914). Includes 80 different galleries with thousands of paintings, sculptures, objets d'art, architectural models, furniture, and photographs. Here you'll find such famous French impressionist and post-impressionist painters as Cézanne, van Gogh, and Monet as well as cubist, expressionist, and abstract painters. Look for the famous *Whisler's Mother* along with paintings by Degas, Renoir, and Manet. If you've ever studied 19th and early 20th century art history, you'll recognize many of the great painters in this museum. One of the loveliest settings for a museum. Includes two good restaurants and a museum shop.

❑ **George Pompidou Centre**: Place Georges-Pompidou, 4th arr., Tel. 44-78-12-33. *Open Monday and Wednesday-Friday, noon-10:00pm; and Saturday-Sunday, 10:00am-10:00pm. Admission 60F adults, 40F ages 18-24 and over 60, under 18 free; Museum of Modern Art 35F adults, 24F ages 18-24, under 18 free. Free admission on Sunday.* Housed in a controversial building that looks more like a huge boiler system than a museum, this is Paris' major cultural center for 20th century art. It consists of four major centers: Musée National d'Art Moderne (National Museum of Modern Art), Public Information Library, Center for Industrial Design, and the Institute for Research and Coordination of Accoustics/Music. The major attraction is the Museum of Modern Art that displays the works of major 20th century artists such as Kandinsky, Bonnard, Chagall, Dufy, Léger, Calder, and Epstein. Includes special exhibits in the Grande Galerie. If you want to get a good idea of what's in the museum, visit the bookstore which has an extensive collection of postcards, each representing a major art work found in the Museum of Modern Art. The Centre now draws larger crowds than the Eiffel Tower.

After visiting these "big three" museums, you might want to visit a few of these popular museums:

❑ **Musée Picasso**: Hôtel Salé 5, Rue de Thorigny, 3rd arr, Tel. 42-71-25-21. *Open April-September, Wednesday-Monday, 9:30am-5:30pm; and October-March, Wednesday-Monday, 9:30am-5:30pm. Admission 27F adults, 17F ages 18-25; free under 18.* Houses the largest collection of Picasso art: 203 paintings, 158 sculptures, 16 collages, 19 base-reliefs, 88 ceramics, 1,500 sketches, 1,600 engravings, and 30 notebooks. Acquired by the state in lieu of $50 million in estate taxes.

❑ **Musée de l'Armée:** Hôtel National des Invalides, 51 Boulevard de Latour-Maubourg, 7th arr., Tel. 44-42-37-67. *Open 10-00am-5:00pm (April 1-September 30, 10:00am-6:00pm). Admission 35F (also gives admission to two other adjacent sites—Napoléon's Tomb and the Musée des Plans-Reliefs).* A favorite museum for those interested in the glory of the French Army. Probably the largest and most extensive military museum in the world and one of the most overlooked museums in Paris. Fantastic collection of uniforms, weaponry, and battle plans. Even includes Napoléan's stuffed horse and dog! Go directly from the museum to the adjacent Dôme Church where you can view Napoléan's impressive crypt.

❑ **Musée National du Moyen-Age:** 6 Place Paul-Painlevé, 5th arr., Tel. 43-25-62-00. *Open 9:15am-5:45pm. Closed Tuesday. Admission 27F.* Previously known as the **Musée de Cluny**, this is Paris museum of Roman and medieval art. Displays an impressive collection of religious relics, paintings, stained glass, furniture, jewelry, sculptures, ceramics, and textiles.

❑ **Musée Rodin:** Hôtel Biron, 77 Rue de Varenne, 7th arr., Tel. 47-05-01-34. *Open 10:00am-5:45pm (5:00pm in winter). Closed Monday. Admission 27F.* One of Paris' most popular museums housed in the elegant mansion that served as the home and studio of the revolutionary 19th century sculptor Auguste Rodin. Includes sculptures, plans, and drawings. Look for his famous *The Thinker* in the courtyard. Beautiful gardens.

❑ **Cité des Sciences et de l'Industrie:** 30 Avenue Corentin-Cariou, 19th arr., Tel. 36-68-29-30. *Open 10:00am-6:00pm, Tuesday-Sunday. Admission 45F.* The world's largest science and industry museum. Great for kids.

❑ **Musée de la Marine:** Palais de Chaillot, 17 Place du Trocadéro, 16th arr., Tel. 45-53-31-70. *Open 10:00am-6:00pm, Wednesday-Monday. Admission 31F.* This is the world's largest maritime museum. Includes navigational instruments, weaponry, and scale-model ships. Popular with young people.

❑ **Musée National des Arts d'Afrique et d'Océanie:** 293 Avenue Daumesnil, 12th arr., Tel. 44-74-84-80.

Open 10:00am-noon and 1:30pm-5:30pm (Saturday and Sunday 12:30pm-6:00pm), closed Tuesday. Admission 27F. The former French colonial museum, it houses an interesting collection of African and Pacific artifacts as well as an aquarium. A little worn but the aquarium is popular with children.

❑ **Musée des Arts Asiatiques-Guimet:** 6 Place d'Iéna, 16th arr., Tel. 47-23-61-65. *Open 9:45am-6:00pm. Closed Tuesday. Admission 27F. Closed for two-year renovation beginning in late 1995.* Terrific collection of Asian art: Cambodia (Khmer), China, Tibet, Japan, India, and Nepal. Includes everything from paintings and sculptures to ceramics and furniture.

If these aren't enough to get you started, keep in mind that there are over 100 more museums you can visit in Paris!

MONUMENTS, BUILDINGS, AND VIEWS

Paris has numerous monuments and buildings that display some of the world's most interesting architecture and afford terrific views of the city. Not included here, but equally important, are Notre Dame Cathedral and Sacré Cœur Basilica which are summarized in the section on churches.

❑ **Tour Eiffel (Eiffel Tower):** Champ-de-Mars, 7th arr., Tel. 45-50-34-56. *Open September-June, 9:30am-11:00pm; July-August, 9:00am-midnight. 20F to first landing; 38F to second landing; 55F to third landing; 12F to second floor by stairs.* Nothing symbolizes Paris better than the Eiffel Tower. Built in 1889, this 1,056 foot structure provides a panoramic view of Paris. You can visit three different levels, each providing a more spectacular view of the city the higher you go. One of the city's best restaurants, Jules Verne, is located on the first level. You'll need reservations several weeks in advance to secure a seat.

❑ **Arc de Triomphe:** Place Charles-de-Gaulle-Etoile, 16th arr. (but also in the corner of the 8th and 17th arrondissements), Tel. 43-80-31-31. *Open April-September, 9:30am-4:30pm; October-March, 10:00am-4:30pm. Admission only for taking the elevator to the top: 32F adults, 21F ages 18-24 and over 60, 10F children 12-17; free for 11 or under.* Another great symbol of Paris and France, the

Arc de Triomphe was completed in 1836. It has come to symbolize France's military greatness with most military parades and ceremonies centering here. Includes an interesting museum and the tomb of the unknown soldier. Twelve streets, including the western end of the Champs Élysées converge at this monument. Be sure to take the elevator to the 163 foot top of the Arc where you can get a panoramic view of Paris. Access to the Arc is by way of two underground walkways. Don't try reaching the Arc by crossing the busy street!

❏ **Hôtel des Invalides (Napoléon's Tomb):** Place des Invalides, 7th arr., Tel. 44-42-37-72. *Open October-March, 10:00am-5:00pm; and April-September, 10:00am-6:00pm. Tomb open June-August until 7:00pm. Admission 35F adults, 24F children 7-18, children 6 and under free.* Valid for two consecutive days, the ticket admits holders to the Musée de l'Armée, Napoléon's Tomb, and the Musée des Plans-Reliefs. The impressive tomb, made of red Finnish porphyry set on a slab of green granite, is surrounded by the tombs of his son and brother as well as other war heros. An impressive and grand site well worth visiting for both history and architecture.

❏ **Panthéon:** Place du Panthéon, 5th arr., Tel. 43-54-34-51. *Open 10:00am-6:30pm, April-September; 10:00am-5:30pm, October-March. Admission 27F adults, 18F ages 18-24, 10F ages 12-17, free under 12.* Formerly a church constructed in 1783, this imposing domed building now stands as the burial site for many local notables—Victor Hugo, Jean-Jacques Rousseau, Emile Zola, Louis Braille, Voltaire, Soufflot. Includes many fine frescos.

❏ **La Grande Arche (La Défense):** Pont de Neuilly, at the west end of Avenue Charles de Gaulle, Tel. 49-07-26-26. *Open April-September: Monday-Friday 9:00am-8:00pm; 9:00am-9:00pm Saturday, Sunday, and holidays; October-March: 9:00am-7:00pm, Sunday-Friday and holidays; 9:00am-8:00pm Saturday.* Constructed in 1989 as part of the city's La Défense high-rise office development, this hollow cube structure offers an excellent view of Paris. Includes and exhibition gallery.

❏ **Opéra de Paris Garnier:** Place de l'Opéra, 9th arr,, Tel. 47-42-57-50. *Open 10:00am-4:30pm (until 5:30pm in August). Admission 30F adults, 18F students and senior* *citizens.* Boasting the world's largest stage (11,000 square yards), this opulent building was completed in 1875. Unusual architectural design incorporating everything from Classical to Baroque styles. Be sure to see the Grand Staircase, Grand Foyer, and false ceiling painted by Marc Chagall in 1964. Building now used for ballet.

SQUARES

Some of the most important landmarks are the city's numerous squares. Each square has its own distinct character. Some are rich in history (Concorde, Bastille) whereas others function as major hotel and shopping areas (Vendôme). Squares with churches at their centers (Madelaine, Saint-Germain-des-Pres) are summarized in the section on churches.

❑ **Place Vendôme:** 1st arr. This grand, elegant, but stark square has a 120 foot stone column, similar to Trajan's column in Rome, at its center topped by a statue of Napoléon as Caesar. Surrounded by the Ritz Hotel and Paris' top jewelry stores.

❑ **Place de la Concorde:** 8th arr. This massive square, with the Luxor obelisk standing at its center between two fountains, affords terrific views of the Louvre, Arc de Triomphe, Madeleine, and Palais Bourbon. Huge statues of horses stand at the entrance. Lots of history was made here during the Revolution when some of France's most notable figures lost their heads at the guillotine assembled at this square.

❑ **Place des Vosges (Place Royale):** 4th arr. A landmark square for the Marais section of the city. One of the most beautiful squares in Paris boasting some of the most pleasant architecture from the early 17th century. With a park at its center, the square is surrounded by 36 red bricked town houses that have retained their original architectural symmetry. Includes several shops and restaurants. House #6, which was the home of Victor Hugo, is now a museum.

❑ **Bastille:** Place de la Bastille, 11th arr. This is where the French Revolution began in 1789 when mobs attacked the Bastille. Torn down long ago, today the Bastille is a square most noted for the newly constructed (1989)

Opéra d'Bastille at its southern end. The former work-class neighborhood is undergoing major redevelopment with new restaurants, shops, and night spots springing up along several adjacent streets—Rue du Faubourg Saint-Antoine, Rue de la Roquette, Rue de Lappe, Rue de Charonne, and Avenue Daumesnil.

❑ **Place du Tertre:** 18th arr. Located in Montmartre at the foot of Sacré Cœur Basilica, this square is a popular center for artists, restaurants, and shops.

CHURCHES

Several churches are popular attractions for visitors to Paris. While all of these churches have interesting histories, they are especially popular because of their architecture as viewed from the outside. The most popular churches include:

❑ **Sacré Cœur Basilica:** Montmartre, 18th arr. *Open 7:00am to 10:00pm. Admission 15F to dome; 15F for crypt.* Perched on the tallest hill overlooking Paris at Montmartre, this imposing white church with five domes is one of the great landmarks of Paris. For a wonderful view of Paris, take the elevator (from the basement level) to the top and continue walking the narrow staircase to the base of the largest dome.

❑ **Notre-Dame Cathedral:** 6 Place du Parvis Notre-Dame, 4th arr., Tel. 42-34-56-10. *Cathedral open 8:00am-6:45pm; towers and crypt open 9:30am-7:30pm (10:00-am-4:30pm, October-March); museum Wednesday and Saturday-Sunday 2:30-6:00pm; treasury Monday-Saturday 9:30am-5.45pm. Masses celebrated on Saturday, Sunday, and four weekdays. Free organ concernts Sunday at 5:30pm. Free entrance to cathedral but entrance fees to towers: 35F adults, 20F ages 18-24 and over 60, 10F children 7-17. Separate fees for treasury.* One of the great symbols of Paris, Notre Dame Cathedral sits majestically along the banks of the river Seine on the Ile de la Cité. Its unique architecture, with the distinctive flying buttresses, is one of the most photographed structures in Paris.

❑ **Sainte-Chapelle:** Palais de Justice, 4 Boulevard du Palais, 1st arr. (Ile de la Cité), Tel. 43-54-30-09. *Open April-September 9:30am-6:30pm; and October-March 10am-*

5:00pm. Admission 27F adults, 18F ages 18-25 and over 60, 10F ages 12-17. Set within the grounds of two other major attractions, Conciergerie and the Palais de Justice. Built in the 13th century, this is one of the most impressive chapels with its incredible stained glass windows. Consisting of two chapels—the lower level for palace servants and the upper level for the king and his courtiers—the upper level is the most impressive. Be sure to take the narrow spiral staircase to the upper level where you can spend the afternoon counting the windows and contemplating each scene!

❏ **Saint-Germain-des-Prés Church:** 3 Saint-Germain-des-Prés, 6th arr., Tel. 43-25-41-71. *Open 8:00-7:30pm.* This is the oldest church in Paris standing at the center of one of its most popular and vibrant squares. This is truly a people center. Surrounded by some of Paris' most popular cafés and shops in the heart of the Latin Quarter with its abundance of nearby art galleries, antique shops, and chic boutiques.

❏ **La Madeleine:** Place de la Madeleine, 8th arr. *Open Monday-Saturday 7:00am-7:00pm, and Sunday 3:30-7:00pm.* Built in 1764 with a colonnade of 52 Corinthian columns, this church resembles a Greco-Roman temple. The church and square is surrounded by two of Paris' best gourmet shops (Fauchon and Hédiard), several restaurants, a shopping center (Les Trois Quarters), and the beautiful glass and crystal showrooms of Lalique and Baccarat.

Several other churches dot the Parisian landscape and are popular sightseeing destinations for individuals interested in church history and architecture. Some of the most popular are:

❏ **St-Séverin:** 3 Rue-des-Prêres-St-Séverin, 5th arr., Tel. 43-25-96-63. Beautiful Gothic church begun in the 13th century and finally completed in the 16th century.

❏ **St-Paul—St. Louis:** 99 Rue St-Antoine, 4th arr., Tel. 42-72-30-32. Jesuit church built in 1627. Includes Delacroix's masterpiece, *Christ in the Garden of Olives*.

❏ **St-Eustache:** Place du Jour, 1st arr., Tel. 42-36-31-05. A beautiful Gothic church decorated in the Renaissance style. Built between 1532 and 1637.

❑ **Dôme Church:** Hôtel National des Invalides, Avenue de Tourville, 7th arr., Tel. 45-55-37-69. Enshrines Napoléon's tomb.

OTHER ATTRACTIONS

Paris abounds with other attractions, from famous gardens, parks, and zoos to cemeteries and sewers. Here are a few you may find interesting:

❑ **Cimetière du Père-Lachaise:** 16 Rue du Repos, 20th arr., Tel. 43-70-70-33. *Open March 15-November 5: Monday-Friday 8:00am-6:00pm, Saturday 8:30am-6:00pm, Sunday 9:00am-6:00pm; November 6-March 14: Monday-Friday 8:00am-5:30pm, Saturday 8:30am-5:30pm, Sunday 9:00am-5:30pm.* This is Paris' most famous cemetery occupying a 40 acre site. You'll need a map to visit the various graves (10F at the entrance for 10F). Look for the graves of Oscar Wilde, Delacroix, Balzac, Chopin, Colette, Proust, Isadora Duncan, Gertrude Stein, and the most popular site of all, rock star Jim Morrison.

❑ **Jardin de Tuilerie:** Directly west and adjacent to the Louvre, 1st arr. These popular gardens link the Louvre to the Place de la Concorde, Champs Élysées, and the Arc de Triomphe. Other popular gardens worth visiting are the **Jardin du Luxembourg** (Boulevard St-Michel, 6th arr.) and **Jardin du Palais Royal** (Place du Palais Royal, 1st arr.).

❑ **Boating on the River Seine:** While the river Seine is a working river with commercial barges, it's also a pleasure boating river. Several tour companies operate large tour boats (*bâteaux-mouche* and *vedettes*) which carry from 80 to 400 passengers up and down the Seine between the hours of 10:00am and 10:00-11:00pm. Making a 60 minute run, most of these boats start near the Eiffel Tower (Pont de Grenelle), pass by the Musée d'Orsay, Musée du Louvre, and Conciergerie, and circle the two islands (Ile de la Cité and Ile St-Louis), passing Notre Dame Cathedral, before returning. Many also operate lunch and dinner cruises which may last 2½ hours. If the weather is nice, this is great cruise to take early in your visit to Paris. Commentary provided in both English and French on sites along the way.

❑ **The Sewers (Les Egouts):** Pont de l'Alma, 7th arr., Tel. 47-05-10-29. *Open Saturday-Wednesday, 11:00am-6:00pm (May-October) or 11:00-5:00pm (winter).* This popular attraction takes visitors into an underground city consisting of a maze of huge tunnels. Tour includes viewing a movie on the sewer system, visiting a museum, and taking a brief look at a few tunnels.

ENTERTAINMENT AND NIGHTLIFE

Paris stays alive until the wee hours of the morning. For many visitors, dining out at regular Parisian restaurant hours (8:30pm to 10:30pm) occupies most of the evening; it can easily become one's entertainment for the evening. For others, Paris in the evening offers all kinds of options, from high culture (opera, theater, dance, music) to popular Parisian nightlife institutions (cabarets, nightclubs, and bars).

The high culture end of evening entertainment very much reflects Paris' reputation for being a center for art, culture, and education. While the city does not boast the same quality and variety of theater, opera, and music as New York, London, or Milan, nonetheless, it offers first-rate productions. Expect most of them to be presented in French.

For information on what's happening in entertainment, contact the **Paris Tourist Office** at 127 Avenue des Champs-Élysées, or its branch offices at the railway stations and Eiffel Tower, or call their 24-hour hotline for information (Tel. 49-52-53-56). Several of the tourist magazines, such as *Where*, *Allo Paris*, and *Clefs de Paris*, have entertainment or nightlife sections announcing on-going or upcoming activities for the month. Also, check weekly magazines such as *Figaroscope*, *L'Officiel des Spectacles*, and *Pariscope* or the biweekly *Boulevard* to find out what's playing during your visit to Paris.

If you need tickets, contact the box offices directly (usually open from 11:00am to 7:00pm) or ask your hotel concierge or reception desk for assistance. **Virgin Megastore** (52 Avenue des Champs-Élysées) does sell theater and concert tickets. For half-price theater tickets, contact the **Kiosque Théâtre** near 15 Place de la Madeleine (Tuesday-Saturday 12:30-8:00pm and Sunday 12:30-6:00pm; no credit cards) and in the RER station at Châtelet-Les Halles (12:30-6:00pm, Tuesday-Saturday). If you're in the underground shopping arcade, Forum des Halles (1 Rue Pierre-Lescot, 1st arr.), check the **FNAC** department store booth (Tel. 40-41-40-00) on the third level for tickets to some events. FNAC also has branches elsewhere in the city

(136 Rue de Rennes, 6th arr., Tel. 44-09-18-00 plus others).

The following places are the major centers for various types of evening cultural activities. They usually have something going on:

ORCHESTRA

❏ **Sale Pleyel:** 252 Rue du Faubourg St-Honoré, 8th arr., Tel. 45-61-53-00. Look for performances of the Paris Symphony Orchestra at the city's top concert hall.

❏ **Theatre des Champs Élysées:** 15 Avenue Montaigne, 8th arr., Tel. 49-52-50-50.

❏ **Museum performances:** Check for mid-day and evening concerts at the auditoriums of The Louvre and Musée d'Orsay.

❏ **Opera L'Opéra Bastille**: Place de la Bastille, Tel. 44-73-13-00. Recently replaced the L'Opéra Garnier as the main opera house.

DANCE

❏ **L'Opéra Garnier:** Place de l'Opéra, 9th arr., Tel. 47-42-53-71. Home for the Paris Ballet. Numerous foreign dance troops perform here.

THEATER

Theaters are spread throughout Paris in the 1st, 4th, 5th, 8th, 10th, 14th, and 18th arrondissements. Each tends to specialize in different types of productions. Most are in French. Some of the best include:

❏ **Comédie-Française:** 2 Rue de Richelieu, 1st arr., Tel. 40-15-00-00.

❏ **Theatre National de Chaillot:** 1 Place du Trocadéro, 16th arr., Tel. 47-27-81-15.

CABARETS

Parisian cabarets are second to none. Expect to pay US$120-150 per person for dinner and a show at most major cabarets.

You'll see lots of female flesh in these places. The best of the best in cabarets include:

❏ **Le Crazy Horse:** 12 Avenue George V, 8th arr., Tel. 47-23-32-32.

❏ **Les Folies Bergère:** 32 Rue Richer, 9th arr., Tel. 44-79-98-98.

❏ **Le Lido:** 116 Bis Avenue des Champs-Élysées, 8th arr., Tel. 40-76-56-10.

❏ **Le Moulin Rouge:** Place Blanche, 18th arr., Tel. 46-06-00-19.

NIGHTCLUBS

Parisian nightclubs remain popular with the jet-set. Most have cover charges, minimums, and serve dinner. Many are private membership clubs which you may or may not be able to get into. When in doubt, ask your concierge for assistance. You may still be able to get in.

❏ **L'Arc:** 12 Rue de Presbourg, 16th arr., Tel. 45-00-45-00.

❏ **Les Bains:** 7 Rue du Bourg-l'Abbé, 3rd arr., Tel. 48-87-01-80.

❏ **Regine:** 9 Rue Ponthieu, 8th arr., Tel. 43-59-21-13. Members only, but if you're insistent, you might get into this very exclusive club.

CASINO

❏ **Casino d'Enghien:** Located 20 minutes north of Paris by the lake at Enghien-les-Bains, Tel. 34-12-90-00.

Paris also has over 100 movie houses and hundreds of bars, wine bars, pubs, and jazz clubs that stay open until the early morning hours. For information on these places, consult the weekly, biweekly, and monthly entertainment and tourist publications we identified at the beginning of this section.

PART III

The French Riviera

9

The Treasures and Pleasures of the French Riviera

After Paris every place else is different. The art, culture, and architecture that make Paris so distinctive becomes replaced by other treasures and pleasures found in other parts of France.

Let's head southeast to the what is variously called, Provence, Côte d'Azur, and the French Riviera. Technically speaking, **Provence** extends from the French-Italian border in the east to Montpellier in the west (beyond Marseille). A smaller geographic area, the **Côte d'Azur** area extends from the French-Italian border in the east to Bandol in the west (east of Marseille). The **French Riviera** normally encompasses the area from Monaco in the east to St. Tropez in the west.

Consisting of several luxurious seaside resorts and a series of quaint perched villages, **our French Riviera** encompasses a 60 mile stretch of coastline from Monaco in the east to Cannes in the west. This is the area of the famed cities of Monte Carlo, Nice, Cannes, and Antibes. It's a glamorous area frequented by the rich and famous and the not so famous wannabes. Nearly 8 million visitors flock to this area each year to enjoy its many treasures and pleasures. This is where celebrities come; where the wealthy dock their yachts and work the casinos; where writers and artists congregate; where international conferences and festivals take place; and where the sea and hills meet in forming one of the world's most delightful resort areas. It's truly a decadent area for enjoying the treasures and pleasures of southern France.

AN APPEALING AREA

Like Paris, the French Riviera is an area of unique art and culture. But unlike Paris, this is the south, it's close to Italy, it's an upscale resort area, and it attracts a different type of traveler. The lifestyle, culture, and architecture are different in many ways. The pace of life is slower, less stressful, and more spontaneous. The sidewalk cafés are here but so too are the million dollar yachts, fabulous hotels and restaurants, chic shops, crowded casinos, and fine museums, art galleries, and craft shops. The delightful climate and beautiful scenery make this an ideal place to visit and stay awhile. Like Paris, the French Riviera will not disappoint you.

But the French Riviera is not all sun and surf, hedonism and high prices in an expensive resort setting. Beyond the famous beaches and palm tree and café lined streets lie another less well known French Riviera. Serious business of the big city variety gets done here in addition to hosting 8 million visitors each year. In recent years this area has also become a surprising business and technological center. The area around Nice, for example, is France's high tech center, comparable to the Silicon Valley in the U.S. Cannes is the country's major convention center, attracting thousands of French and international visitors year-round to its convention facilities that are second to none in Europe. Monaco is one of Europe's major banking centers.

While the images of the French Riviera may be those million dollar yachts, fancy restaurants, golden beaches, crowded casinos, and relaxing celebrities, the reality is much more complex and explains why our French Riviera functions well twelve months a year whereas other parts of this area, especially St. Tropez, close down for five months a year. These are working resorts with major non-resort economic infrastructures. To a very large extent, the business of the French Riviera today is business.

In recent years the French Riviera has received some bad press for being overcrowded, overpriced, and over-hyped. For some old French Riviera hands, the place is not like it used to be twenty or thirty years ago. But the same can be said for Paris and most other destinations that inevitably experience change. But the crowds keep coming and the area continues to offer numerous attractions for visitors. For many other visitors, the French Riviera continues to get better and better, especially after the crowds leave from the peak months of May, June, July, and August. Indeed, October, November, and April in the French Riviera can be very delightful.

Today's French Riviera offers numerous treasures and pleasures for those who know where to go and what to do. Whether you explore its major cities or wander into its famous perched villages of artists and craftspeople, you'll discover a wonderful area you'll want to return to again and again. Before long you'll get a sense of why this alluring area has appealed to so many famous writers and artists, such as Picasso, Matisse, Chagall, Renoir, and Chagall, who became captivated by the luminous Mediterranean light and exciting lifestyle that was so conducive to their creativity. And you'll discover why, despite the crowds and high prices, you may want to come back here as much as you want to return to Paris. The area is addictive in its own special way.

GETTING THERE

The French Riviera is easily accessible by air, rail, or road. Nice, for example, has the second largest airport in France. It's regularly serviced by most major airlines, including Delta which has a daily New York to Nice flight. Train connections between Paris and Nice, or even between Italy and Nice, are excellent. However, you may want to arrange your train tickets before arriving in France.

We normally rent a car, stopping in the French Riviera as part of a longer drive between Paris and Italy. The roads are excellent and a car is the most convenient way of getting around this area. It's especially convenient if you want to visit the many villages outside the major cities in this area. Be sure to arrange your car rental before arriving in France. If not, you're likely to pay two or three times more. Rental cars are readily available in Nice, Cannes, and Monte Carlo.

THE TWO RIVIERAS

We like to approach the French Riviera as consisting of two major but very different parts—the cities and villages. The cities stretch along as well as cling to a narrow coastline of beaches bounded by hills whereas the villages are found in the hills five to 30 miles from the beaches. Each of these two Rivieras has its own distinct pattern of treasures and pleasures. For some visitors, it's the expansive beaches, bright lights, designer shops, and fabulous hotels, restaurants, and casinos of the beachfront cities that are most appealing. For others, it's the charming villages with their numerous art galleries and craft shops that are the real pleasures of the French Riviera. They would rather stay in a lovely small hotel and dine at a quaint restaurant in a friendly and peaceful perched village than in the hectic resort cities along the Mediterrean. As you will quickly discover, these are two different worlds which appeal to different types of travelers.

For us the real treasures and pleasures of the French Riviera are found in both the cities and villages. We enjoy both and feel fortunate to visit an area that offers such delightful alternatives. But it's the play between city and village that makes this area so appealing to many visitors. To come here and only stay in a resort, or visit one or two major cities, would be unfortunate. For there is much more to the French Riviera. You'll need a car, a good map, intelligible directions, and a sense of adventure to really explore the many treasures and pleasures found along and beyond the beaches of the French Riviera. In so doing, you'll get a sense of why so many famous writers and artists have fallen in love with this area. Many have made it their home, occasionally coming down from the hills to participate in the cosmopolitan culture of the beachfront cities.

THE CITIES

The French Riviera is most famous for four major cities that dominate this area: Monte Carlo, Nice, Cannes, and Antibes. This is where the action is, the hotels, restaurants, shops, casinos, beaches, and yachts. Each city has its own distinctive character. These are nonstop cities for visitors in search of everything but peace and quiet. Extremely crowded during most summer months, these cities offer numerous attractions and opportunities for individuals interested in visiting an upscale resort area. These are not stereotypical resort areas offering lots of cheap T-shirts, beachwear, and fast-food restaurants. Most are working cities that disproportionately offer excellent quality hotels, restaurants, and shops in response to their upper-class clientele. These also are charming cities with lots of history and character. Like Paris, they are walking cities. And after you encounter the traffic, walking will be the only sensible way to get around!

THE VILLAGES

Numerous famous villages constitute a lesser-known but equally important part of the French Riviera. Found in valleys as well as perched on hills, many of these villages are famous for arts and crafts. Several have become centers for famous artists and craftspeople who operate galleries in and around the villages. They offer unique shopping opportunities for individuals interested in arts and crafts. The three most interesting and rewarding such villages are Biot, Saint-Paul-de-Vence, and Vallauris, all within an hour's driving distance of the major coastal cities. And then there's Grasse, the world's most famous perfume center, with is numerous factories open to the public. Other villages offer a variety of museums and interesting sites. After visiting a few of these villages, you might want to cancel your hotel reservations in Monaco, Nice, Cannes, or Antibes and move to the hills where you will find some lovely hotels in the heart of the perched villages!

SELECTING THE BEST PLACE TO STAY

Where you stay along the French Riviera depends on what you wish to do here. If you're primarily interested in the casinos, bright lights, and nightlife, plan to stay in Monte Carlo or Cannes. If you're looking for relative peace and quiet, consider Antibes or one of the perched hill villages. If you want a big city with lots of shopping and sightseeing, look toward Nice. If you want to be centrally located along the Riviera, Nice would be a good choice. However, given the short driving distances between the various cities and villages, any of these places would be appropriate. The longest driving distance will be from Monte Carlo to Cannes. When we drive in from Italy, we usually stay in Monte Carlo for a few days and then move on to Nice, Cannes, Antibes, or a village for the remainder of our stay. While the driving distances are not great, we find making two or three hotel moves to be most convenient for exploring the separate areas of the Riviera. Staying in Monte Carlo and driving to Cannes, for example, takes a lot of time, especially during the busy tourist season. You're best off finding a place close to where you want to visit. Staying at the Negresco Hotel in Nice, the Carlton Hotel in Cannes, or the Eden Roc in Antibes are excellent, although very expensive, choices for experiencing three of France's finest hotels as well as being centrally located for enjoying Nice, Cannes, and nearby villages. Monte Carlo tends to be a world unto its own.

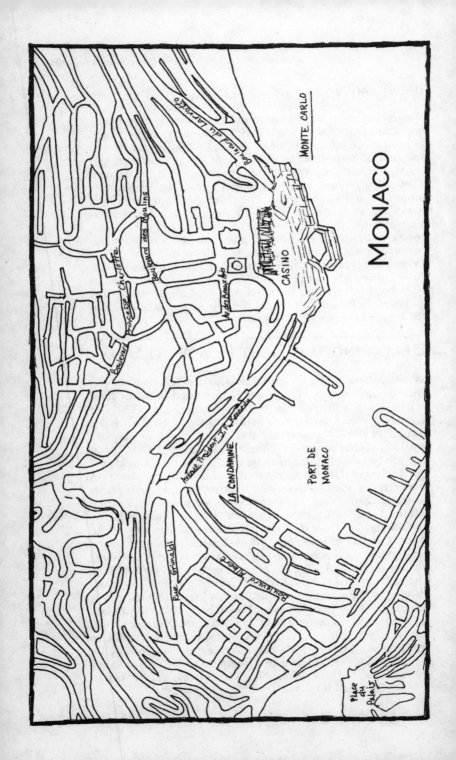

Monaco/Monte Carlo

L ocated in a majestic setting just 12 kilometers west of the
French-Italian border and 18 kilometers east of Nice,
wedged between a gorgeous blue sea and high-rise
buildings buttressing steep cliffs, Monaco both is and
isn't a part of France. Indeed, it's somewhat of a political
anomaly. On the one hand, it's an independent principality or
sovereign state, meaning it is politically and economically
independent of France. On the other hand, it depends on
France for defense, security, foreign affairs, water, and
electricity. In fact, all of Monaco's smartly dressed police are
French citizens (some say this is purposeful to prevent any local
insurrections). French is the official language, most French laws
apply in Monaco, and the French franc is accepted currency.
Obviously, Monaco has a very close relationship with France.

MONACO AND MONTE CARLO

Monte Carlo, the most famous section of this city/principality,
is sometimes mistakenly equated with the principality of
Monaco. "Monaco" officially refers to the independent
principality which is made of four *quartiers*: Fontvieille, Monte-
Ville, La Condamine, and Monte-Carlo. All of the principality

can be referred to as the city of Monaco since it Is 100 percent urbanized; Monte Carlo is one section, the most upscale and glittering, of the city.

Just a bit larger than the Vatican, at .74 square miles (1.9 square kilometers) or 482 acres, Monaco is actually smaller than New York City's Central Park. It's home to nearly 28,000 residents of whom 3,000 are citizens of the principality. The rest hang around to enjoy their money or make more money, or do both. Monaco's residents have the world's highest per capita income. Best of all, they pay no income taxes. For a city so small, Monaco has managed to develop an unusually larger international presence, based on a mixture of mystique and money, than its population numbers would seem to justify.

FROM ADDICTION TO BOREDOM

Monaco is both a small and large city. Its permanent population of 28,000 hosts over 1 million visitors each year. An extremely compact and densely populated city built along the ocean and at the foot of steep cliffs, Monaco is a spectacular city-state. Its picture-postcard manicured lawns, well maintained buildings, and neat, clean, and orderly streets impress first-time visitors: this city pays attention to the details of fine living. Walk past the waterfront with its large sailboats and power boats, window-shop for exquisite jewelry and designer-label clothes, step into the famous Monte Carlo Casino, and observe the many banks that line Monaco's major commercial area and you immediately sense this city is all about money and how to spend it. Observe the city at night from the towering cliffs overlooking the principality and you will view one of the most beautifully lighted cities in the world. Stay here very long and you may get addicted to its upper-class lifestyle. On the other hand, some short-term visitors may become quickly bored with such an antiseptic city that doesn't look like it's having much fun living the ostensible good life.

REAL MONEY ON THE MED

Monaco is famous for many things, from its tax-free status and glittering casinos to its celebrity status as a prime destination for the rich and famous. Above all, it's about real money, not the stuff that's flaunted in Hollywood. Neat lawns and gardens, clean streets, tidy sidewalks, freshly painted high-rise buildings lining narrow winding streets, and million dollar yachts bobbing in the harbor give this city an almost Disneyland-like, and sometimes boring, appearance. It has long had a fairy-tale mystique. It's the home for one of Europe's major banking establishments ($25 billion in local deposits), the annual Monte Carlo Grand Prix (offered in May concurrently with the Cannes Film Festival), and the ever-popular, shrewd, and sometimes controversial ruling family, the Grimaldis (Prince Rainier, Princess Grace, Prince Albert, Princess Caroline, Princess Stephanie).

Contrary to its casino image, casino revenue makes up less than 5 percent of the principality's income. This place is all about banking and finance. More precisely, as you will quickly discover, it's all about money—making it, managing it, spending it, and recycling it through the casinos, shops, and local banking establishment before investing it elsewhere.

❏ French is the official language, most French laws apply in Monaco, and the French franc is accepted currency. Monaco also receives its security, water, and electricity from France.

Like so many other places along the French Riviera, Monaco is best enjoyed by people who have lots of money and are willing to spend it. Without money, there's not much to do here. You'll quickly discover this fact of life in Monaco's many first-class casinos, hotels, restaurants, and shops. There's nothing poor or shabby about this place—other than perhaps an occasional tourist trying to gain entry into the luxurious but selective Hôtel de Paris—and the Monégasques are content in keeping it that way.

❏ Just a bit larger than the Vatican, at .74 square miles (1.9 square kilometers) or 482 acres, Monaco is actually smaller than New York City's Central Park.

❏ Monaco is home to nearly 28,000 residents of whom 3,000 are citizens of the principality. They host over 1 million visitors a year.

❏ Contrary to its casino image, casino revenue makes up less than 5 percent of the principality's income. This place is all about banking and finance.

They would like to become the Hong Kong of the Mediterranean, but only represent the upper 10 percent of Hong Kong's population.

THE BASICS

While heavily into making money through finance and banking, Monaco's 28,000 residents host over 1 million visitors a year with style and efficiency.

As long as you've gained entry into France, you're automatically qualified to enter Monaco. Since there are no border check points, no one asks for a passport except at the casinos, hotels, and banks where you'll need one to conduct business.

You might want to get more information on Monaco before leaving home. In the United States, contact the **Monaco Tourist Offices** at the following addresses:

845 Third Avenue
New York, NY 10022
Tel. 212/759-5227

542 S. Dearborn Street
Suite 550
Chicago, IL 60605
Tel. 312/939-7863

1001 Genter Street
Suite 4E
La Jolla, CA 92037
619/459-8912

Once you arrive in Monte Carlo, you might want to stop at the **Monaco Tourist Office** at 2a Boulevard des Moulins (Tel. 92-16-61-66). They have a map of the city as well as some brochures advertising places where you can spend your money; they will help with room reservations. While housed in a nice building with lots of personnel, this is one of the least helpful offices we've encountered. You'll have to take lots of initiative here!

Transportation to Monaco is relatively convenient. You can reach Monaco directly by rail or road. If you fly into the French Riviera, you'll land at the Nice-Cote d'Azur International Airport which is located 15 miles west of Monaco. From the airport to Monaco, you can take a taxi (US$75) or bus (US$15.00) as well as rent a car. Two trains from Paris will take you to Monaco: the overnight train takes 12 hours and arrives early morning in Monaco; the high speed train (TGV) takes 7 hours and stops in Nice from where you can take a local train to Monaco. If you drive to Monaco, the major highway linking Monaco with other major cities along the French Riviera is A8. The 955 kilometer drive from Paris to Monaco takes about nine hours, depending on your driving habits. Once in Monaco, taxis and buses are readily available, although you can easily walk to most places. The city even has ten public elevators and four escalators for overcoming the worst effects of Monaco's steep terrain.

While French is the official **language**, English is widely spoken and many signs are in English. You'll have no difficulty

❑ Monaco is best enjoyed by people who have lots of money and are willing to spend it.

❑ Monte Carlo is only one section, albeit the most famous and upscale, of the principality of Monaco.

❑ The 955 kilometer drive from Paris to Monaco takes about 9 hours.

❑ If you drive into the city, look for underground parking garages which are well marked on the official tourist map.

getting around with English, French, or even Italian.

Monaco follows the same **tipping** rules as elsewhere in France—a service change is included in the price of menu items; leave an "extra tip" if you are especially impressed with the service or if you want to impress others with your seeming wealth. But don't feel obligated to leave anything extra behind.

Unlike Paris but similar to other places along the Mediterranean, most **shops close** in Monaco for two hours in the afternoon, usually from 12:30pm to 2:30pm. This is the traditional lunch period, so plan your shopping life accordingly.

THE STREETS OF MONTE CARLO

Given the small size of Monte Carlo, you can easily navigate the streets on foot as long as you have a good map and don't mind 15 minute walks. If you drive into the city, look for underground parking garages which are well marked on the official tourist map. Otherwise, you'll have difficulty finding parking along the congested streets.

Monaco's basic geographic fact of life is that it is sandwiched between the ocean and mountain cliffs. In addition, this is the only city along the French Riviera that permits the construction of tall buildings. The result is a long narrow city following the east-west coastline with high-rise buildings backing up to the cliffs. The overall visual effect is very dramatic, reminiscent of a miniature Hong Kong Island. The city is most spectacular, and romantic, viewed from the hills on a clear night when the city lights blaze from the harbor to the hills.

Most major streets run east to west and follow the contour of the hilly terrain. The city actually has four major centers, each with its own particular character and attractions. It's best to view Monaco in terms of these four parts and plan your schedule accordingly. The first one, **Monte Carlo**, is centered at the Place du Casino (between Boulevard des Moulins and Avenue de Monte-Carlo) and is famous for the Monte Carlo Casino, major hotels (Hôtel de Paris and Hôtel Hermitage) and chic shops. A second area, **La Condamine** (between Boulevard Albert 1ᵉʳ and Rue Grimaldi), is located off the major harbor and includes numerous shops and restaurants. Another major area, known as **Monaco-Ville**, is the old medieval city with the palace, cathedral, and museums perched on Le Rocher ("The Rock") overlooking the two major harbors (Port de Fontvielle and Port de Monaco). The final area, **Fontvieille**, is located west of the Monaco-Ville and includes a stadium and shopping center. These areas are within 15-30 minute walking distance of each other.

ACCOMMODATIONS

Monaco offers many fine hotels that are nicely located either within Monte Carlo or overlooking the principality. The two major hotels within Monte Carlo are:

❑ **Hôtel de Paris:** Place du Casino, Tel. 92-16-30-00, Fax 92-16-38-49. 200 rooms including 40 suites and 19 junior suites plus a new spa and health center. Overlooking the Casino, Cáfe de Paris, and the ocean, this is Monte Carlo's grand dame hotel and most prestigious address in Monaco. Built in 1864 and exuding the gilded Belle Epoque style, it has hosted every conceivable celebrity, statesman, and royalty to pass through Monaco. Comfortable rooms but nothing exceptional to write home about. Opulent lobby but difficult to get in unless you are a guest. The doorman only admits bonafide guests or those with restaurant reservations. Includes the famous Louis XV Restaurant which draws even more celebrities, statesmen, and royalty. Very expensive. F1,750-3,000.

❑ **Hôtel Hermitage:** Square Beaumarchais, Tel. 92-16-40-00, Fax 93-50-47-12. 260 rooms. Located just around the corner and up the street (Avenue des Beaux-Arts) from the Hôtel de Paris, this is another one of Monte Carlo's landmark hotels. Built in 1900, it boasts beautiful Edwardian architecture, opulent public areas, and spacious rooms. Very expensive. F1,500-3,000.

Our favorite hotel lies outside the city proper and has one of the most incredible views of the principality from the hills:

❑ **Vista Palace Hôtel:** F-06190 Roquebrune/Cap Martin, Tel. 92-10-40-00, Fax 93-35-18-94. Located about 10 minutes northwest from Monte Carlo but conveniently serviced by a hotel shuttle bus that regularly takes guests back and forth from the hotel to Place du Casino. This is a deluxe hotel with 68 spacious and well appointed rooms, junior suites, and apartments. The views here are simply breathtaking. If the winds are cooperative, skydivers leap off the cliffs and circle in front of your room which overlooks the sea. Each room has a balcony or a terrace with a gorgeous view of the sea. Spectacular views of Monaco from the La Corniche Restaurant, bar, and pool. Very conveniently located in reference to several nearby villages, especially the medieval town of Roquebrune and the adjacent Cap-Martin and Menton. Expensive.

Other hotels worth considering include:

❑ **Le Metropole Palace:** 4 Avenue de la Madone, Tel. 93-15-15-15, Fax 93-25-24-44. 170 rooms with 30 suites and 45 junior suites. This relatively new hotel constructed in the Belle Epoque style is located near the Place du Casino and above the Metropole Gallerie, Monaco's major shopping arcade. Expensive but offers specials.

❑ **Loews Monte Carlo:** 12 Avenue ds Spelugues, Tel. 93-50-65-00, Fax 93-30-01-57. Tel. 800-235-3697 (US reservations). 650 rooms and suites. A convention and resort hotel with casino all rolled into one. Spacious, comfortable, and very American. Has several rooms with terraces overlooking the sea. Very expensive.

❑ **Hôtel du Louvre:** 16 Boulevard des Moulines, Tel. 93-50-65-25. 34 rooms. Centrally located for shopping and the Casino. Moderate.

❑ **Hotel le Siecle:** 10 Avenue Prince Pierre, Tel. 93-30-25-56, Fax 93-30-03-72. 35 rooms. Located across from the railway station. Good value. Moderate.

❑ **Hôtel de France:** 6 Rue de la Turbie, Tel. 93-30-24-64. 26 rooms. Near the train station. Basic but inexpensive.

RESTAURANTS

Restaurants catering to the rich and famous must deliver what's expected of them. Indeed, Monaco offers some excellent restaurants at prices that will definitely remind you of the best of the best in Paris. But you also will find French bistros, brasseries, pizzerias, creperies, American, Japanese, and fast-food eateries at reasonable prices. Here are some of the very best that may or may not bust your dining budget:

- ❑ **Le Louis XV:** Place du Casino, Hôtel de Paris, Tel. 92-17-30-01. Open noon-2:30pm and 8:00pm-10:00pm Wednesday-Monday. Monaco's most famous restaurant. Oppulent dining room serving outstanding cuisine fit for a king. This is where the stars come. Very expensive.

- ❑ **Le Grill:** Place du Casino, Hôtel de Paris, Tel. 93-50-80-80. Open daily for lunch and dinner. Rooftop harbor-view restaurant serving excellent grilled meat and fish dishes. Favorite of celebrities. Very expensive.

- ❑ **Café de Paris:** Place du Casino, Tel. 93-50-57-75. Open 8:00am-2:00am. This is the people-watching spot in Monte Carlo. You can dine inside or outside all day long and watch the world go by. Beautifully renovated in 1920s style. Watch for specials. We think US$4 coffees, US$6 ice creams, and US$20 hamburgers puts this place in our very expensive column. Consider these prices part of a built-in cover-charge for occupying a table at this famous eatery. Popular center for watching people enter and exit the casino as well as for watching many others being rejected by the doorman for entrance into the Hôtel de Paris.

- ❑ **Rampoldi:** 3 Avenue de Spelugues, Tel. 93-30-70-65. Open daily but closed in November. A favorite for many local and international celebrities. The place to see and be seen. Serves grills and Italian dishes. Expensive.

- ❑ **Polpetta:** 2 Rue Paradis, Tel. 93-50-67-84. This hard to find restaurant is well worth finding (near the French border). Monaco's most popular Italian restaurant with locals who can find it. Serves excellent pasta in cozy surroundings. Good value. Moderate.

- ❑ **Le Périgordin:** 5 Rue des Oliviers, Tel. 93-30-06-02. Open noon-2:30pm, 8:00pm-10:00pm. Located on a small side street near the Casino, this rather small and nondescript bistro serves excellent specialties (duck) from the Périgord region of southeastern France. Very friendly service. Inexpensive.

If you're hankering for a **McDonald's** hamburger, head for the Centre Commercial de Fontvieille, Salle Climatisee, or Aire de Jeux. For other American dining experiences, try **Stars N Bars Sports Bar and Restaurant** (6 Quai Antonieler, Tel. 93-

50-95-95, blues bar) and **Le Texan** (4 Rue Suffren Reymond, Tel. 93-30-34-54, Tex-Mex cuisine).

SHOPPING

If you've already been to the top money-is-no-object shops in Paris or Milan, shopping in Monaco may not be all that impressive. You've seen it all, and you've already been sensitized to high prices. But if you've not been to such places, Monaco's shopping is impressive. Best of all, it's concentrated in two major areas of Monte Carlo, both within easy walking distance.

Shops in Monaco disproportionately offer top quality jewelry and designer-label clothes and accessories. Major jewelers and clothing designers are well represented here. You'll also find a few excellent quality art and antique shops. Overall, shops in Monaco offer luxury products brought in from other parts of France and Italy. In this sense, there is nothing particularly unique about shopping in Monaco other than the physical setting.

Monaco follows the same value-added tax system as France. Tourists are entitled to a 16 percent tax refund on purchases over 1200F. Be sure to check with the shop about the procedure for claiming the refund before you finalize the purchase.

The best place to start your shopping adventure is at Place du Casino. Face the entrance to the Hôtel de Paris. If you go around the left side of the hotel, you'll discover some of the

- ❑ Monaco's best shopping is concentrated in two major areas of Monte Carlo, both within easy walking distance. Two other shopping areas are found near the harbor in the La Condamine *quartier* and in the far western Fontvieille *quartier*.

- ❑ Shops in Monaco disproportionately offer top quality jewelry, accessories, and designer-label clothes, reflecting the tastes of their upscale clientele.

- ❑ Monaco follows the same value-added tax system as France. Tourists are entitled to a 16 percent tax refund on purchases over 1200F.

- ❑ Monaco's top shops are found along both sides of the Hôtel de Paris in Monte Carlo. Start your shopping adventure here.

finest shops in Monaco—**Tabbah** for quality watches, **Lalique** for beautiful glassware, and **Hermes** and **Valentino** for fine quality designer clothes and accessories. Turn around and return to the front of the hotel. Along the way, just across the street on your right (Casino building), is a branch shop of one of the world's top jewelers, **Van Cleef & Arpels**.

Facing the front of the hotel again, go to your right and then turn left at the corner onto **Avenue des Beaux-Arts**. This short street, which leads to the Hôtel Hermitage at Square Beaumachais, is lined with fine shops. Starting at the corner on the left, the street begins with **Cartier** with its beautiful watches, rings, bracelets, and necklaces. Next door is **Louis Vuitton** with its signature luggage and leather bags. For a real treat, stop next door at **Sora Sio**. This shop has beautiful bouquets of dried roses which supposedly last about five years. They look so real you'll probably want to touch them, which the posted signs in English warn against doing. The shop can ship for you. Next door is **Adriano Ribolzi** which offers nice quality antique furniture.

But the real stand-out shop on this street, and for most of Monaco, is located next door—**Gianmaria Buccellati** (Tel. 93-50-90-10). This famous Italian jeweler produces some of the world's most exquisite jewelry in gold and silver. Based in Milan, but with shops in Paris, Venice, New York, Beverly Hills, Tokyo, and Hong Kong, Gianmaria Buccellati's creations are unique one-of-a-kind pieces. His work is very expensive but he represents the "best of the best" in jewelry.

Look for two other nice shops on the left side of this street—**Jacques Fath** for nicely tailored women's clothes and **Piaget** for watches in glittering diamonds. At this point you should cross to the other side of the street where you will find several designer label clothing and accessory stores (**Yves Saint Laurent, Christian Dior, Celine**) and the fine jeweler **Bvlgari**.

Returning to Place du Casino, turn left and you'll be in front of one of Monaco's small but top quality shopping centers, **Galerie du Sporting d'Hiver**. We say small because there are only a few shops here. If you are a collector of fine art, including old masterpieces, be sure to visit **Monaco Fine Arts** on your left. This is a serious collector's gallery offering many 50 to 200 year old oils depicting scenes of the French Riviera. We especially like the beautiful bronze sculptures of wolves, elephants, and camels offered in this shop by American sculptor Robert Glenn. Across the hall is an antique shop, **Fersen**, which offers a good selection of furniture and paintings. **Czarina**, located across the hall from Haagen-Daas Ice Cream, is a nice eclectic home decorative shop offering lots of odds and ends; they have a good selection of tableware. At the front is **Lanvin** offering upscale men's and women's clothing.

If you exit this shopping arcade at the Place du Casino entrance, turn left and enter the adjacent pedestrian street on your left—**Allee Serge de Diaghilev**. Here you will find more upscale clothing and jewelry shops: **Chanel, Hanae Mori,** and **Odibe** for clothes and accessories; and **Ciribelli** for jewelry, especially Chopard watches.

After completing this area, walk across the street and through the carefully manicured park toward the Metropole

Palace Hotel at 4 Avenue de la Madone. Here you will find Monaco's largest shopping center which extends three levels underground and includes 150 shops—**Le Metropole Shopping Center**. You'll see a sign and an escalator that takes you to the lower level which is the entrance to the shopping center. Compared to other cities you've visited, this is a small shopping center. Nonetheless, it offers a few interesting shops. Look for **l'Art Venitien** for Venetian glass (on your right as soon as you get off the escalator on the first level); **Yves Delorme Paris** for linens and bedding; **Noor Arts** for antique furniture and estate jewelry; **Comtesse du Barry** for a terrific selection of wines and chocolates. The second level includes several major clothing stores (**Max Mara, Ermenegildo Zegna, Boss, Guy Laroche**); jewelry shops (**Burma, Henri Martin, Au Castel d'Or**); and a nice shop offering a good selection of neckties and scarves (**Cravatterie Nazionali**). The third level has a **Yves Saint Laurent** shop for men but not much else.

The next major shopping area is just a three minute walk away. **Boulvard des Moulins** is Monaco's major shopping street. Running east to west, the major shopping area is found along a long five block area extending east of the tourist office at 2a Boulevard des Moulins. Across from the tourist office is the Monte Carlo Palace Hotel which has a few nice shops offering designer clothes and accessories by **Gucci, Burberrys**, and **Paloma Picasso**. You'll also find **Pollini** for nice leather goods and **Escada** and **Laurel** for clothes and accessories. If you walk east along this street, you'll come to the exclusive **Louis Sciolla** for men's clothing and **Galerie des Moulins** (#4), an antique shop offering lots of small collectible items. At this point you may want to turn left and head up to Avenue Saint-Charles. Here you will find **La Difference** (3 Avenue Saint-Charles, Tel. 93-50-61-57), a much advertised factory outlet shop offering men's and women's designer clothes. Since this shop puts its own label (La Difference) on the clothes, it's difficult to compare apples to oranges. Silk neckties go for US$33 and men's leather coats go for US$700. While you may find this place interesting, we think we can buy much better quality clothes back home for half the price! But have a look. The selections are constantly changing.

Returning to Boulevard des Moulins, turn left and continue east until you come to a large concentration of shops on both sides of the street. This is Monaco's major shopping area. Look for **Sapjo** (antique furniture and jewelry); **Monique, Trussardi, La Coste, Benetton**, and **Old River** (clothes); **De Wan** (beautiful glass); **Christofle** (tableware); **Galerie 41** (Asian ceramics and screens); **Claris. A** (jewelry); and **La Jolie Bou-**

tique (unique gift items). Interspersed between the shops are numerous real estate firms offering property at astronomical prices. You can easily spend a couple of hours visiting the many interesting shops along this street.

If you return to the Place du Casino, you'll discover a seemingly small shop to the left of the Casino entrance. Called **Würz** (Tel. 93-25-10-40), this is a classy second hand and pawn shop. The second hand items are on display. They normally are acquired through estate sales (heirs have difficulty dividing heirlooms and come here to settle their disputes for cash). The pawned items are stored in back and are not for sale. They periodically go to auction. As one might expect, second-hand items, especially jewelry, silver serving pieces, books, and coin collections, are of the finest quality.

A second major shopping area is found just off the Port de Monaco in the **La Condamine** *quartier*, Monaco commercial harbor area of businesses and apartments. Approximately a 10-15 minute walk west of Monte Carlo (take Avenue de Monte Carlo from Place du Casino, which also becomes Avenue d'Ostende and then turns into Boulevard Albert). The area, bordered by Rue Grimaldi, Boulevard Albert, and Avenue du Port, is densely populated with restaurants, bistros, pizzarias, small shops, travel agencies, real estate agencies, banks, and grocery stores. One of the best streets for shopping is the pedestrian mall area, **Rue Princesse Caroline**. Here you will find several restaurants and small shops. Monaco's best English-language bookstore is here, **Scruples** (9 Rue Princess Caroline). A small and cramped bookstore, it offers a good selection of fiction and nonfiction. As you will quickly discover, imported English-language books can be expensive: US$5.99 paperbacks sell for US$20.00 here. If you go to the end of this street and turn right onto Rue Grimaldi, you'll find several small shops selling clothes and home decorative items. The quality here is very different from the what was represented in the many shops of Monte Carlo. This is definitely not the best of the best, but —you may find the shopping here more interesting and fun.

The final shopping area is located further west in the newly developing Fontvieille *quartier* which is Monaco's industrial area largely created from 20 acres of reclaimed land. Look for **Fontvieille Shopping Plaza** (*Centre Commercial de Fontvieille*) which has 36 boutiques along with a MacDonald's and a good supermarket from which you may want to stock up on soft drinks and snacks or perhaps organize a picnic: **Carrefour**.

ENJOYING YOUR STAY

There's much to see and do in Monaco in addition to shopping. Monaco's major attractions are found in the following *quartiers*:

MONACO VILLE/LE ROCHER (THE ROCK)

This is the old medieval city which stands majestically overlooking the sea and principality. The views are breathtaking and the sights are interesting. The major highlights include:

❑ **Prince's Palace (Palais Princier)**: Place du Palais, Tel. 93-25-18-31. *Public Rooms open June-October, 9:30am-6:30pm. Admission 25F.* The colorful Changing of the Guard takes place each day at 11:55am. Perched on a hill overlooking the Principality, this is the official residence of the ruling Grimaldi family. A flag is raised when Prince Rainier is in residence. The palace is open to the public in the summer during which time you can view the Central Courtyard, State Apartments, and the Throne Room. The new wing of the Palace remains open all year long, except November, and houses the Napoleonic Museum (Napoleonic mementos) and the Palace Archives (admission 15F). The archieves includes historic documents, uniforms of the palace guards, and Monegasque postage stamps and currency.

❑ **Cathedral of Saint-Nicolas**: 4 Rue Colonel-Bellando-de-Castro. Architectural styles combine Romanesque on the outside and Byzantine on the inside. Princess Grace and Princes of the Grimaldi family are buried in the crypt. Famous children's choir (*les Petits Chanteurs de Monaco*) performs at the 10:00am Sunday mass.

❑ **Oceanographic Museum and Aquarium (Musée Océanographique et Aquarium)**: Avenue-Saint Martin. *Open 9:00am-7:00pm. Admission 50F for adults and 20F for children.* Founded in 1910 by Prince Albert I, this is one of the world's finest aquariums which also functions as a scientific research center that has been directed for many years by Jacques Cousteau.

MONTE CARLO

This is the hedonistic area for those wishing to gamble, attend the opera, stay in luxurious hotels, dine in fine restaurants, shop for exquisite jewelry and clothes, and see and be seen.

❑ **Place du Casino:** This complex consists of the Monte Carlo Casino and the Opera House. If gambling is on you mind, here's the best of the best places to enjoy the sport. And even if you're not a gambler, you should at least view the ostentatious architecture and gilted rococo ceilings of these excessively decorated buildings. Designed by Charles Garnier (architect of the Paris Opera House), the building was completed in 1879. You'll need to be at least 21 years of age and present your passport at the desk on the left in order to gain entrance into the gaming rooms (American Room and Salles Privées). You'll also need to dress appropriately (coat and tie for back rooms); this is not sleazy Las Vegas nor Atlantic City. The casino opens at noon and closes after the last die is thrown. The opulent Opera House is home for the Monte Carlo Ballet, Monaco's Philharmonic Orchestra, and the Opera Company.

❑ **Loew's Casino:** 12 Avenue des Spélugues, Tel. 93-50-65-00. *Open 4:00pm on weekdays, 1:00pm on weekends.* Located in the huge Loews Monte-Carlo hotel-casino complex just east of Place du Casino, this is a favorite casino for serious gamblers.

❑ **National Museum of Fine Arts (Musée National de Monaco):** 17 Avenue Princesse Grace, Tel. 93-30-91-26. *Open 10:00-6:30pm (Easter to September); 10:00-12:15pm and 2:30-6:30pm (September to Easter). Admission 26F for adults and 15F for children.* A unique showcase of 300 dolls and mechanical toys made in Paris in the latter half of the 19th century and collected by Madelaine de Galéa. Presented in period furniture, chinaware, and everyday objects for replicating the historic period. Housed in a 19th century villa designed by Charles Garnier, the architect of the Paris and Monte Carlo Opera Houses.

❑ **Casino Gardens:** Located in front of Place du Casino and extending from Avenue des Beaux Arts to Boulevard des Moulins. This delightful park/gardens consists of an impressive fountain and sculpture by Bottero (black cat) and carefully manicured gardens with numerous species of tropical plants all nicely labeled. A very pleasant place to stroll and sit.

LA CONDAMINE

This harborfront commercial and residential area includes several additional attractions:

❑ **The Zoological Gardens (Centre D'Acclimatation Zoologique):** Place du Canton, Tel. 93-25-18-31. A small but interesting zoo near Place des Armes. Includes a lion, tigers, a rhinocerous, a hippopotamus, oranguatangs, and chimpanzees.

❑ **SeaBus:** Societe Monegasque de Tourisme Sous-Marin, 11 Boulevard Albert 1st, Tel. 92-16-18-19. Adults 270F, children 140F. This 44-seat submarine dives 100 feet to tour simulated shipwrecks, artificial reefs, and colorful flora and fauna.

❑ **Open-Air Market:** Located at Place des Armes, this colorful early morning market offers fruits, vegetables, and flowers. Great place for people-watching. Open from early morning until noon.

FONTVIEILLE

❑ **Exhibition of H.S.H. The Prince of Monaco's Private Collection of Classic Cars (Collection de Voitures Anciennes de S.A.S. Le Prince de Monaco):** Les Terrasses de Fontvieille, Tel. 92-05-28-56. *Open 10:00am-6:00pm every day except Friday. Closed in November. Admission 30F adults and 15F children ages 8-14 years.* A display of nearly 100 antique cars collected by Prince Rainier III, from a 1903 De Dion Bouton to a 1956 Chrysler Imperial. Includes some of the most important models from Maserati, Jaguar, Mercedes, and Rolls Royce.

ELSEWHERE

❑ **Exotic Gardens (Jardins Exotique):** 65 Boulevard du Jardin-Exotique, Tel. 93-30-33-65. *Open 9:00am to 7:00pm (May 15-September 15) and 9:00am to 6:00pm (remainder of year). Admission 39F adults, 26F senior citizen, and 16F children.* Located a half-hour walk northwest of the palace (western entrance to Monaco), these unique gardens cling to 300 foot high cliffs overlooking the sea and principality. Includes 7000 species of cacti and succulents. You'll find two other attractions at the base of this cliff: the prehistoric Observatory Caves (*Grott de l'Observatoire*) and the Museum of Prehistoric Anthropology (*Musée d'Anthropologie Préhistorique*).

SPECIAL EVENTS

❑ **The Grand Prix:** This internationally acclaimed Formula One race takes place each year during May, in conjunction with the Cannes International Film Festival. The racing circuit begins near the harbor in La Condamine and runs to Place du Casino in Monte Carlo and back. Over 100,000 people attend and compete for 35,000 seats along the circuit. Needless to say, Monaco is extremely crowded at this time with hotels and restaurants bursting at the seams. Many hotel rooms are reserved years in advance and hotel prices tend to skyrocket during May. To get tickets, contact the Monaco Automobile Club well in advance (6-12 months) to get on their mailing list: Automobile Club de Monaco, 23 Boulevard Albert 1st, MC 98000 Monaco. You'll receive a order form requiring prepayment (500F to 1200F, depending on whether you're standing or sitting). You also can purchase tickets in Monaco the week before the race (look for special kiosks dispensing tickets).

❑ **Other:** If you're in Monaco during February, July, August, and November, look for these special fairs and festivals: **International Circus Festival** (first week of February), **International Fireworks Festival** (July and August), and **The Prince's Fair** (three weeks in November). Check with the Monaco Tourist Office for specific details.

Monaco also has its share of **nightlife**. Much of it centers around the casinos (Monte Carlo Casino at Place du Casino and Loews Casino at 12 Avenue des Speluges), restaurants, bars, discotheques, cabarets, nightclubs, and cinemas. Contact the Monaco Tourist Office for information on what's going on in various night spots during your visit.

Cannes

The fact that Cannes' sister city is Beverly Hills, California tells you a lot about what you might expect to encounter in this small (population 78,000) but popular resort town 16 miles southwest of Nice. Cannes appears to be all about money, fancy cars, expensive yachts, chic boutiques and cafés, celebrities and wannabes by the dozen, suntans, and a decadent lifestyle by the sea. It's a sophisticated city content with its upper-class draw. It's a wonderful place for those who can afford it.

A SPECIAL PLACE

Cannes occupies a very special place in France. Especially famous for its glamorous annual International Film Festival usually held in May (some years in April), which brings over 50,000 journalists, producers, directors, actors, distributors, and businessmen to this oceanfront city, chic Cannes primarily appeals to the rich and famous. Throughout the year, except for the quiet month of November, Cannes always seems to have something going on, be it more festivals, galas, shows, and international regattas: video, dance, horses, fireworks, music, golf, game, and audiovisual communication. At the same time,

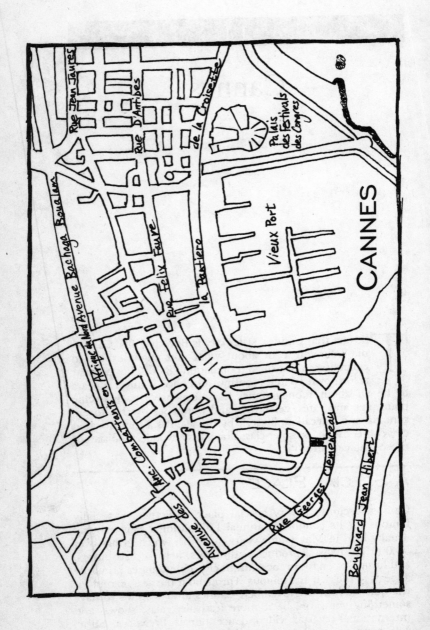

Cannes is France's second largest convention city. Each year it attracts numerous conferences and conventions throughout the world. The **Palais des Festivals**, Cannes' huge convention facility with 17 auditoriums, can accommodate most large groups in search of an ideal mix for work and play.

But it's the **play** that attracts the crowds to Cannes. Drive into the hills for a panoramic view of the city and sea; stroll down its handsome well-manicured flower and palm tree-lined promenade (Promenade de la Croisette) ringing the beach; view the picturesque harbor with its expensive yachts; dine at one of the many open-air restaurants lining the beach front Boulevard de la Croisette; step into the famous Carlton Hotel; spend the evening in its casinos and discos; or shop the many boutiques lining Boulevard de la Croisette and Rue d'Antibes; and you'll quickly discover why so many people flock to this charming seaside resort. They are here to primarily play in its many restaurants, hotels, shops, casinos, and discos and lie on its inviting beaches.

Despite the massive crowds that descend on this place during the International Film Festival as well as the peak season months of July and August, Cannes still retains its unique seaside charm. While many seaside resorts, such as St. Tropez, close down between mid-October and the first of March because of the sharp drop in visitors, Cannes keeps busy most of the year.

THE BASICS

Located 562 miles south of Paris, 101 miles east of Marseille, and 16 miles southwest of Nice, Cannes is easily accessible by air, rail, and road. If you fly in, you'll arrive at the **Nice-Côte d'Azur Airport** (see Chapter 12 on Nice) which is 20 minutes northeast of Cannes. A taxi from the airport to Cannes is very expensive—350F. A much cheaper (70F) bus service departs every hour from the airport and stops at the Hôtel de Ville terminus in Cannes. An even cheaper (30F) and faster (20 minutes) hourly train service runs from the airport to Cannes. Trains from other parts of France stop frequently in Cannes each day as part of the rail service that links the major cities and towns along the French Riviera.

If you drive into Cannes, please be forewarned that parking can be very difficult. It's best to put your car in a parking garage or lot, or drop it off at one of the hotels that will park it for you.

Cannes' main **tourist office** (Office du Tourisme) is located in the Palais des Festivals (1 Boulevard de la Croisette, Tel. 93-39-24-53); a branch office is located in the train station (Place Semar, Tel. 93-99-19-77). The main office is open daily in May, July, and August but closed on Sundays from September through April and in June; the branch office is closed on weekends. This office provides maps and brochures, arranges tours, and offers a free accommodations service.

- ❑ Cannes is a sophisticated city content with its upper-class draw, a wonderful place for those who can afford it.

- ❑ Cannes is France's second largest convention city.

- ❑ The 20-minute taxi ride from the airport to Cannes is very expensive—350F (US$75).

- ❑ Parking can be very difficult. Put your car in a parking garage or lot or drop it off at one of the hotels that will park it for you.

- ❑ Make hotel reservations well in advance because many hotels are fully booked during much of the year, especially the grand hotels along the Croisette.

Except for taking trips into the surrounding hills, you should have no problem **getting around** Cannes on foot. After all, this is a relatively small resort town where most hotels, restaurants, shops, markets, beaches, and entertainment establishments are all within a short walking distance of each other.

Do make sure you make **hotel reservations** well in advance, especially if you plan to stay in one of Cannes' grand hotels. Most of these hotels are fully booked several weeks in advance because of the many conferences, conventions, galas, regattas, and festivals being held in Cannes. The easiest month to get reservations is November, the only relatively quiet month for Cannes.

THE STREETS OF CANNES

The resort section of Cannes of most interest to visitors is relatively compact and easy to get around in. It consists of a long and narrow rectangular area about one kilometer in length and one-eight of a kilometer in width. Facing the ocean, this area is bounded by Boulevard de la Croisette on the South, Rue d'Antibes on the north, the Martinez Hotel on the East (Rue Latour Maubourg), and Rue Louis Blanc on the West. An extremely crowded and congested area, it's difficult to find parking along the narrow streets. While you will find a few parking garages, it may be best to leave your car with a parking attendant at one of the major hotels along Boulevard de la Croisette (assuming you are not staying in one of these properties).

Boulevard de la Croisette is the major street to stay, shop, gamble, and be seen on. The street faces the ocean and is ringed by a delightful walkway, the promenade, which altogether follows the bay for three kilometers and is filled with nicely manicured flowered gardens and lawns planted with palm trees and umbrella pines. Here you will find five of Cannes' best hotels—Carlton, Majestic, Gray d'Albion, Noga Hilton, and the Martinez. Toward the western end of this street is the huge convention center, Palais des Festival, which is the site for the International Film Festival and numerous conventions held throughout the year. It also houses a major casino, disco, and the Tourist Information Office. You'll also find numerous restaurants lining this street and facing the harbor, great places from which to people-watch and enjoy the oceanfront scenery. Interspersed between the hotels and restaurants are some of Cannes' best quality shops. Here's where you will find the designer boutiques and fine jewelry stores: Chanel, Piaget, Gucci, Hermès, Van Cleef & Arpels, Valentino, Ungaro, Yves Saint Laurent, Gianfranco Ferre, and Celine. The shopping emphasis here is definitely on upscale and expensive. This is also the street for Cannes' major shopping center, Les Boutiques de Gray Street, which primarily has upscale shops facing the Boulevard de las Croisette side of the center. You also will find a few other shops along this street worth visiting—Jean-Louis Scherrer for clothes and accessories, Varouj (#3) for well tailored women's jackets and blouses, Burma for "almost perfect" costume jewelry, and Galerie Arpe (#5) and the Picture Gallery (#66) for paintings, prints, lithographs, and sculptures.

- ❑ Boulevard de la Croisette is the main street to stay, shop, gamble, and be seen on.

- ❑ The Old Town is located on a cliff (Le Suquet) and is characterized by narrow and winding streets and charming fishermen's houses.

- ❑ Rue Meynadier, once Cannes' main street, is now a pedestrian zone with numerous classy food shops and open-air boutiques.

- ❑ Expect to pay US$400 or more per night for a double in one of Cannes' grand hotels along Boulevard de la Croisette.

- ❑ The emphasis here is definitely on luxurious designer jewelry, clothes, and accessories at prices that will remind you of the "best of the best" in Paris.

- ❑ The best shops in Cannes' largest shopping mall are found on the Boulevard de la Croisette side, especially the ones facing the street (Gucci, Hermès, Jean-Louis Scherrer).

Cannes' second major street is **Rue d'Antibes** which parallels Boulevard de la Croisette. If you walk east along Boulevard de la Croisette, go all the way to the corner of Rue Latour Maubourg where you will see the Martinez Hotel. Turn left at **Rue Latour Maubourg** and within a few minutes you'll reach the eastern end of Rue d'Antibes. Turn left onto this street and continue walking for approximately one kilometer, until you come to **Rue du Maréchal Joffre**. Turn left again and you'll be at Place de Gaulle and within three minutes back on Boulevard de la Croisette. The Palais des Festivals et des

Congrés will be across the street to your left.

Once you've completed this two kilometer circuit—encompassing Boulevard de la Croisette, Rue Latour Maubourg, Rue d'Antibes, Rue du Maréchel Joffre—you will have passed by most of Cannes' major hotels, restaurants, and shops. You'll see where all the money is going!

If you want to go beyond the chic resort atmosphere, you should visit the charming Old Town section of Cannes which is located west of the main resort area and Vieux Port. Located on a cliff known as **Le Suquet**, the town has narrow and winding streets and charming fishermen's houses. The easiest way to get to this hill is to take **Rue St-Antoine** off of Rues Georges Clemenceau (this is the western extension of Rue d'Antibes which changed its name to Rue Felix Faure before becoming Rues Georges Clemenceau) and then take Rue des Abbesses. Here you can visit the 16th-17th century church **Eglise Notre-Dame de l'Espérance**, the 12th century **Saint Anne Chapel**, and the **Musée de la Castre**. At the foot of the cliff is **Rue Meynadier**, once Cannes' main street but now a pedestrian zone lined with 18th century buildings and numerous classy food shops and open-air boutiques. Come here for fine wine, cheeses, pasta, and other food delicacies you'll want to, and most of which can easily, ship home. The covered food market (*Marché Forville*) near the Vieux Port is open everyday except Monday.

If you have a car, you may want to drive to **Super-Cannes**, a hill to the northeast overlooking Cannes and the harbor. This is one of the loveliest views of Cannes, and it's especially romantic at night. The easiest way to get there is to take **Boulevard de la Républic** to **Avenue de Vallauris**. Turn right and take this road until you come of **Chemin des Collines**. Turn left onto this road and you'll have a stunning view of the area.

Another interesting place on the outskirts of Cannes is **Le Cannet**, a pleasant hillside village located directly north of the town via Boulevard Carnot. Here you can get a panoramic view of Cannes, the Bay of Cannes, the islands, and the Estéral.

ACCOMMODATIONS

While Cannes has 114 hotels offering 5183 rooms for all budget categories, it also has a disproportionate number of expensive hotels that cater to its upmarket clientele. Indeed, you'll think you are in Paris when it comes to paying the bill. Expect to pay US$400 or more per night for a double in one of

Cannes' grand hotels along Boulevard de la Croisette that face
the Bay of Cannes. Many of these places maintain private
beaches across the street. If you plan to stay in Cannes during
the film festival in May, expect to pay much more, that's if you
can find a room. Since this is a popular resort and convention
center, be sure to make your hotel reservations well in advance.
Many visitors to Cannes prefer staying in less expensive Nice or
other nearby areas and thus avoid both the high prices and
extreme congestion of Cannes. If you decide to stay in Cannes,
here are some of the best places to stay:

❑ **Carlton Inter-Continental:** 58 Boulevard de la Croisette, Tel. 93-68-91-68, 800-327-0200 from the U.S.,
Fax 93-38-20-90. 354 rooms, including 30 suites. This
is Cannes' grandest and one of France's most famous
hotels, similar in prestige to the famous Negresco in
Nice. Its twin domed white facade stands out as one of
the city's landmarks. Spared by both the Nazis and the
Allies from destruction during World War II, the
Carlton has seen lots of history since being built in
1912. Just about every celebrity and notable that has
passed through Cannes claims to have stayed here.
Luxurious rooms with nice views of the bay and the Iles
de Lérins. 930-2890F; seaview rooms are more expensive
(1650-3690F). Very expensive.

❑ **Majestic:** 14 Boulevard de la Croisette, Tel. 92-98-77-
00, Fax 93-38-97-90. 262 rooms, 25 suites. Another one
of Cannes' grand hotels centrally located (across the
street from the Palais des Festivals et des Congrès) with
gorgeous views of the old harbor, the Suquet, and the
Esterel Mountains. 650-3580F. Very expensive.

❑ **Martinez:** 73 Boulevard de la Croisette, Tel. 92-98-73-
00, Fax 93-39-67-82. 418 rooms and 12 suites. Another
one of Cannes' grand landmark hotels built in an art
deco style. Luxurious and comfortable built rooms. 720-
3,500F. Very expensive.

❑ **Noga Hilton:** 50 Boulevard de la Croisette, Tel. 92-99-
70-00, Fax 92-99-70-11. 180 rooms, 45 suites. This
relatively new luxury hotel (1992) was built on the
former site of the Palais des Festivals. Centrally located
with all amenities expected for a luxurious Hilton
property. 850-3190F. Very expensive.

❑ **Gray d'Albion:** 38 Rue des Serbes, Tel. 92-99-79-79, Fax 93-99-26-10. 172 rooms, 14 suites. Superb location in the heart of Cannes' shopping district. In fact, it's attached to the city's major shopping center, **Les Boutiques de Gray Street**. Luxurious, spacious, and comfortable rooms. Includes the popular disco **Jane's** and one of Cannes best restaurants, **Le Royal Gray**. 1200-1,550F. Expensive to very expensive.

❑ **Victoria:** Rond-point Duboys-d'Angers, Tel. 93-99-36-36, Fax 93-38-03-91. 25 rooms. A small modern hotel with quiet and comfortable rooms. Some rooms have terraces overlooking a park and swimming pool. 400-1,200F. Moderate to expensive.

❑ **Fouquet's:** 2 Rond-point Duboys-d'Angers, Tel. 93-38-75-81, Fax 92-98-03-39. 10 rooms. Closed October 28-December 26. Centrally located near the Croisette, this comfortable hotel offers attractive rooms and amenities. 440-1,400F. Moderate.

❑ **Mondial:** 7 Rue d'Antibes and 1 Rue Teïsseire, Tel. 93-68-70-00, Fax 93-99-39-11. 56 rooms. This modern six-storey hotel is centrally located along Cannes' major commercial street. Some rooms have a sea view while others face the mountains. A basic good value hotel. 530-740F. Inexpensive to moderate. No credit cards.

❑ **Saint-Yves:** 49 Boulevard d'Alsace, Tel. 93-38-65-29, Fax 93-68-50-67. 8 rooms, 5 suites. This attractive villa with lovely gardens offers good value for those planning to spend a week or month in Cannes. A few rooms and suites may be rented for shorter periods. 250-450F. Inexpensive.

❑ **Hotel du Cap-Eden Roc:** Boulevard J. F. Kennedy, Cap d'Antibes, Tel. 93-61-39-01, Fax 93-67-76-04. 130 rooms, 10 suites. Closed mid-October to mid-April. Located about 20 minutes from Cannes at the exclusive Cap d'Antibes peninsula, this is the ultimate luxury resort on the French Riviera; some travel professionals rank it as the number one resort in the world. Classy and elegant. Indeed, many rich and famous arrive by luxurious yacht and remain on the incredible 22 acres of grounds throughout their stay. Others venture beyond, especially heading for the bright lights and noise of

Cannes. Built in 1870, Eden Roc has hosted many celebrities, from F. Scott Fitzgerald, Charlie Chaplin, Ernest Hemingway, and Clark Gable to Clint Eastwood, Bill Cosby, Johnny Carson, and Madonna. If you want to go all out and be truly pampered in one of the world's most exclusive resorts, this is the place. Fabulous grounds worthy of an exclusive château or grand country estate, excellent views of the Mediterranean, and an outstanding restaurant (Pavillon Eden Roc). Rooms which lack basic four-star hotel amenities (no mini-bar—just call room service; no hairdryer—visit the hair salon; no television—how proletarian) can be disappointing given the hefty rack rate. Be sure to bring lots of money because this place is extremely expensive and does not accept credit cards! 2500-5400F. Very, very, very expensive.

RESTAURANTS

The restaurant scene in Cannes reflects its upscale clientele. You'll find lots of good restaurants, many of which are in the grand hotels, that also are very expensive. Some of Cannes' finest include:

❏ **La Palme d'Or:** Hôtel Martinez, 73 Boulevard de la Croisette. Tel. 92-98-74-14. *Open Wednesday-Sunday, 12:30-2:00pm and 7:30-10:30pm; Tuesday, 7:30-10:30pm.* Popular with celebrities, this award-winning restaurant run by chef Christian Willer serves outstanding seafood dishes. Very expensive.

❏ **Le Royal Gray:** Hôtel Gray-d'Albion, 38 Rue des Serbes, Tel. 93-68-54-54. *Open October-May, Tuesday-Saturday, noon-2:00pm, 8:00pm-10:30pm; June-September, Tuesday-Saturday, noon-2:00pm, Monday-Saturday, 8:00pm-10:30pm; closed Sundays and February.* Long revered as one of Cannes' finest restaurants offering innovative dishes under the careful hand of chef Jacques Chibois. Since his recent departure to open his own restaurant in Grasse, the kitchen has been taken over by chef Michel Bigot. Early reports are that the restaurant has retained its reputation for excellence. Very expensive.

❏ **La Belle Otéro:** Hôtel Carlton, 58 Boulevard de la Croisette, Tel. 93-39-09-06. *Open until 12:30am but* *closed Sunday and Monday during the off-season, February 1-March 7 and November 2-15.* Chef Francis Chauveau produces innovative Provençal dishes in one of Cannes' most prestigious addresses. Try the truffled salad of langoustines, lobster tourte, and veal. Offers a 260F fixed-price lunch (except Sundays). Expensive to very expensive.

❑ **La Mère Besson:** 13 Rue des Frères-Pradignac, Tel. 93-39-59-24. *Open Monday-Friday, 12:15-2:00pm, 7:30-10:30pm; Saturday, 7:30pm-10:30pm.* Offers home-style Provençal dishes at affordable prices. A friendly and popular bistro frequented by locals. Casual dress. Moderate.

❑ **Le Relais des Semailles:** 9 Rue St-Antoine, Tel. 93-39-22-32. *Open for dinner only, 7:00-11:30pm; closed November and March 15-31.* Located in Le Suquet area (Cannes' Old Town neighborhood), this casual dining spot offers fresh market fare at reasonable prices. Try the stuffed pigeon, foie gras lasagna, and grilled sea bass. Moderate.

❑ **Au Bech Fin:** 12 Rue du 24-Août, Tel. 93-38-35-86. *Open Monday-Saturday, noon-2:30pm and Monday-Friday, 7:00pm-10:00pm; closed December 20-January 20.* This popular bistro offers excellent meals at relatively inexpensive prices. Try the fish soup, salad niçoise, and duckling. Inexpensive to moderate.

SHOPPING

Cannes offers lots of upscale shopping opportunities for those who want to engage in this resort sport and who have sufficient credit limits on their credit cards. The emphasis here is definitely on luxurious designer jewelry, clothes, and accessories at prices that will remind you of the "best of the best" in Paris and several chic shops in Monte Carlo. Indeed, Cannes' major shopping streets are mini-versions of Paris' Rue du Faubough-St.-Honoré and Avenue Montaigne. All the major clothing designers, as well as many leading jewelers, are well represented in the many upscale shops that are interspersed amongst the grand hotels lining Boulevard de la Croisette. It's the hotels and their wealthy clientele that are largely responsible for such a heavy concentration of luxury shops in this area.

In contrast to shopping in Nice or Paris, you won't find

much in the way of art and antiques in Cannes and, if you do, the prices will be extremely high, reflecting the resort location of these places. If you're looking for unique products, you're in the wrong place!

Cannes' shopping district is largely confined to the downtown area we previously defined as encompassing a two kilometer circuit bordered by four streets—**Boulevard de la Croisette, Rue Latour Maubourg, Rue d'Antibes**, and **Rue du Maréchel Joffre**. Further northwest of this area, at the foot of Le Suquet, is **Rue Meynadier** a pedestrian zone lined with classy food shops offering wine and delicacies (most will ship the goodies abroad) as well as several open-air boutiques. Up on the cliff in the Old Town area of **Le Suquet**, a market is held every morning except Sundays and several shops are found under the medieval arches.

It's best to start your shopping adventure along Boulevard de la Croisette. If you start at Place de Gaulle—across the street from the Palais des Festivals et des Congrès—and head east passing the Majestic, Noga Hilton, and Carlton hotels and reaching the Martinez Hotel (corner of Rue Latour Maubourg), you'll have covered most of Cannes' upscale shopping. Along the way you'll pass **Varouj** (#3) for nice women's clothes, **Galerie Arpe** for paintings, **Chanel** (#5) for leather bags and accessories, **Henri Martin** (#7) for jewelry, and **Piaget** for quality watches. At the Majestic Hotel (#14), look for the famous jeweler **Bulgari**.

❑ Rue d'Antibes is Cannes' second major shopping street, a very long and narrow one-way street.

❑ Lalique (87 Rue d'Antibes) has a beautiful collection of glass and crystal as well as clothing, jewelry, and accessories.

❑ Atelier de Provence (72 Rue de'Antibes) offers lovely dried flowers, trees, fruits, and vegetables that make attractive home decorative pieces.

❑ Cannes has two museums you may want to visit.

❑ If you want to escape the crowds of Cannes, head for peaceful Iles de Lérins—the islands of Ste-Marguerite and St. Honorat.

❑ Casinos charge admission fees and men need to wear a coat and tie. The one exception is for the slot machine section of the Casino Croisette.

This area also has a large shopping mall, **Les Boutiques de Gray Street**, which is attached to the Hôtel Gray d'Albion. Cannes' major shopping arcade, it includes clothing and leather accessory shops such as **Bally, Lancel, Façonnable, Gucci, Hermès, Jama, Claude Bonucci, Soleiado**, and **Jean-Louis Scherrer**; and jewelry shops such as **Carla, Ferret**, and **Au Castel d'Or**. While the other end of this shopping arcade opens to Rue d'Antibes, the best shops are found on the Boulevard de la Croisette side of the arcade, especially the ones facing the street (Gucci, Hermès, Jean-Louis Scherrer).

Continuing east along Boulevard de la Croisette you'll pass

Burma (#20) for faux jewelry and **Alexandra Reza** (#33) for fine jewelry. The **Nogo Hilton** (#50) has a small shopping arcade. As you get closer to the Carlton Hotel, you'll pass several familiar name-brand shops such as **Christian Dior**, **Louis Vuitton**, and **Cartier**. On the other side of the Carlton Hotel, look for **Van Cleef & Arpels** (#61) for fine jewelry, **Alma** and **Gianfranco Ferre** (#67) for quality clothes. At the front of the Miramar Hotel you'll find **Valentino**, **Ungano**, and **Yves Saint Laurent** for designer-label clothes.

When you reach the Martinez Hotel (73 Boulevard de la Croisette), turn left onto Rue Latour Maubourg. In about five minutes you'll reach **Rue d'Antibes** which is Cannes' second major shopping street. Entry onto this street may be a bit confusing because of Avenue Général Vautrin at Pont des Gabres. You may need to jog to your left, onto Rue du 14 Jullet, and then right onto Rue Pasteúr to get to Rue d'Antibes. You won't get lost if you turn left and then turn right.

Rue d'Antibes is a very long and narrow one-way street. It may take you two to three hours to shop it well. These are not the same quality shops you've just passed on Boulevard de la Croisette. Nonetheless, you will find a few excellent shops worth spending some time browsing for treasures. The east end of this street includes several antique and home decorative shops, such as **Marc C. Francl**. One of our favorite clothing stores is on the corner of Rue d'Antibes and Rue d'Oran, **Dūrrani** (121 Rue d'Antibes, Tel. 93-38-61-23). Further down this street you'll come to **Galerie de Cannes** (#111) for interesting paintings. **Benito & Fils** (#109) has a terrific collection of nicely displayed crystal, tableware and porcelain, including such names as Christofle and Haviland. **Galerie Gantos** (#105) and **Galerie Robin** (#101) offer a good selection of unique paintings. You'll also find a fashionable **Façonnable** clothing store here. One of our favorite shops is **Lalique** (#87) with its beautiful collection of glass and crystal as well as clothing, jewelry, and accessories (uniquely designed scarves, purses, pendants, and brooches). If you're familiar with Lalique crystal, this shop will give you a much broader range of quality Lalique products.

If you're interested in the lovely dried flowers, trees, fruits, and vegetables that make attractive home decorative pieces, be sure to stop at **Atelier de Provence** (#72). This large shop has an extensive inventory of beautiful pieces and they will ship for you. Also, look for **Louis Julian** (#71), one of Cannes' well established jewelers since 1862. The remainder of the street includes the **Les Boutiques de Gray Street** shopping arcade between Rue de Estats-Unis and des Serbes and several boutiques, leather stores, and decorative shops, including **Bally** (#36), **Lancel** (#34), **Geraci** (#22), and **Pavillion Christofle** (#9). Most of the quality shopping is centered in and around the shopping arcade. The Rue d'Antibes entrance to the arcade includes a few jewelry (**Carla**, **Ferret**, **Au Castel d'Or**) and clothing stores (**Façonnable**). The better quality shops, such as **Gucci** and **Hermès**, are located at the Boulevard de la Croisette entrance to the arcade. If you continue walking west along Rue d'Antibes, you may want to turn left at Rue du Maréchal Joffre and return to Boulevard de la Croisette. Alternatively, you may want to continue going west along Rue d'Antibes, which now becomes Rue Felix Foure, and passes **Allées de la Liberté** on the right; this area becomes a flea market (*Marché aux Puces*) on Saturday. Take a right at the next intersection and go one block to **Rue Meynadier**. Turn left on Rue Meynadier and walk east to the foot of the **Le Suquet**. As noted at the beginning of this section, this area has numerous food shops and boutiques along the pedestrian walkway. From here you can go directly to the Old Town or return to Boulevard de la Croisette from where you started your shopping adventure.

While you will find a lot of shopping in Cannes, we frankly have difficulty getting excited about the choices. Because of the large concentration of name-brand designer boutiques and famous jewelers, who maintain small branch shops in Cannes to cater to rich socialites, we've seen it all before in Paris and other parts of the French Riviera. If you're looking for something unique to buy—only available in Cannes—you'll have difficulty finding it. Except for a few art galleries representing artists from the French Riviera, most everything comes from outside Cannes. But that's what you might expect in such a resort area. After all, this is a money-is-no-object crowd in Cannes that seeks the "best of the best" in shopping. They are not into buying cheap handicrafts and souvenirs that often plague other resort areas. When they shop, they want to step into the haute couturiers along Boulevard de la Croisette or the designer boutiques found along Rue d'Antibes. Understandably, shops have been most accommodating to the tastes of this social group.

Enjoying Your Stay

If you've planned to visit Cannes, you probably know exactly what you want to do here—probably very little. In addition to attending one of its major festivals, galas, or conventions, the pleasures of Cannes center around the beaches, the casino, and the nightlife. During the day many people spend their time on the beach soaking up the sun, browsing through shops, and or sitting in sidewalk cafés and restaurants whiling the day away on coffee, wine, conversation, and people-watching.

There are a few other things to do in Cannes, many of which involve escaping from the tourist crowds along the promenade and absorbing some of Cannes' history and local character. As mentioned earlier, you may want to drive up to **Super-Cannes**, the village of **Le Cannet**, or the Old Town at **Le Suquet** to get a panoramic view of Cannes, the Estéral range, the outlying islands, and the coastline.

In addition to a couple of historic churches in the Old Town section (**Notre-Dame-d'Espérance** and **Chapelle Ste-Anne**), Cannes has two museums you may want to visit. These include:

❑ **Musée de la Castre**: Château de la Castre, Le Suquet (Old Town), Tel. 93-38-55-26. *Open October-June, Wednesday-Monday, 10:00am-noon and 3:00pm-7:00pm; October-June, 10:00am-noon and 2:00pm-5:00pm; closed January. 10F.* Housed in an old castle built by the Lérins monks in the 11th and 12th centuries. Eclectic displays of sculptures, ceramics, weavings, paintings, weapons, masks, and instruments from all over the world, including Mediterranean and Middle East artifacts, pre-Columbian sculptures, Asian art, African masks, Japanese military uniforms, and costumes from the South Sea Islands.

❑ **La Malmaison**: 47 Boulevard de la Croisette, Tel. 93-99-04-04.*Closed Tuesdays and holidays. 20F.* Housed in a charming Italianate building along with Cannes' directorate of cultural affairs. Look for temporary art exhibits which go up here every six weeks.

You also may want to visit the two islands in the bay (**Iles de Lérins**): Ste-Marguerite and St-Honorat. You can catch the boats to these islands from the Cannes Harbor (Gare Maritime), located alongside the Palais des Festivals (across from the tourist office), which leave daily between 7:30am and 6:00pm. The ferry to Ste-Marguerite takes 15 minutes and costs 40F for a round-trip ticket; the ferry to St-Honorat takes 30 minutes and costs 45F for a round-trip ticket.

❑ **Ile Ste-Marguerite**: This is the larger of the two islands (3.2 kilometers long and 950 meters wide). A good place for peaceful walks along the many paths of the wooded interior as well as for visiting Fort Royal (also known as Fort Vauban) and Fort Ste-Marguerite. The Man With the Iron Mask was imprisoned in Fort Royal from 1687 to 1698 and then sent to the Bastille where he died in 1703. The Fort Ste-Marguerite has a marine museum (**Musée de la Mer**) on its ground floor. Admission. 10F. Tel. 93-43-18-17. Open Wednesday-Monday, 10:30-noon and 2:00pm-4:30pm (6:30pm in summer). Closed in January.

❑ **Ile St. Honorat:** Only 1.5 kilometers long and 400 meters wide, this island is famous for its old fortified monastery (Abbaye de Lérins) which many centuries ago was one of the great power centers in this part of the world. It takes about two hours to walk to the monastery which is on the other side of the island. The working monastery next door sells handicrafts and locally produced honey and Lérina liqueur. Open 9:00am-noon and 2:00pm-4:45pm. Tel. 93-48-68-68.

You'll find a variety of **water sports** available in Cannes from scuba diving and sport fishing to windsurfing and boating. For information on what's available, where, and with whom, contact the **tourist office** or the **Office Municipal de la Jeunesse** at 2 Quai St-Pierre (Tel. 93-38-21-16).

Cannes' nightlife goes on until the wee hours of the morning. The most popular discos are **La Jane's Club** in the Hôtel Gray d'Albion (38 Rue des Serbes, Tel. 92-99-79-59) and **Le Jimmy'z de Regine** in the Casino Croisette (Palais des Festivals, Tel. 93-68-00-07). Like most discos, both of these places have cover changes at around 120F per person, which include the first drink, and with additional drinks costing about 70F. Opens at 11:00pm, but the action doesn't get started until after midnight.

If you haven't spent all your money yet, or if you're feeling lucky, Cannes offers a few opportunities for **casino gambling**: **Casino Croisette** (Palais des Festivals, Tel. 93-38-12-11, 5:00pm-4:00am), **Carlton Casino Club** (Carlton Hotel, Tel. 93-68-00-33, 4:00pm-4:00am), and the **Casino Riviera** (Noga Hilton Hotel, Tel. 93-68-43-43, 7:00pm-4:00am). Each casino charges admission and men need to wear a coat and tie. Be sure to bring your passport. One exception to these rules is the **Casino Croisette** which operates its slot machines separate from the rest of the casino. Here you can play the slots from 11:00am to 4:00am and men need not wear a coat and tie to do so. But don't lose your shirt!

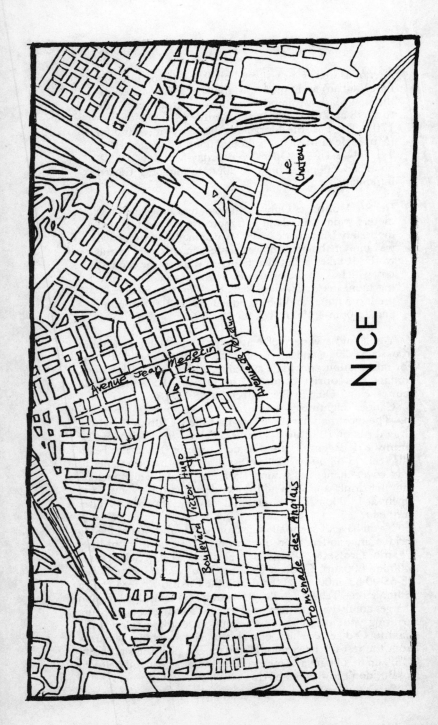

Nice

Located in the heart of the French Riviera, Nice is the Riviera's unofficial capital. An old yet charming Italian-style city of over 400,000 people who host 8 million summer visitors, the city is set along the Mediterranean with a dramatic range of mountains as its backdrop. This is where the Alps meet the Mediterranean.

Once the favorite destination for wealthy Englishmen and Russian princes, today Nice is an important center for tourism, business, and reputedly the French Mafia. Even the Russians, including their Mafia, are returning to indulge in Nice's many treasures and pleasures. Everyone seems to have a good time here. Despite the hordes of tourists, the city has not lost its unique character and charm.

Nice has a distinctive character unlike any other city along the French Riviera. Close to Italy, it has a definite Italian character about it, from architecture to food and attitudes. It is France's largest tourist resort and it's fifth largest city. Often referred to as the "Queen of the Riviera," it has been aging gracefully. Somewhat worn like a fading Miami Beach, its long pebbly beach (big rocks, not sand) adjacent to a wide sidewalk along Promenade des Anglais makes for pleasant strolls, jogging, or just lying on the beach in front of an impressive facade of buildings that line this delightful promenade which, in turn, circles the beautiful Bay of Angels. Add to this the charming Old Town, pastel Italianate buildings along narrow streets, major shopping streets, parks, gardens, fountains, museums, and art galleries, and you have a city exuded a wonderful ambiance and offering lots of things to see and do.

Indeed, no other city along the French Riviera has as much to offer as does Nice. While other cities are primarily organized for tourists, Nice seems to have it all, with lots of French charm and Italian character to satisfy travelers in search of unique experiences.

GETTING TO KNOW YOU

But Nice is much more than just an old charming resort city stretched along the Mediterranean. It's one of France's most important cities for business and culture. It's home for France's second busiest airport and it boasts the largest number of banks, museums, and art galleries outside Paris. And much of France's developing high tech industry is centered in and around Nice. Its thriving business park next to the airport testifies to continuing business growth.

This is one of our favorite cities along the French Riviera. It has real character that goes beyond typical tourist attractions. It's surprisingly less expensive than Monte Carlo and Cannes. It's also ideally located for visiting these other cities as well as nearby villages. Best of all, the shopping in Nice is some of the best in all of the French Riviera.

THE BASICS

Nice is the easiest place to get to on the French Riviera. Regularly scheduled international and domestic airlines fly into Nice's airport which services all of the French Riviera. In fact, nearly 6 million passengers come through this airport each year. A major gateway airport to Southern Europe, it handles 41 airlines that fly to more than 90 cities in 33 countries. Over 220 flights from Paris arrive each week, making this one of the heaviest trafficked corridors in Europe. Each day 20 trains from other cities in France and 11 trains from abroad pass through Nice's train station. The TGV express travel from Paris takes seven hours. An extensive network of national highways lead to Nice: Routes Nationales 7, 98, 202; Route Napoléon and A8 Motorway. If you drive into Nice, you'll probably want to park your car while visiting the city since the streets cannot accommodate many cars. You can use any of several underground parking garages that are clearly marked on maps. However, expect to pay 60-100F a day for this privilege.

The **airport** (Aéroport Nice-Côte) serves both international and domestic flights. It's located approximately 4 miles west of the city and is connected to the city by taxis (150-200F), an airport shuttle bus (25F), and a regular bus (8F). The shuttle bus (*navette*) leaves every 20 minutes and goes between Place Leclerc (departs Avenue Félix-Faure and returns Boulevard Jean-Jaurès) and the airport.

Once you arrive in Nice, you may want to stop at one of the **tourist offices** for a map and literature on the city and surrounding area. Be sure to pick up a copy of "Nice Practical Guide" which includes a wealth of useful information on the city. These offices are found in Terminal 1 of the Nice-Côte d'Azur Airport (Tel. 93-21-44-11), Avenue Thiers (beside the train station, Gare SNCF Nice-Ville, Tel. 93-87-07-07), 2 Rue Massenet (near the beach, Tel. 93-87-60-60), and Nice Feber (près aéroport) Promenade des Anglais (Tel. 93-83-32-64). Most of these offices are open daily 8:00am-8:00pm (September 16-June 30, Monday-Saturday, 8:00am-7:00pm, Sunday 8:00am-noon and 2:00pm-6:00pm). These are very helpful offices that have information on just about everything you ever wanted to know about Nice. Most publications are available in English although some of the most useful tourist newspapers are only in French.

While much of Nice can be covered on foot, taxis and buses are readily available for getting around. If you use a **taxis**, make sure the meter is engaged or you agree on the price before departing. **Buses** (Sunbus) are very convenient for getting around to the various museums. You can pick up a bus map at one of the tourist offices. You also can purchase a 1-day bus pass for 23F, a 5-ticket *carnet* for 34F, a 5-day pass for 87F, or a 7-day pass for 110F.

The best **seasons** to visit Nice are in the spring or fall, especially the months of April-May and October-November, when the weather is pleasant and the crowds are least oppressive. During the hot summer months of July and August the city is wall to wall tourists, hotel rooms are hard to find, and the streets are jammed with cars and people.

THE STREETS OF NICE

Nice is best approached via **Promenade des Anglais**, the main thoroughfare that runs approximately three miles east to west along the beachfront. This eight-lane highway, lined with palm trees, manicured flower beds, a broad beachside walkway, and a pebbly beach, is usually congested with cars, joggers, roller skaters, strolling pedestrians, and beach sitters and bathers. Immediately off this street you'll find three of Nice's major museums: **Musée International d'Art Naïf Anatole Jakovsky** (at Avenue Val Marie), **Musée des Beau-Arts** (33 Avenue des Baumettes), and **Musée Masséna** (65 Rue de France). You'll also find Nice's major casino along this street, the **Casino Ruhl**.

But one of the best places to start exploring the city begins at the famous **Negresco Hotel** which is located at the corner of Rue de Rivoli and Promenade des Anglais, just across the street from the back entrance of the Musée Masséna. Most of the city center for restaurants, shops, and department stores is located north and east of this hotel in a relatively compact area bordered by **Rue de France, Rue Masséna,** and **Rue de la Liberté** (north) and **Promenade des Anglais, Avenue de Verdun,** and **Avenue Jean Medecin** (east and reaching Place Masséna). **Rue Paradis**, for example, is Nice's most upscale shopping street which has been turned into a pedestrian mall. Nearby **Rue de Longchamp, Rue de la Liberté,** and **Rue Masséna** are lined with interesting boutiques, art shops, and sidewalk cafés and restaurants. The broad and pleasant gardens, parks, and fountain surrounding **Place Masséna** (Avenue de Verdun/Avenue Felix Faure and Boulevard Jean Jaures), which functions as the city's center, extends northeast to the Acropolis which is Nice's arts and congress center. You can easily spend the day exploring this vibrant area.

A second city center is located immediately east of this area and is known as the **Old Town**. It has a very different character from the first city center and the rest of Nice. This pedestrian zone (no cars) is characterized by narrow lanes and plazas lined with 17th and 18th century buildings that lead to numerous bistros, Niçois restaurants, art galleries, junk shops, boutiques, and Baroque churches as well as the famous flower market (Cours Saleya) and the Palais de Justice. The area is bordered by **Boulevard Jean Jaures** (northwest) and **Quai des Etats Unis** (south), and buttresses **le Château**. The best way to enter this area is to go to Place Masséna at Jardin Albert 1er (look for the fountain) and cross the street going south into Rue de l'Opera. This short street deadends into Rue Saint-François de Paule. Turn left and you will quickly come to **Cours Saleya**, the Flower Market, which is lined with small restaurants on both sides of the street. This area also becomes a flea market on Monday. If you walk north of this area via Rue L. Gassin, you'll come to Place du Palais and the impressive **Palais de Justice**. Other interesting architectural landmarks to visit here are Sainte-Réparate Cathedral, the Churches Gésu, Saint-Augustin, and Sainte-Rita, and the Palais Lascaris. This whole area is interesting to explore on foot. You can also take a public elevator to the top of the hill that overlooks the Old Town. Known as **la Château**, this hill includes lovely public gardens and breathtaking views of the city, the Bay of Angels, and the Alps.

Another important area of the city is in the north. Called **Cimiez**, this area includes the **Roman ruins**, the Franciscan monastery of **Notre-Dame-de-l'Assumption**, the **Musée Archéologique**, and two of Nice's best art museums: **Chagall Museum** (Musée National Message Biblique-Marc Chagall, Boulevard de Cimiez) and the **Matisse Museum** (Musée Matisse, 164 Avenue des Arènes).

Several other attractions, found in other parts of the city, are best reached by bus or taxi. The **Musée des Beau-Arts** (33 Avenue des Baumettes), for example, with its 17th, 18th, and 19th century paintings, is located several blocks west of the Negresco Hotel. The **Musée International d'Art Naïf Anatole Jakovsky** (Château Ste-Hélène, Avenue Val Marie) is located further west of the Musée des Beau-Arts. And the beautiful Russian cathedral, the **Cathédrale Orthodoxe Russe St-Nicolas**, is located at Avenue Nicolas II, a few blocks west of the train station (Gare Nice-Ville)

Overall, you should be able to cover most of Nice's major attractions on foot. The shopping areas are relatively compact and well-defined. The museums tend to be spread out in various areas of the city.

ACCOMMODATIONS

Nice is noted for offering a good range of accommodations that are more affordable than comparable places along other towns of the French Riviera. If you want to save some money on hotels, find a place in Nice rather than Monte Carlo or Cannes. Some of Nice's best accommodations include the following:

❏ **Le Négreso:** 37 Promenade des Anglais, Tel. 93-88-39-51, Fax 93-88-35-68. 131 rooms. Founded in 1868 by the Romanian immigrant Henri Negresco, this hotel has been restored to its former glory. Classified by the French Government as a National Historic Monument, the hotel has played host to every conceivable celebrity and dignitary to pass through the French Riviera, from Queen Elizabeth, Prince Rainer, Sir Winston Churchill, and President Truman to Elizabeth Taylor, Orson Wells, Marlon Brando, Frank Sinatra, and Sophia Loren. Its distinctive Belle Epoque style is both opulent and ostentatious, although some might say gaudy. Boasting a huge glass dome designed by Gustave Eiffel, the world's largest carpet (600 square yards), and a one-ton crystal chandelier created by Baccarat for the Tzar of Russia (its duplicate hangs in the Kremlin), this is the hotel to see and be seen in. The rooms are spacious, quiet, and retrofitted with conveniences normally expected of four-star hotels. The history and central location of this classic hotel make it one of the most sought-after addresses on the French Riviera. The hotel also houses several upscale boutiques and one of France's best restaurants, **Le Chantecler**. The impressive piano bar, **Le Relias**, was once the favorite rendezvous for Hemingway, Coco Chanel, Jean Cocteau, Marlene Dietrick, Scott Fitzgerald, Valentino and others. There's lots of history here and the hotel continues to wear it well. Its helpful management also provides a special travel guide as well as a shopping guide for its guests (ask the concierge). A unique experience you'll remember for years. If you don't stay here, at least walk through the lobby, view the circular gallery with its crystal chandelier, and perhaps stop for a drink. 1,250-2,250F. Very expensive.

❑ **Beau Rivage:** 24 Rue St-François-de-Paule, Tel. 93-80-80-70, Fax 93-80-55-77. 110 rooms. Includes its own private beach. Located in the Old Town section, near the Cours Saleya and the Opera, the hotel also has the noted restaurant, **Le Relais**. Expensive.

❑ **Abela Hotel Nice:** 223 Promenade des Anglais. Tel. 93-37-17-17, Fax 93-71-21-71. 320 rooms. A large and comfortable hotel with great views. 790-1,395F. Moderate to expensive.

❑ **Élysée Palace:** 59 Promenade des Anglas, Tel. 93-86-06-06, Fax 93-44-50-40. 121 rooms. Deluxe rooms and nice amenities. 750-1,050F. Moderate.

❑ **Le Pérouse:** 11 Quai Rauba-Capeu, Tel. 93-62-34-63, Fax 93-62-59-41. 62 rooms. A nice hotel with terraces and ocean view rooms. 350-1,180F. Moderate.

- ❏ **Méredien:** 1 Promenade des Anglais, Tel. 93-82-25-25, Fax 93-16-08-90. 290 rooms. Great location for this modern hotel overlooking the sea. 1,020-1,650F. Expensive.

- ❏ **Petit Palais:** 10 Avenue E.-Bieckert, Tel. 93-61-19-11, Fax 93-62-53-60. 25 rooms. Located on a hill overlooking the city, this small hotel boasts nice rooms and attentive service. 490-740F. Inexpensive to moderate.

- ❏ **Vendôme:** 26 Rue Pastorelli, Tel. 93-62-00-77, Fax 93-13-40-78. 56 rooms. A small but pleasant hotel that used to be a townhouse. 590-685F. Inexpensive to moderate.

- ❏ **Windsor:** 11 Rue Dalpozzo, Tel. 93-88-59-35, Fax 93-88-94-57, 60 rooms. This small and elegant hotel in the heart of Nice includes frescos in the room, a lovely garden, and a fitness club. Good value at 360-695F. Inexpensive to moderate.

RESTAURANTS

Restaurants in Nice are famous for their seafood and Italian specialties along with standard Provençal fare. Some of Nice's best include these:

- ❏ **Don Camillo:** 5 Rue Ponchettes, Tel. 93-85-67-95. *Open Tuesday-Saturday, noon-2:30pm; 7:00pm-10:00pm.* Located at the foot of le Château, the kitchen of Chef Franck Cerutti is renowned for its tasty dishes. Try the rabbit stuffed with Swiss chard, ravioli, red mullet, and fresh breads. Moderate.

- ❏ **L'Acchiardo:** 38 Rue Droite, Tel. 93-85-51-16. *Open Monday-Friday, noon-1:30pm and 7:00pm-9:30pm; and Saturday, noon-1:30pm.* Serves authentic Niçois cuisine in a charming setting. Try the *soupe de poisson.* Moderate.

- ❏ **La Florian:** 22 Rue Alphonse Karr, Tel. 93-88-86-60. *Open until 10:00pm. Closed Saturday lunch, Sunday, and July 25-August 25.* Serves excellent prepared seafood, meat, and ravioli dishes in elegant art deco surroundings. Moderate.

- ❏ **Le Chantecler:** Le Négresco, 37 Promenade ds Anglais, Tel. 93-88-39-51. *Open 12:30pm-2:30pm and 7:30pm-10:30pm. Closed mid-November to mid-December.* Considered one of France's top restaurants. Opulent dining room with attentive service. Everything here is good, especially the seafood dishes. Very expensive.

❏ **Le Grand Pavois:** 11 Rue Meyerbeer, Tel. 93-88-77-42. *Open noon-2:30pm and 7:00pm-10:30pm.* Considered by many to be Nice's finest seafood restaurant. Expensive.

❏ **Le Mélisande:** 30 Boulevard M.-Maeterlinck, Tel. 92-00-72-00. *Open until 10:00pm, closed Sunday dinner and Monday.* Elegant dining and outstanding service accompany the fine dishes of Chef Jean-Marc Thivet. Try the avocado with duck breast and the lamb navarin. Expensive.

❏ **Les Préjugés du Palais:** 1 Place du Palais, Tel. 93-62-37-03. *Open until 10:00pm. Closed Sundays and October 15-November 10.* Dine on the terrace in front of the Palais de Justice and enjoy the tempting dishes of Henri Scoffier, one of Nice's top chefs. Includes a 150F fixed-price menu. Moderate to expensive.

SHOPPING

Shopping is one of Nice's major strengths. As a large city catering to the resort crowd, Nice offers numerous shopping alternatives, from luxury products found in upscale boutiques to local consumer products found in department stores and shopping centers. Half the fun of shopping in Nice is window-shopping along its major downtown streets.

Most shopping in Nice is centered along seven adjacent streets in the congested downtown area which radiate west and northwest of Place Masséna: **Rue de France, Rue Masséna, Rue Paradis, Rue de Longchamp, Avenue de Verdun, Avenue Jean-Médecin,** and **Rue de la Liberté.** Two streets are essentially pedestrian malls with restricted automobile traffic—**Rue Masséna** and **Rue Paradis.** The street offering the most upscale shopping is **Rue Paradis.**

We recommend beginning your shopping adventure at the Négresco Hotel or at Place Masséna. Let's begin with the hotel and work our way east along Promenade des Anglais to Place Masséna. The Négresco Hotel itself has a few fine boutiques (Gucci) offering quality jewelry, clothes, and accessories. As you leave the front entrance, turn left and begin walking down Promenade des Anglais. You'll initially pass the back entrance to the Musée Massena (front entrance is along Rue de France) and then you'll come to **Galerie des Antiquaires** (7 Promenade des Anglais) which includes 30 art galleries and antique shops; some, such as Yves Bruck, are branch shops of ones found in the much larger antique emporium in Paris, Le Louvre des Antiquaries. From here, the remainder of Promenade des Anglais is lined with restaurants, including McDonald's, and Nice's major casino, Casino Ruhl. You may also want to stop at the nearby tourism office which is located just off this street at 2 Rue Massenet.

As soon as you reach **Avenue de Verdun** (just after Casino Ruhl), turn left. You now enter one of Nice's major shopping streets, which is adjacent to Jardin Albert 1er and Place Masséna. The real shopping begins at the corner of **Rue Paradis**. If you continue east on Avenue de Verdun, you'll pass several nice clothing, jewelry, home accessory, art, and antique shops: **Henri Martin**, **Barichella**, **Burma**, **Remaine**, **Barclay**, **Benetton**, and **P.E. Lacrampe & Fils** (jewelry); **Hermes**, **Tiktiner**, and **Machin Chose** (clothes and accessories); **Soleil en Ville** (home accessories); **Lord Byron** (antiques); and **Galerie Longchamp** (paintings, sculptures, glass art). If you turn left at the end of this street, you'll be on **Avenue Jean Medecin** which has **Pécha** (3 Place Masséna) for beautiful glass and tableware, **Galerie Lafayette** department store, and **Nice Etoile**, a four-level mall at the corner of Avenue Jean Medecin and Boulevard Victor Hugo. We'll return to this street in a few moments. For now, let's return to the corner of Avenue de Verdun and Rue Paradis where the "good stuff" is.

Rue Paradis is Nice's most upscale shopping street. Turned into a pedestrian walkway, this street has it all: **Louis Vuitton** (luggage and handbags); **Electra** (elegant women's clothes); **Jama** (sweaters and leather and fur coats under the Christian Dior and Nina Ricci label); **Sonia Rykiel** (elegant clothes and accessories); **Glady Falk** (designer clothes and accessories); **Sport House** (men's clothes); **Bonpoint** (children's clothes); **Chanel** (leathergoods); **Christian Dior** (clothes); **Alain Figaret** (shirts and ties); **Jacques Andreous** (home accessories); **Kenzo** (clothes); **Peter Hadley** (country-style men's clothes); and **Façonnable** (men's clothes).

At the end of Rue Paradis, you come to an intersection where you can turn right or left onto Rue de Massena. Alternatively, you can go straight ahead and cross Rue de la Liberté and onto Rue Longchamp. The best quality shopping will be found along Rue Longchamp and Rue de la Liberté, although several excellent quality shops are found to the right where Rue de Massena becomes Rue de France. Let's head for Rue de la Liberté where we will turn right. The whole street is lined with boutiques, jewelry shops, and restaurants. You will find Laura

Ashley, Les Copains, and Max Mara for clothes. At the end of this street, you'll come to the intersection with Avenue Jean Medecin. **Galeries Lafayette** is directly across the street on your right. There's nothing much to recommend here; it's not the equivalent of Galeries Lafayette in Paris. If you turn left onto Avenue Jean Medecin and go two blocks to the intersection with Boulevard Victor Hugo, you'll see the **Nice Etoile**, the city's largest shopping mall. Consisting of four levels, it's filled with numerous shops and restaurants which are of most interest to local residents. Nonetheless, you may find a few shops worth visiting. **Lanvin**, for example, has two adjacent shops with the latest in handbags, luggage, and accessories. You'll also find Habitat and Pier Imports for home furnishing as well as several jewelry, electronic, home decorative, bedding, beauty, optical, and food shops. We like to hang out at the Baskin-Robbins refreshment stand where we can get some ice cream and cold drinks!

After leaving the mall, cross the street and walk west along Boulevard Victor Hugo for just a few feet. Turn left onto Rue de Longchamps. You'll find a few interesting clothing stores here. However, our favorite shop is set back from the corner of Rue de Longchamps: **Un Jardin en Plus** (7 Rue Maréchal Jeffre). This is an attractive home accessory shop offering silk and paper flowers, tableware, pillows, lamps, bouquets of dried roses, placemats, carpets, and candles. You'll find branches of this shops throughout Italy as well as in Paris.

Keep walking south along Rue de Longchamps, cross over Rue de la Liberté, and continue on to Rue Massena. Turn right onto Rue Massena and walk west. If you turn left, you'll pass by several nondescript shops offering clothes and accessories and your end up at Galeries Lafayette again; along the way you'll find a real extreme mix of shops, from a large **Cartier** shop for jewelry and handbags, **Mélonie** for dried flower arrangements, and **Galerie Jacqueline Soisson** for an unusual mix of ethnic jewelry, paintings, and artifacts to a sleazy porno shop.

As you walk west along Rue Massena, the street changes its name to Rue de France. Essentially a pedestrian walkway, you'll find lots of outdoor restaurants and small shops lining both sides of the street. On your left, at the corner of Rue de France and Rue Massenet, you'll come to Nice's top boutique—**Pink** (7 Rue de France, Tel. 93-16-26-56). It doesn't get any better along the French Riviera than Pink. The two floors of this attractive and expansive shop are filled with the latest in haute couture and designer label clothes for women. You'll find lots of formal dresses, suites, and coats here designed by Christian

Lacroix, Ungano, Fontana, and Valentino.

Just around the corner, along **Rue Massenet**, are two excellent quality clothing shops: **Claude Bonucci** (10 Rue Massenet, Tel. 93-87-48-87) for the best in men's clothes and accessories and **Dūrrani** (8 Rue Massenet, Tel. 93-87-26-34) for lovely women's suits, coats, and accessories.

If you return to Rue de France, continue west until you come to the next intersection and turn left onto **Rue du Congrès**. Here you'll find one of Nice's most interesting art galleries for paintings and sculptures, **Galerie Ferrero** (2 Rue du Congrès, Tel. 93-88-34-44). From here, turn around and go back to Rue de France, turn left, and walk several blocks to Rue de Rivoli which takes you back to the Negresco Hotel. Along this section of Rue de France you'll find several quality art and antique shops: **Stratos** (colorful art and jewelry), **Galerie Marie Christine** (antiques), **Galerie St. Michel** (antiques), and **Recamier** (antiques).

Congratulations, you've just completed a quick shopping tour of Nice. You will find a few art shops in the Old Town section, but most of Nice's quality shopping is found along the streets we've just visited.

Some of our favorite shops in Nice, all offering top quality products, include these:

❑ **Pink:** 7 Rue de France, Tel. 93-16-26-56. This is Nice's top boutique for women's clothes and accessories. In fact, nothing comes close to this unique shop on the French Riviera. Two floors of this elegant shop are packed with the latest designer fashions, from suits to cocktail dresses and coats, from Christian Dior, Valentino, Ungaro, Christian Lacroix, Karl Lagerfeld, Bernard Perris, and others. Attentive service in a relaxing setting.

❑ **Claude Bonucci:** 10 Rue Massenet, Tel. 93-87-48-87. Attached to Pink's building and has a distinctive "CB" awning. Nice's best shop for men's clothes and accessories. Small but exclusive shop. Literature about the shop is now available in Russian for its growing Russian clientele that seeks the "best of the best" in menswear. Also has a small sale shop around the corner (Rue de la Paix) as well as two shops in Cannes.

❑ **Dūrrani:** 8 Rue Massenet, Tel. 93-87-26-34. Nice designer dresses, jackets, coats, and furs. Expensive but good value compared to other shops. Look for sale items in the basement. Also has a shop in Cannes.

❑ **Galerie Ferrero:** 2 Rue du Congrès, Tel. 93-88-34-44. A wonderful art gallery displaying unique paintings and sculptures by César, Arman, Spierri, Combas, Farhi, Venet, and Ben. Arman's bronze and wood sculptures depicting broken instruments (violins, French horns, trumpets) are especially fascinating. One of our favorite galleries in France. Also has two other shops at 24 Rue de France (Boutique Ferrero, Tel. 93-87-41-50) and 7 Promenade des Anglais (Tel. 93-88-34-44).

❑ **Galerie des Antiquaires:** 7 Promenade des Anglais, open Tuesday-Saturday, 10:00am-12:30pm and 2:30pm-7:00pm; closed Sunday and Monday. This emporium includes 30 art and antique shops. If you like Asian antiques, **Kubera**, for example, has excellent selections from China, Japan, and Southeast Asia.

❑ **Pécha:** 3 Place Masséna, Tel. 93-16-28-08. Offers a wonderful collection of glass and tableware produced by Christofle, Baccarat, Lalique, Daum, Sèvres, Saint-Louis, Haviland, Bernardaud, Coquet, and Etains du Manoir.

❑ **Un Jardin en Plus:** 7 Rue Maréchal Jeffre, Tel. 93-87-82-40. Located just off Rue Longchamps near Boulevard Victor Hugo, this shop offers a wonderful selection of colorful tableware, silk and paper flowers, pillows, placements, carpets, candles, and dried bouquets of roses and fruit displays.

ENJOYING YOUR STAY

As soon as you arrive in Nice, you might want to do two things to get oriented to the city:

❑ **Take a walk along the Promenade** near the Negresco Hotel (also go in to see this landmark property with its huge crystal chandelier). The walk is especially pleasant at night.

❑ **Join a 40-minute tour of the city** (flower market, old town, castle gardens) by way of the cute little white tourist train, **Les Trains Touristiques de Nice**, (departs every 30 minutes, from 10:00am to 7:00pm, from the "Albert the First" Esplanade on the sea front, opposite the Centenary Monument and the Le Meridian

Hotel; 30F; Tel. 93-18-81-58 for reservations) to the top of le Château where you'll get a panoramic view of Nice.

MUSEUMS AND CHURCHES

Make no mistake about it, most visitors to Nice come here to enjoy typical resort pleasures. That means beaches, restaurants, discos, and shops. But Nice offers some extra bonuses normally not found in most beach resorts—numerous quality museums, art galleries, historic churches and sites, and special festivals. Indeed, Nice's long history as a haven for artists has resulted in some of France's finest museums. The best news of all is that museums in Nice are free, with the exception of Musée Matisse and Musée d'Art Moderne et d'Art Contemporain which charge for exhibitions during the busy summer months. The most interesting and popular ones include:

❑ **Musée Matisse:** 164 Avenue des Arènes, Cimiez, Tel. 93-81-08-08. *Open April-September, 11:00am-7:00pm; October-March, 10:00am-5:00pm. Closed on Tuesdays.* Exhibits the paintings, drawings, and engravings of Matisse who lived in Nice from 1917 to 1954 and bequeathed his collection for the creation of this museum. One of the best art museums in France.

❑ **Musée National Message Biblique Marc Chagall:** Avenue du Docteur Ménard (Boulevarde Cimiez), Tel. 93-81-75-75. *Open October-June, 10:00am-12:30pm and 2:00pm-5:30pm; July-September, 10:00am-7:00pm. Closed on Tuesdays.* Includes the largest collection of Chagall's paintings, drawings, and engravings.

❑ **Palais Masséna:** 65 Rue de France, Tel. 93-88-1134. *Open October-April, 10:00am-noon and 2:00pm-5:00pm; and May-September, 10:00am-noon and 3:00pm-6:00pm. Closed on Mondays.* Covers the history of Nice from the 6th to the 19th century. Includes religious art, pottery, weapons, garments, and jewels.

❑ **Musée d'Art Moderne et d'Art Contemporain:** Promenade des Arts, Tel. 93-62-61-62. *Open 11:00am-6:00pm and until 10:00pm on Fridays. Closed on Tuesdays and some public holidays.* Exhibits more than 100 European and American avant-garde works from the 1960s to the present, including Andy Warhol and Roy Lichtenstein and Ecole de Nice artists César and Yves Klein.

❑ **Musée des Beaux-Arts:** 33 Avenue des Baumettes, Tel. 93-44-50-72. *Open October-April, 10:00am-noon and 2:00pm-5:00pm; May-September, 10:00am-noon and 3:00pm-6:00pm. Closed Mondays and some public holidays.* Once the villa of a Ukrainian princess, this museum houses three centuries of art including the works of noted Impressionists and Post-impressions Bonnard, Dufy, and Vuillard.

❑ **Palais Lascaris:** 15 Rue Droite, Tel. 93-62-05-54. *Open 9:30am-noon and 2:30pm-6:00pm. Closed on Mondays and in November.* This former 17th century palace is noted for its grand open Genoese-style staircase lined with 17th century paintings and statues of Mars and Venus. Includes an 18th century pharmacy on the ground floor. Hosts temporary exhibitions.

❑ **Musée International d'Art Naïf Anatole Jakovsky:** Château Ste-Hélène, Avenue Val Marie, Tel. 93-71-78-33. *Open May-September, 10:00am-noon and 2:00pm-6:00pm, and until 5:00pm from October-April. Closed on Tuesdays and some public holidays.* Includes permanent collections of paintings, graphic works, sculptures, and pieces of pottery.

❑ **La Cathédrale Orthodoxe Russe St-Nicolas:** Avenue Nicholas II, Tel. 93-97-88-02. *Open 9:30am-noon and 2:30pm-5:00pm; closed Sunday mornings.* Beautiful Russian Orthodox church constructed in 1912 with pink bricks, grey marble, and colorful ceramics. Includes six onion-shaped cuppolas with important icons, wood paneling, and frescos housed inside.

SITES WORTH VISITING

Nice also boasts numerous historic buildings, gardens, and walkways worth visiting if time permits:

❑ **Le Palais de Justice:** Place du Palais (Old Town). Palace of Justice on a lovely pedestrian square.

❑ **Le Palais de la Préfecture:** Rue de la Préfecture. Built in the 16th century, this building once served as the royal palace. Home of the President of the General Council.

❑ **L'Opera:** Rue Saint-François de Paule. The city's working opera house rebuilt in 1885 after being destroyed by a fire in 1881.

❑ **Le Cours Saleya:** Old Town. *Daily from 6:00am to 5:30pm, except Monday and Sunday afternoons.* This is the famous flower market (all day) that starts out as a fruit and vegetable market every morning except Monday when it becomes a flea market for antique dealers. Surrounded by numerous restaurants.

❑ **La Jardin Albert 1ᵉʳ:** Located just southwest of Place Masséna, these public gardens extend northeast. A great place for relaxing and taking walks.

❑ **La Promenade des Anglais:** This wide seafront boulevard encompasses the Bay of Angels (*Baie des Anges*). Built in 1820 by the Englishman Reverand Lewis Way. Now a popular place to jog, roller skate, stroll, or just sit and watch the people, beach, and sea.

SPECIAL EVENTS

There always seems to be something special going on in festive Nice. Some of the major such events include:

❑ **Carnival:** February. This celebration of spring brings out lots of merrymaking in the streets with costumes, song, and dance. One of Europe's most famous Mardi Gras celebrations draws visitors from all over Europe. Procession on Shrove Tuesday at Place Masséna, Avenue Jean Médecin.

❑ **Festin Des Cougourdons:** April. Held at the Gardens of Cimiez. Includes procession and stalls set up on the square offering gourds and containers.

❑ **La Fete des Mai:** May. One of the oldest celebrations in Nice. Celebrates the 'Merry Month of May' with balls, picnics, folk dancing, and entertainment every Sunday in the Gardens and Arenas of Cimiez.

❑ **Festival de Jazz:** July. International jazz festival with major jazz soloists and famous jazz-bands playing at the Arenas and Gardens of Cimiez.

❑ **Nikaia:** July. International sports competition with 20,000 spectators at the Charles Ehrmann Stadium.

❏ **Bataille de Fleurs**: August. This annual flower festival, complete with carnival floats decorated by Nice's leading florists, takes place along Promenade des Anglais where grandstands are set up for the festive occasion.

Nice doesn't stop until the wee hours of the morning. If you're looking for things to do at night, consider the many restaurants, piano bars, and pubs found in the city as well as these popular places:

CASINO

❏ **Casino Ruhl**: 1 Promenade des Anglais, Tel. 93-87-95-87

DISCOS

❏ **Alizé**: 73 Quai des Etats-Unis, Tel. 93-92-37-08.

❏ **Factory**: 26 Quai Lunel, Tel. 93-56-12-26.

❏ **La Végas**: 8 Rue Maréchal Joffre, Tel. 93-88-75-00.

❏ **Gatsby**: 11 Rue Alexandre Mari, Tel. 93-62-61-96.

❏ **Le Quartz Underground**: 18 Rue du Congrès, Tel. 93-88-88-87.

CABARETS

❏ **New Cha-Cha Club**: 19 Rue Masséna, Tel. 93-87-82-60.

❏ **Charlot**: 8 Rue Saint-François-de-Paule, Tel. 93-13-84-13

NICE IS NICE

Whatever you do, spend some time in Nice. It has a great deal to offer visitors who might otherwise think of coming here just to visit the beaches. As you'll quickly discover, the rocky beaches aren't that great to walk or lie on. They are best appreciated when viewed with the backdrop of the city and hills. Better still, use Nice as your base for exploring less diversified areas of the French Riviera. You'll save some money here on your "travel essentials" as well as soon discover why so many people refer to this city as the "Queen" and "Capital" of the Riviera.

The Villages
and Towns

s we noted at the very beginning of this book, there are
two Frances—one city, the other village. Nowhere is this
more apparent than along the French Riviera. While
millions of people flock to the beach resorts, thousands
of them also have discovered the pleasures and treasures of this
area's many nearby villages and towns. Some of these places are
perched villages noted for their scenic beauty whereas others are
famous art colonies or towns producing unique products. And
still others are perched villages that also function as art centers.
Most are charming places offering interesting cultural and
shopping experiences.

Whatever you do during your stay on the French Riviera,
make sure you literally "head for the hills." The villages and
towns in this area are some of the most charming and rewarding
you'll find anywhere in France or, for that matter, in Europe.

SPECIAL PLACES

While you can find hundreds of villages and towns in hills
beyond the coast, only a few are of interest to visitors. Most of
our villages and towns are located within a half hour driving
distance from Monaco, Nice, or Cannes and are easily reached

by car via good two-lane paved roads. Some are surprisingly urban, such as Vallauris, Grasse, and Antibes, whereas others are quaint and charming, such as Biot and St. Paul de Vence (St. Paul). All have something special to offer visitors.

We've selected three villages because of our interest in shopping. If you've seen all the pricey designer boutiques and haute couturiers you ever wanted to see in Paris and in the cities along the beachfront French Riviera and you're interested in learning about as well as acquiring unique arts and crafts, you're in for a treat. Our villages and towns offer some wonderful arts and crafts that are not generally available elsewhere.

We've selected the following villages and towns, in order of interest, for our arts, crafts, and specialty shopping adventure: Biot, Saint-Paul, and Vallauris. You'll also find several other villages and towns that offer excellent cultural experiences.

For now, all you need is a car, a good map, comfortable clothes and walking shoes, and a sense of adventure. You might also want to practice your French since fewer people in these places speak English as compared to the major resort cities and towns you have visited. In some villages, such as Saint-Paul, you'll need to walk some distance from the parking area into the medieval perched village with its cobblestone streets. We recommend setting aside one or two days to explore these places. While you can visit all four of our villages in one day, the pace may be too hectic for really enjoying each village, especially since many shops don't open until 10:00am and most close between noon and 2:30pm. You might want to visit Biot and Saint-Paul in one day and Vallauris and Antibes on another day. This plan would combine the two most interesting art and craft villages on one day (Biot and Saint-Paul) and the two towns on the other day. Better still, you may want to stay in one of the villages for a couple of nights. Our recommendation: head for a lovely hotel in the quaint village of Saint-Paul. You won't be disappointed. In fact, this may well become the highlight of your visit to France!

BIOT

Biot is an ancient walled village located four miles northwest of Antibes. Once the region's main pottery center, today Biot is famous for its glass blowing factories, arts and crafts shops, and village ambience. You'll still find some of Biot's distinctive yellow and green pottery here, but pottery making long ago shifted to Vallauris with the help of Pablo Picasso who was responsible for reviving the industry and taking it into new art forms. Today, Biot is most noted for producing bubble-flecked glassware which is abundantly produced at the area's most famous glass factory, **La Verrerie de Biot** (Chemin des Combes, Tel. 93-65-03-00), located on the outskirts of town.

Biot actually consists of two sections. A **central town/ village area**, which includes a large concentration of shops, restaurants, tourist office, and a traditional medieval village area and an **outlying area** that includes Biot's most noted glass blowing and ceramic factories as well as the famous **Musée National Fernand Léger**.

Let's begin in the central town/village area. Since Biot has become a very popular tourist destination, parking can be a problem inside the town. On many busy days you'll have difficulty parking along Biot's narrow streets. Depending on the traffic situation, it may be best to park south of the village and walk into Biot. Once in the village, go directly to the **tourist office** on Rue St. Sébastien for a map of the village and information on restaurants and shops. You will see large ceramic maps posted on various street corners of the town which provide information on restaurants and shops. You should have no difficulty getting around the village by following the main street and these maps.

Biot is a charming old medieval village now preserved by art galleries, craft shops, and restaurants that attract thousands of visitors to its three major streets each year. The main shopping areas include Rue Saint Sébastian, Chemin Neuf, and Place des Arcades. It's best to start at the tourist office on the main street, **Rue Saint Sébastian**. Along this street you'll find several attractive arts and crafts shops. **Reflets d'Art** (18 Rue St. Sébastian, Tel. 93-65-18-10), for example, offers an excellent selection of beautiful glass bottles and glass decorative pieces produced in Biot, Vence, and elsewhere in France. **Galerie Saint Sébastian** (11 Rue St. Sébastian, Tel. 93-65-11-50) has a nice selection of ceramics and jewelry, a good place for discovering some unique gift items. We especially like **La Cigaline** (3 Rue St. Sébastian, Tel. 93-65-02-36), located just two doors from the tourist office, with its wide range of quality glassware, ceramics, clothes, and dolls.

If you go to the end of Rue St. Sébastian, you'll come to the second major shopping area, **Place des Arcades**. This is a small plaza which includes several shops, a good restaurant, and an old church. The most important shop here is **Galerie le Patrimoine** (2 Place des Arcades, Tel. 93-65-60-23) which represents the glassworks of J.C. Novaro, one of France's most famous glass artists. Next door is **Terra Terre** which offers attractive blue ceramic tableware. Behind Place des Arcades is the old village area with narrow cobblestone lanes leading down steep hills. This is a very charming residential area which also includes a few galleries. One of our favorites is **Galerie "H"** (12 Rue de la Caroute, Tel. 93-65-06-13) which represents the unique stoneware and porcelain works of artist Alain Rech. This small shop is well worth the effort to find in this area.

The third major shopping area is along Chemin Neuf, which intersects with Rue St. Sébastian. Here you'll discover one of Biot's best pottery and home decorative shops, **Poterie du Vieux Biot** (4 Chemin Neuf, Tel. 93-65-10-40). This is one of our very favorite shops in the French Riviera with its distinctive sand floors and attractive displays. Housed in a two-storey historic building, it's filled with lovely pottery, ceramics, tableware, and furniture. You'll find the traditional yellow and green Biot pottery and ceramics here along with selections from other parts of southern France. We especially like their gorgeous selection of large paper flowers, dried roses, and ceramic figures. The upstairs area is devoted to painted furniture. The shop is very experienced in shipping abroad. Best of all, they have a parking area. You'll probably find something here to take home to remind you of southern France. Next door to this shop is another one of Biot's best shops, **La Verrerie de Biot**. It offers attractive glass, ceramics, and tableware.

The rest of downtown Biot has numerous small restaurants and shops. You can easily spend two to three hours browsing through the shops and enjoying a leisurely lunch at one of its charming restaurants.

Biot's second major area is located just south of town. You'll find several glass blowing factories along Route de la Mer and Chemin des Combes. The largest and most famous glass factory is **La Verrerie de Biot** (Chemin des Combes, Tel. 93-65-03-00). This is a "must see" stop in southern France. In addition to offering a glass blowing factory with typical tourist demonstrations and a factory shop offering a wide selection of factory products, this place also has two outstanding museum-galleries for serious art lovers. If you don't know much about glass art, this is the place to get a real education on this unique art form. If you do know a lot, you're still in for an education. The Serge Lechaczynski family that owns the factory has been instrumental in promoting fine glass art from all over the world. Be sure to visit their international glass gallery—**Galerie Internationale du Verre**—which is housed in a separate building. This is one of the most interesting galleries we have encountered in all of France; it attracts visitors from all over the world who come here just for this gallery. The beautifully displayed works of glass art are all for sale, ranging in price from 10,000F to

250,000F; most sell in the 30,000-40,000F range. They are literally the "best of the best" one-of-a-kind collector pieces. Representing several major international artists, including noted Americans Kreg Kallenberger and Steven Weinberg, the gallery is very interesting. Even though you may not buy anything here, at least you will leave this gallery with a new appreciation for glass art. Be sure to ask questions of the English-speaking gallery personnel who are most helpful in explaining the individual works of art.

The building that houses the glass factory and shop also has a museum-gallery representing the glass art of Jean Claude Novaro's—**Galerie Jean Claude Novaro**. Known as France's "Picasso" in glass art, Novaro's works are very pretty, colorful, and interesting but not of the intellectual quality and diversity of those found in the international gallery. Nonetheless, this is one of France's best glass artists, and you might find something you fall in love with. Most of Novaro's pieces are for sale. You should also visit the adjacent glass blowing factory with its huge furnaces and glass blowing demonstrations and the factory shop that sells a large selection of glass and ceramics.

You'll find several other glass and ceramic factories along nearby roads which are all part of the Biot community. **Verrie d'Art Michèle Luzoro** (1520 Route de la Mer, Tel. 93-65-62-18), for example, represents the works of glass artist Michèle Luzoro. **La Poterie Provençale** (1689 Route de la Mer, Tel. 93-65-63-30) produces attractive ceramics. **La Verrerie du Val de Pome** (Tel. 93-65-03-78) produces colorful handcrafted glassware from the hands of artists Daniel and Marcel Saba.

Another highlight of the Biot area is the **Musée National Fernand Léger** (Chemin du Val-de-Pome, Tel. 93-65-63-61; open April-October, Wednesday-Monday, 10:00am-noon and 2-6:00pm; November-March, Wednesday-Monday, 10:00am-noon and 2:00pm-5:00pm; admission 30F) which displays the colorful paintings, ceramics, mosaics, and tapestries of Fernand Léger who lived in Biot from 1881 to 1955.

SAINT-PAUL

Saint-Paul, also referred to as Saint-Paul de Vence, seems to be everyone's favorite village. One of the best examples of an occupied and working perched village, this walled medieval village continues to attract crowds of tourists who come here to shop and enjoy its village ambience. Shopping, however, seems to be its primary function.

Located 19 miles north of Nice and 17 miles east of Cannes,

Saint-Paul is real gem of a village. While it may at times appear overrun by busloads of tourists, it still retains its charm and continues to be a working village as residents go about their daily chores and observe local customs. The village has functioned as part artist colony since the 1930s.

Since you cannot drive into the village, you'll need to park outside the walls, along the road if you can find space, or further down the hill in a parking lot next to the buses and across from the famous art museum-gallery, The Fondation Maeght. It's only a 10 minute walk from there to the village's main street, Rue Grande.

As soon as you enter the village walls through the narrow stone archway, look for the **tourist office** on your right. This small office has a map, brochures, and other information on the various shops, restaurants, and hotels in the village. From here you can easily cover the cobblestone streets of the village. There's basically one main street, Rue Grande, and a few side streets. Armed with brochure/map from the tourist office, you can't get lost for very long since this is such a small and compact village. And if you do get lost, you'll probably discover an interesting shop, meet some local residents, or get a wonderful view of the village and surrounding area.

The streets of Saint-Paul are lined with numerous art galleries, studios, gift shops, restaurants, and hotels. The quality of the shops varies greatly, from those offering T-shirts, souvenirs, and postcards to studios displaying top quality paintings, sculptures, ceramics, and jewelry. The best way to shop this village is to start at the tourist office and work your way shop by shop through the main street and side streets. Don't come too early: most shops don't open until 10:00am or 10:30am, although some do open as early as 9:30am. Look for **Cristallier d'Art** (across the street from the tourist office) for a large collection of glass and crystal; **Stratos** for unique and colorful sculptures (also in Nice); **Galerie du Vieux St-Paul** for paintings and sculpture; **J. S. Labret** for all blue crystal jewelry; **L'Air du Sud** (56 Rue Grande, Tel. 93-32-56-50), one of our favorite shops with three floors of unique home decorative items, from ceramics, pillows, paintings to lamps and furniture; **Galerie Frederic Gallong** (59 Rue Grande) for high quality paintings and sculptures; **Asteroide** (47 Rue Grande, Tel. 93-32-56-65) for a good selection of gifts and home decorative items; and **Galerie Isthar** (Près de la Grande Fontaine, Tel. 93-32-64-14) for beautiful art glass work by Eric Laurent, Y. Braun, and others. Just across the street from the village entrance, near the popular Café de la Place, is **Galerie L'Orangeraie** (838 Route de la Colle, Tel. 93-32-80-13) which offers one of the most extensive collections of contemporary paintings and sculptures by Arman, César, Chagall, Léger, Mendjisky, Picasso, Rapp, Verdet, and Volti.

Saint-Paul also offers some good restaurants and hotels right in the heart of the village. Indeed, many people love to stay in this village rather than in the resort towns and cities along the coast. Saint-Paul's most famous hotel and restaurant, is one numerous noted artists (Braque, Chagall, Dufy, Picasso, Miró) frequented and contributed to the decor: **La Colombe d'Or** (1 Place du Général-de-Gaulle, Tel. 96-32-80-02, Fax 93-32-77-18); 15 rooms, 11 suites; closed November 5-December 20; 1255F-2200F). The popular restaurant is open daily noon-2:30-pm and 7:00pm-10:30pm and also is closed during much of November and December. **Le Saint-Paul** (86 Rue Grande, Tel. 93-32-65-25, Fax 93-32-52-94) is another gem of a hotel-restaurant, a four-star Relais & Chateaux property, located in the heart of the village with 18 rooms, including three small suites (600F-1900F). Guests rave about this charming hotel and its excellent restaurant (open Friday-Wednesday, noon-2:00pm and 7:30pm-10:00pm, but closed for lunch on Wednesday). This is where we'll stay next!

One of the real treats of Saint-Paul for art lovers is the famous **Fondation Maeght** (Tel. 93-32-81-63, open July-September, 10:00am-7:00pm; October-June, 10am-12:30pm, 2:30pm-6:00pm; admission 45F adults, 30F children). If you visit only one museum on the French Riviera, make sure it's this one (try to also include the Matisse Museum in Nice). Located near the parking lot just down the hill from the village, this is one of Europe's most important modern art museums. The peaceful setting, with its avant-garde building and courtyard, houses sculptures, ceramics, mosaics, and paintings by such noted artists as Giacometti, Chagall, Braque, Miró, Ubac, Bonnard, Kandinsky, Léger, Matisse, and Hepworth. The museum-gallery also includes a library, cinema, and cafeteria. You can purchase original lithographs by Chagall and Giacometti and some limited-edition prints here.

Whatever you do along the French Riviera, put the perched village of Saint-Paul on your travel itinerary. If you're looking for peace and quiet, as well as a unique cultural experience set in the midst of some wonderful art galleries and shops, we highly recommend staying a night or two in the village. The hotels and restaurants are first-rate, and you'll most likely enjoy the village ambience. However, be sure to make reservations well in advance. These are small and popular hotels that may be fully booked weeks in advance.

VALLAURIS

Vallauris is a good sized town made popular by Pablo Picasso who settled here after World War II and revived the pottery industry. You may or may not enjoy this place. It tends to be overrun by tourists and lots of tacky tourist shops offering tasteless ceramics and souvenirs. Nonetheless, Vallauris is a very popular place to visit, and it does yield some excellent quality shopping and attractions. It's somewhat of a shopping mecca for arts and crafts.

Located 4 miles east of Cannes, Vallauris is easy to get to. Once you arrive, go to the **tourist office** at Square du 8 Mai 1945 (Tel. 93-63-82-58). This office is well stocked with good maps and brochures on the town. It also has a large parking lot where you may want to leave your car and walk into the main part of the town.

The main shopping area is found along **Avenue Georges Clemenceau**. If you walk directly north of the tourist office, you'll find numerous art, craft, home decorative, and clothing stores lining both sides of this long street. Be sure to walk the length of the street. Once you come to the intersection with Avenue du Tapis Vert, keep to your left as you continue to follow Avenue Georges Clemenceau to the north.

The majority of shops along this street offer a disproportionate amount of tourist kitsch, especially in the ceramics department. However, you will also find some nice art galleries and numerous shops offering olive wood products. Some of the highlights include these galleries and shops:

❑ **Galerie Madoura (Poterie Boutique):** Tel. 93-64-66-39. Located just to the west of Avenue Georges Clemenceau, along d'A.F.N, this attractive gallery is the exclusive agent licensed to sell reproductions of a special line of uniquely designed ceramics by Picasso. His copyrighted works are nicely displayed in two rooms along with ceramics by other noted artists. Be sure to examine the plexiglass boards that function as a catalog for ordering his ceramics. Yes, you can still own a Picassso, at least ones he designed and licensed here for reproduction! This gallery alone is well worth the visit to Vallauris.

❑ **Madoura Boutique:** Tel. 93-64-66-39. Located in the heart of town and more convenient to other shops, this is a branch shop of Galerie Madoura. It includes a limited selection of Picasso ceramics, postcards, and ceramics products by other artists. Also has the same plexiglass catalog for examining your Picasso shopping alternatives!

❑ **Galerie Sassi-Milici:** Tel. 93-64-65-71. 65 Avenue Georges Clemenceau (near the intersection with Avenue du Tapis Vert). This large art gallery has regular exhibitions of paintings, sculptures, and ceramics by leading artists in the area. Excellent quality. Make this one of your first stops before shopping in other galleries.

❑ **Exposition de Poteries:** Salle Jules Agard. Tel. 93-63-23-91. Avenue J. Gerbino. Located near Galerie Modoura, this gallery represents the works of many different ceramic artists in the area. Excellent quality. A good place for identifying local talent and developing contacts.

❑ **Galerie Valdoria:** Tel. 93-64-65-76. 59 Avenue Georges Clemenceau. Includes numerous oil paintings and poster prints along with a few sculptures.

❑ **Galerie Jean Marais:** Tel. 93-63-85-74. Avenue des Martyrs de la Résistance. Located just off the southern section of Avenue Georges Clemenceau, this popular gallery displays the unique paintings, prints, and bronze sculptures of Jean Marais. Also includes his line of designer perfume and scarves. A large but very crowded gallery that attracts hundreds of curious visitors each day.

❑ **Blue Banana:** Tel. 93-63-20-08. 54 Avenue George Clemenceau. Looking for something blue to add to your home decor? This shop includes a large selection of uniquely designed bedding, linens, ceramics, rugs, and carved wood pieces all done in blue.

❑ **Carbou:** Tel. 93-63-60-07. 69 Avenue George Clemenceau. This distinctive gallery produces attractive jewelry and figures (masks, birds, sculptures) in metal.

❑ **Atelier K:** Tel. 93-63-90-01. 69 Avenue George Clemenceau. Lots of fun ceramic pieces including lamps and vases.

❑ **Galerie 52**: Tel. 93-63-10-12, 52 Avenue George Clemenceau. Good quality gallery representing the bold and colorful abstract paintings of Gavazzi. Be sure to visit the second floor which also includes some sculptures.

You can easily spend three to four hours visiting the many shops and galleries in Vallauris. While your initial reaction may be to move quickly through the town because of all the tourist shops, if you're patient and walk the streets carefully (watch where you step since doggie do-do is especially prevalent on the sidewalks), you will find a few gems in the midst of all the tourist kitsch. Indeed, you may find Vallauris to be a most rewarding stop along the French Riviera.

Index

More Treasures
and Pleasures

The following "Impact Guides" can be ordered directly from the publisher. Complete the following form (or list the titles), include your name and address, enclose payment, and send your order to:

IMPACT PUBLICATIONS
9104-N Manassas Drive
Manassas Park, VA 22111 (USA)
Tel. 703/361-7300 or Fax 703/335-9486
E-mail: impactp@impactpublications.com

All prices are in U.S. dollars. Orders from individuals should be prepaid by check, moneyorder, or Visa, MasterCard, or American Express number. If your order must be shipped outside the U.S., please include an additional US$1.50 per title for surface mail or the appropriate air mail rate for books weighting 24 ounces each. We accept telephone orders (credit cards). Orders are shipped within 48 hours. For information on the authors and on our travel resources, visit our site on the Internet's World Wide Web: **http://www.impactpublications.com**.

Qty.	TITLES	Price	TOTAL
__	Shopping and Traveling in Exotic Asia (5 countries)	$16.95	_____
__	Shopping the Exotic South Pacific	$16.95	_____
__	Treasures and Pleasures of the Caribbean	$16.95	_____
__	Treasures and Pleasures of Hong Kong	$14.95	_____
__	Treasures and Pleasures of Indonesia	$14.95	_____
__	Treasures and Pleasures of Italy	$14.95	_____
__	Treasures and Pleasures of Paris and the French Riviera	$14.95	_____

__ Treasures and Pleasures of Singapore
and Malaysia $14.95 _____
__ Treasures and Pleasures of Thailand $14.95 _____

Coming in 1997

__ Treasures and Pleasures of Australia
and Papua New Guinea $15.95 _____
__ Treasures and Pleasures of India $14.95 _____
__ Treasures and Pleasures of Morocco $14.95 _____
__ Treasures and Pleasures of the
Philippines $14.95 _____

SUBTOTAL $ _____

Virginia residents add 4.5% sales tax $ _____

Shipping/handling ($4.00 for the first
title and $1.00 for each additional book) $ _____

Additional amount if shipping abroad $ _____

TOTAL ENCLOSED------------- $ _____

SHIP TO:

Name _____

Address _____

_____

_____

PAYMENT METHOD:

❑ I enclose check/moneyorder for $ _____
made payable to IMPACT PUBLICATIONS.

❑ Please charge $ _____ to my credit card:

❑ Visa ❑ MasterCard ❑ American Express

Card # _____

Expiration date: _____/_____

Signature _____